P9-BYT-428

Nick Ward

The Present 'confirms the author of *The Strangeness of Others* as a theatrical poet.' Irving Wardle, *Independent on Sunday*

Nick Ward was born in Geelong, Australia, in 1962. His first plays as writer/director were seen at the Edinburgh Festival, winning three *Scotsman* Fringe Firsts in 1983/84. His subsequent plays include *Eastwood* in 1985, for which he won a *Time Out* Award in 1986. For *Apart from George* and *The Strangeness of Others* he won the 1988 George Devine Award. His films include *Dakota Road* (1991) for Channel 4/Working Title (screenplay published by Faber) and *Look Me in the Eye* (1994) for the BBC/ Skreba-Creon.

FABER CONTEMPORARY CLASSICS

Alan Ayckbourn
Alan Bennett
Brial Friel
Trevor Griffiths
David Hare
Sharman Macdonald
Frank McGuinness
John Osborne
Harold Pinter
Tom Stoppard
Nick Ward
Timberlake Wertenbaker

NICK WARD

Plays One

The Present
Apart from George
The Strangeness of Others
Trouble Sleeping

Introduced by
the author

faber and faber
LONDON · BOSTON

Apart from George and *The Strangeness of Others* first published in 1988 by
Oberon Books Limited
This collection first published in 1995 by
Faber and Faber Limited 3 Queen Square London WC1N 3AU

Photoset by Parker Typesetting Service, Leicester
Printed in England by Clays Ltd, St Ives plc

Introduction and this collection, © Nick Ward, 1995
Apart from George and *The Strangeness of Others*, © Nick Ward, 1988

The epigraph on p. 236 is taken from *The Complete Stories of Flannery
O'Connor* (Faber and Faber, 1990).

Nick Ward is hereby identified as author of this work in accordance with
Section 77 of the Copyright, Designs and Patents Act 1988

All rights whatsoever in this play are strictly reserved and application for
performance should be made in advance, before the beginning of rehearsals,
to Judy Daish Associates, 2 St Charles Place, London W10 6EG.

*This book is sold subject to the condition that it shall not, by way of trade
or otherwise, be lent, resold, hired out or otherwise circulated without the
publisher's prior consent in any form of binding or cover other than that
in which it is published and without a similar condition including
this condition being imposed on the subsequent purchaser.*

A CIP record for this book
is available from the British Library

ISBN 0–571–17681–X

2 4 6 8 10 9 7 5 3 1

Contents

Introduction, vii

The Present, 1

Apart from George, 75

The Strangeness of Others, 129

Trouble Sleeping, 235

Introduction

We are lost, uncertain, and divided: things are moving too fast for us, so defensively, and with degrees of irony and hysteria, we do our best to keep up appearances. Perhaps this is what the present has always felt like, but the approaching millennium gives it an irrational and heightened edge. Time passing is the only thing we all have in common. Political certainties dissolve and opposing leaders begin to bear an uncanny resemblance to each other, as culture high and low smacks itself in the face. Meanwhile lap-top technocrats gaze with pasty faces at computer screens, intimidating us with visions of an unregulated future, care of that glorified telephone-line, the Internet. Clumsy new words, uncertainty, exclusion, decentralization, and the blind celebrations of a society in denial. These are good times for the playwright.

I was absent from the theatre for the first half of the nineties until *The Present* was staged at the Bush Theatre in 1995. In that time I made two independent films for television, convinced that film, television, home movies and the new technologies held the future of storytelling. There were things about the theatre that I missed: the rehearsal process, the immediacy, the smell, the *liveness*, but on the night bus I would convince myself I was right as I tuned in with a dramatist's compulsion to the twenty-somethings returning home after a night out. Clubs, videos, movies, sexy new chemicals. I rarely heard of a theatre trip, and if I did I assumed it was an out-of-work actor supporting a friend or trying to keep in touch. Never had the theatre been so out of touch with youth, especially youth with no money in its pocket. They craved the new, which is why the theatre seemed to offer them so little and why playwrights had such a rough ride at the end of the eighties and early nineties.

The best theatre had become one part of what it is good at: providing spectacle. The epitome of this trend was Stephen Daldry's Royal National Theatre production of Priestley's *An Inspector Calls*. It was an extraordinary event: here was a trusted old staple of the rep circuit being given a truly remarkable spin. For almost the first time in theatrical history a play's production would take it around the world. Daldry had created a production of a straight play that was behaving like a musical. It sums up the theatrical mood and appetite of the time, which was directly opposed to what became prosaically known as 'text-based' theatre; while Théâtre de Complicité and the extraordinary Lepage were packing them in, new plays were not shifting the tickets.

It was a thrilling, director-driven theatre: improvisation, physical life, design, adaptation and revival. These were the buzz words. Some of it even attracted a few from the night bus, who wouldn't mention the writer unless it was to casually announce his or her death. The wafer-thin avant garde certainly had no place for a living writer, happy instead to exhume the dead. As the director in me was applauding, the writer was feeling a bit left out. 'Can't we work together?' said a small voice, but I silenced the playwright and set off on a different path.

This was the theatre from which I was absent. At its best it had great energy and flair, but beneath the excess there was something missing. Despite an unburiable need for new work, singular new voices and theatrical inner-life, writers were no longer connected to the sources of theatrical energy. Betrayal sounds too premeditated, but there was certainly a loss of faith, and where there is no will, there is no way. The truth is that most directors don't like new plays; they feel inhibited by the singularity and are unable to discover the physical inner-life unless it is applied with attention-seeking force from without. They are unwilling to serve or even co-relate with another authority. There were exceptions. Dominic Dromgoole at the Bush always put playwrights first, but it was a stand against the spirit of the times.

New plays are difficult and the best plays have always been written at times when playwrights have been connected to the epicentre. They represent a financial risk and often the better directed they are the less attention the director gets. The director doesn't get the notices and stars are usually too cautious and self-regarding to make the necessary commitment. More to the point, artistic directors make the decisions about where the shamefully diminishing subsidies go. The result: the theatre loses touch with a generation. The same generation who are interacting with the Internet, dropping E in clubs or learning the MacDonald's dialogue from *Pulp Fiction* by heart. Meanwhile, the cutting edge of newness was in the art galleries, film, music, fiction and in 'performance-based' theatre work; at least the visible edge. It's true that some playwrights continued to pack them in, but it was mainly an audience of Mums and Dads, while others, having nothing to lose, courageously took to the fringe (although the critics rarely followed them) as the Royal National Theatre began to feel like an extension of the West End.

Things are changing now. The escapism born of the theatre establishment's double-headed flirtation with commercialism and false confidence – the after-burn of Thatcherism – has given way to a new-found pluralism. We will always crave great productions of classic plays and the dizzying heights born of improvisation and design, but new plays are also hitting the spot again. There is a demand for what was missing: uncensored perspectives on our troubled and freedom-seeking times. Even the Royal

Shakespeare Company, that bastion of reinterpretation, recently sold its season on the strength of its new plays. Playwrights are getting column inches again. Demand affects supply. Everything comes around. There would be no Tarantino (who has inadvertently done for the dramatist in the nineties what John Osborne did in the fifties) without Harold Pinter. Dialogue has come roaring back into fashion, and paradoxically the cinema has led the charge. But dialogue is only the visible syntax of the playwright's craft. Language is a better word – theatre language – encompassing so much more than simply what the characters say to each other. Writers, directors, designers and actors are working together again. But this was to happen later.

So back in the early nineties, having finished *Dakota Road* for Film on Four and written the first draft of another, *Look Me in the Eye*, for the BBC, I set off to the Western Australian desert to write a film set in the vast and forgotten gold fields. Without knowing it at the time, the further I strayed from theatre, the more I would secretly miss it. Soon after my return I settled down to write the promised screenplay, surrounded by photographs of my journey. There are scores of them, and they are comically repetitive: again and again a dead-straight road stretching ahead into a horizon so distant you can see the shape of the earth, with occasional snaps of strangers encountered on the way, or, more frequently, broken-down cars, discarded domestic objects, a sand-blasted billy-can, a shoe, a gramophone, and the pathetic scarrings of thousands of prospectors' pitches.

I failed to write the screenplay, despite these most cinematic of images. Try as I might, I couldn't find the story. I had a wide-screen landscape bereft of characters, without whom I cannot begin to write. Yet this had been one of the most significant times of my life: a return to the country of my birth. Perhaps the Western Australian desert is a place to project on to, not somewhere to find an independent truth, discounting the most obvious which is that 'this is no place for a white man' (as Danny says at the end of *The Present*, ironically quoting his alter-ego, Luke Murray). For me it became a place to unconsciously follow the traces of my memory. Recent memories of a broken relationship opened doors to other more distant experiences; my time in Melbourne as a teenager and my innocence and fascination in the face of adult sexuality. Through that door a hand reached for still more distant doors, projecting forwards to the road beyond and backwards into my mind, beyond the recent friends and broken trusts, beyond a stubbornly gained education, beyond my troubles with love and money to that shifting place where memory begins: the curious child fastening on to overwhelming questions, without that most adult of prescriptions, 'Am I in the right place at the right time?'. There was a dialogue going on between my present and my past which was refusing to be a film. So I accepted defeat, writing instead a few more drafts of *Look Me in the Eye* and doing radio work.

A year or so later, Stephen Daldry, newly-appointed director of the Royal Court, knowing my preferred working method, invited me to hold a workshop for a new play. It was the invitation I had been secretly craving. I was tired of looking at screens. A single room, committed actors and an opportunity to shape those troubled and confused thoughts.

I have an uncomplicated attitude to actors. They are artists who *do*. If writers have had a bad time of it of late, many actors have been in a hell of frustration: serial auditions for over-researched television or theatrical puppetry. It is unsurprising that journalists who should know better coined the expression 'luvvies' against a profession too battered and self-deprecating to retaliate. When actors are not taken seriously or, worse, don't take themselves seriously, the theatre has gone soft.

For the first two weeks of the workshop I wrote nothing. We told stories together. The actors began to gather in the same emotional space, and when they had done so, I was ready to write. Very occasionally in a writer's life the writing feels easy and right. *The Present* (or 'Danny Rule' as it was called then) was a vessel into which I could pour experience. The characters were real and waiting every morning for the new scene to help me make sense of it. When this begins to happen in the rehearsal room it feels like a miracle – the play exists between the actor and the writer and creates movement both ways. Directing actors on this level has little to do with control. The actors reveal the play to the author and they will risk everything to make the necessary connections: there is 'play' within the play. This is what is known as chemistry. When unlocked, it is a quality unique to theatre: simple actions, words and interactions become inhabited by a mysterious mix of character and personality, intelligence and physicality, giving a density to the work which lurks far beneath the surface of the text. The blend of elements becomes effortless and shifting, as scenes slide from one to another and moods swing as swiftly as an actor's choice.

All the plays in this collection contain and reflect this process. There are two linked scenes in *Apart From George* which appear very thin on the page. Pam is scrubbing the floor, first for her unemployed husband, George, and then for her new employer, John Grey. In Amelda Brown's performance, the scene both unscrambled and amplified her reaction to the frustrated sexuality and potential violence that surrounds her. She knew the audience could read her mind and body, and it did. The same was true of Katrin Cartlidge when she ate a cherry in Danny's face in *The Present* at the Bush. *Trouble Sleeping* would not exist if it were not for the chemistry which developed between Peter-Hugo Daly's Stuart and Sandra Voe's Nancy in *The Strangeness of Others*. The spirit of their characters demanded reincarnation. I have many similar memories of these plays in performance. Above all I hope they are an invitation for directors, actors, designers, lighting designers and composers to seamlessly weave a single texture in time and space – in their own way – for the pleasure of strangers.

After the Royal Court workshop I finally directed *Look Me in the Eye* for the BBC. As we struggled with budgets and schedules to create an unstable dreamscape at odds with the inherent literalness of the medium, I consoled myself with the knowledge that *The Present* was waiting. It would be more than a year before it opened at the Bush, a strange place to make a film set in the desert, but, for me at least, the theatre was again where it was at. I had forgotten its power to create worlds whose only limits are what the imagination lacks.

THE PRESENT

For
Rachel

CHARACTERS

Danny Age eighteen/nineteen. Born in Melbourne, but has lived in England since he was a child.

Michael Age thirty-one. Living in Melbourne, originally from Sydney.

Becky Age thirty-one. Living in Melbourne.

Libby Age thirty-one. Living in Melbourne.

SETTING

Melbourne, Victoria, and in the last scene, Kookynie, Western Australia

TIME

December 1980 and early in 1981

DESIGN NOTE

The main design challenge is to ensure that the flow of the action is not impeded by scene changes.

MUSIC NOTE

Suggested John Lennon and Beatles songs are as follows:

Before play: 'Mother'
Act One
Scene Three: (Danny singing on the telephone) 'I am the walrus'
Scene Four: 'Mind games', followed by 'Tight as'
Scene Five: (On Michael's answer-machine) 'Imagine'
Beginning of the interval: 'Remember'
End of the interval: 'Beautiful boy'
Act Two
Scenes One/Two: Continuous track comprising: 'I am the walrus', 'Strawberry Fields', 'Lucy in the sky with diamonds', 'All you need is love', 'Come together'
Scene Four: (From the end of Danny's monologue in Scene Three): 'Happy birthday'; (for Michael's and Becky's dance): 'Twist and shout'; (Danny singing): 'A day in the life'
End of the play: Reprise from 'Sergeant Pepper'

The Present was first performed at the Bush Theatre, London, on 15 February 1995. The cast was as follows:

Danny Ewan Bremner
Michael Christopher Simon
Becky Katrin Cartlidge
Libby Susan Vidler

Designed by Simon Reynolds
Directed by Nick Ward

An earlier version of the play (*Danny Rule*) was first performed in four private showings at the Royal Court Theatre, London, on 18 and 19 October 1993. The cast was as follows:

Danny John Simm
Michael Christopher Simon
Becky Tessa Humphries
Libby Susan Vidler

Directed by Nick Ward
Technical and creative co-ordination by Simon Reynolds

Act One

SCENE ONE

A street in central Melbourne. Dawn. **Danny** *is in a sleeping bag. Next to him a rucksack and guitar.* **Michael** *is sitting beside him.*

Danny There's a candle and John Lennon . . . and something burning . . . incense . . . Big brown eyes. She's giving me grass, then, God knows what. I'm floating, double vision, drifting. Where is he?

Michael Who?

Danny He's helping me here.

Michael You're in a strange city?

Danny I was born here.

Michael Nothing stranger . . . and besides, how welcome are you? What's your name?

Danny Daniel. Danny Rule.

Michael Good day, Danny Rule. My name's Michael. He's a close friend of the family, from way back, but she's not much older than you, and he's away, so you're all alone.

Danny Except for John Lennon, he's only been dead two weeks and she's got it up really loud. She's dancing at me up close, 'I want to be dead too, Danny-boy.' Danny-boy.

Michael He's a close friend of the family. So, where is he?

Danny He's away for the night.

Michael Away where?

9

Danny He's helping me here. What's happening? An old friend of my mother, he's her age, *she's* much younger.

Michael He knew your mother when she was young. He fucked your mother.

Danny I don't know.

Michael Many years ago.

Danny Did he?

Michael What's she doing now?

Danny She's dancing in my face.

Michael Great arse, yes?

Danny 'I want to be dead too, Danny-boy. Do you think you're capable, Danny-boy, of fucking me?' She's hitting me. I can't see. Her skin is soft. Beautiful smell.

Michael You can still smell her.

Danny She's hitting me and I'm telling her . . .

Michael What are you telling her?

Danny Nothing, I'm not saying anything. I'm trying to stop her. It's so fucking hot, I can't breathe.

Michael You're desperately trying to stop her.

Danny Where's my money? (*He is looking for his wallet. He gets out of the sleeping bag.*)

Michael And you fucked her.

Danny The smell, sweet and strong. And skin. Soft. Brown.

Michael Then you hit her.

Danny I hit her. And she laughs. She's laughing with her teeth. Her shirt is torn. She's laughing and singing along.

Michael She's loving it.

Danny I'm inside her, and she puts my hands around her throat and she's banging her head against the floor.

Michael She's loving it.

Danny No.

Michael But, you don't stop.

Danny No.

Michael You can't stop. On and on. She's screaming.

Danny No, she's stopped screaming. I stop.

Michael Where is she now?

Danny On the floor. She's on the floor and she's not moving.

Michael Her eyes?

Danny Her eyes are closed.

Michael Her head is back. Her body? Her neck? Her tits? Her breathing? She's loving it. Can you see her breathing?

Danny No.

Michael And, you leave her there . . . Here. (*He gives Danny a card.*) Come to this address at four o'clock. I can help you. See you later, Danny.

SCENE TWO

Michael's office.

Michael My name is Jim.

Danny Jim.

Michael Say it.

Danny Jim.

Michael My name is Jim.

Danny My name is Jim.

Michael My name is Luke.

Danny Hello, Luke.

Michael No, say it: 'My name is Luke.'

Danny My name is Luke.

Michael Again.

Danny My name is Luke.

Michael My name is Jim.

Danny My name is Jim.

Michael Luke . . . Murray.

Danny My name is Murray.

Michael No, Luke Murray. My name is Luke Murray.

Danny My name is Luke Murray.

Michael Like you mean it.

Danny My name is Luke Murray.

Michael Again.

Danny My name is Luke Murray.

Michael Better.

Danny My name is Luke Murray.

Michael Good. I'm an artist from England. Repeat.

Danny I'm an artist from England.

Michael I'm in Australia on a grant from the Royal College of Art in London.

Danny I'm in college, Australia, on a grant from the Royal College . . .

Michael For Christ's sake put some feeling into it. I normally pay someone to do what I'm doing for you. You're getting it from the big white chief, mate. You've got to think *fast*. Got me?

Danny OK.

Michael I'm over here from the Royal College of Art in London . . . on a scholarship, to try and capture the exquisite richness and mystery of your Outback in oil; no, just Outback, leave it there, and I was hoping you might be able to spare me a few minutes of your time for me to show you my paintings. No, my landscapes. Got that, Luke?

Danny I think so.

Michael Off you go then.

Danny I'm over here from the Royal College of Art . . .

Michael In London. Come on. Make it real.

Danny On a special scholarship, to explore your Outback and attempt to convey its vast mystery . . .

Michael Too much.

Danny Through my work. In my work. Attempt to convey its exquisite mystery in my work.

Michael Right. Got that?

Danny I think so.

Michael You're a bright one. Now what do you think of these?

Michael takes the paintings out of a portfolio and spreads them out on the floor. Danny looks at them for a while without saying anything.

Look, I know you've got some heavy shit on your mind. Don't worry, we'll soon get you cleaned up and I've got somewhere for you to stay, and if you play your cards right, by the end of the day you'll have some money in your pocket. I'll see you right. So, what do you think of them?

Danny I don't know.

Michael And I don't care. Sell them to me. Here, start with this one.

Danny Um.

Michael Where were you?

Danny The Outback.

Michael The Hammersleys, WA. People want stories. You'd set up camp at the base of the Gorge. You were alone. No, you weren't alone. There was a woman. She's from Perth. No, she was from Perth. Use the past tense. It ended badly. She couldn't handle the solitude – you need to be alone when you paint – so she went bush crazy and left you for a minerologist she met around the pool table in the Grand Hotel in Tom Price. Sums up your life. You offer danger and the denial of convention, he offered security. So there was tension between you, a barrenness, and this painting reflects it. The light is fading, darkness is descending, the sound of your bickering voices is bounced back at you by the thrusting primeval rocks. Where is it?

Danny Um?

Michael A Gorge in the Hammersley Ranges.

Danny The Hammersley Ranges.

Michael Right. Ghost town near Kalgoorlie, called Kookynie. Once a town of thousands, during the Gold Rush of the 1890s. It had banks, hotels, brothels. Fortunes were made and lost. Now, there's nothing. You were alone, you wanted to capture the pioneering tradition of the ordinary man, which is the unsung heritage of all Australians. The old discarded Holden there speaks volumes. What does it speak volumes about?

Danny The pioneering tradition of all Australians.

Michael Water. Or lack of it. No rain to rust it and wash it away. A haunting memorial to the prospectors who died of thirst out there in the desert, who if given the chance would have exchanged their gold for the same weight in water. Make them weep, Danny.

Danny Right. Koo –

Michael Kookynie. Here we are in New South Wales shearing sheep as big as whales. The great and beautiful Murray river, downstream of Mildura. Grapes. You worked the grapes. This place is called Gol Gol. You shared a cabin with a bunch of no-hopers from the city, and they brought the dirt and corruption of the city with them, so you used to head out to Gol Gol to find peace and inspiration. You'd sit beneath the river gums. You wanted to capture the contrasts, you had to refine your technique for the green of the leaves, the white of the bark, the branches; twisted like distorted human limbs, the width of the sky, but at the centre of it all, the river; the great provider, flowing, flowing, like life itself. Get poetic.

Danny Gol Gol, grapes, no-hopers, width of sky, Murray river, life itself.

Michael That's it. Northern Queensland. Tropical rain forest. Somewhere on the Mitchell river. Nothing but green. But, beneath the green, leeches, killer bog spiders and crocodiles. You were camping out in the hut at Farewell Yard, down to your last bottle of Vegemite and bitten to buggery by the mozzies. 'This is no place for a white man,' you thought, you felt like Marlon Brando in *Apocalypse Now*, on the very cusp of insanity. So why were you there? (*Slight pause.*) *Passion*. OK, here we are back in the – guess what? – the desert again. Barrow Creek. Northern Territory. What do you see?

Danny Desert . . . A great emptiness . . . A width of sky.

Michael You've already used width of sky for Gol Gol. A great emptiness is all right. What else do you see?

Danny A pole.

Michael Yeah. What kind of pole?

Danny A lonely pole.

Michael A telegraph pole. Originating from the 1870s. So, this painting is all about communication; a big word for Luke Murray. You want to communicate your message, you want to sell your paintings. You were staying in the old Repeater Station, where the famous, or infamous – depending on your view – and be careful with this one, test the water first. Where the famous Incident occurred. The Aboriginals attacked – almost unheard of – because they put up the station bang slap in the middle of a sacred site. Telegraph lines, song lines, make up your own story.

Danny Got it.

Michael Look at the way you painted the earth.

Danny Red.

Michael Thousands of dots, echoing Aboriginal methods, your humble attempt at a cross-fertilization of cultures. You even incorporated red ochre into your oils for the unique afterglow.

Danny It's a hell of a lot to remember.

Michael You'll be fine. Number one, the Hammersleys –
solitude; number two, Kookynie – tradition; number three,
Gol Gol – technique; number four, Farewell Yard –
passion; number five, Barrow Creek – communication.
The five essential ingredients that make up the artist.
Remember those and you won't go far wrong. I'll jot them
down for you in a minute. We have a wider variety, but it's
best to start with a few until you get the hang of it. The
others will be here in a while, with Keith who's my
Melbourne second in command. He drives the minibus. If
you sell one, Keith will never be far away to replenish your
portfolio, though we're running a bit short of Farewell
Yards, I'm expecting a new consignment from Hong Kong
after the weekend. What else? There's a shower out the
back and a few tubes of paint, mix it well and rub some
into your fingers. Don't overdo it. Remember selling is sex
– always target the woman, unless you get a gay. I'll be
here when you get back, and I'll drive you back to my
place. Any questions?

Danny I don't think so.

Michael So, what do you think of them?

Danny Do people buy them?

Michael They do. By the thousand, mate, and do you
know why?

Danny Why?

Michael Because they like them. See ya later.

*Michael leaves. Danny puts the paintings back in the
portfolio and leaves.*

SCENE THREE

Michael's place. There are numerous abstract sculptures.

Michael So, Danny-boy, what do you think?

Danny I like it.

Michael Welcome back, mate.

Danny I'm sorry?

Michael I thought you said Melbourne was your birthplace. Well, here you are again: you've returned.

Danny Oh right. Thanks, Michael.

Michael And, what's more, I hope you go on returning, Danny . . .

Danny Thanks, I really appreciate . . .

Michael . . . it's like Nietzsche (*he pronounces it 'Nee-chee'*) said, have you read Nietzsche, Danny?

Danny No, I can't say I have.

Michael Jesus! don't they educate you in England? You've got to read him, mate, he was a truly great man. German. Nineteenth century. Here (*he gives him a book*), you can take him to bed with you later.

Danny Thanks.

Michael He put together this theory, right, which he dubbed Eternal Return, which you put me in mind of. It's a winner. In it he says – and I'm paraphrasing, you'll have to read it for yourself later – in it he says that all the important, life-changing moments we live return an infinite number of times. Even if we don't want them to. Especially if we don't want them to. It's like we're haunted by our own experiences. However bad. It's a pretty heavy idea, isn't it? – if you think about it.

Danny It is.

Michael You know, I reckon, if he was alive today he'd be the only one who'd really be able to get behind the idea of the Aboriginal Dreamtime . . .

Danny . . . I'm really looking forward to it . . .

Michael . . . no, listen to me, because if the Dreamtime land of the Aboriginal Ancestors is disturbed – and it's been more than disturbed, Danny, it's been positively raped – raped to buggery – the damage inflicted will return again and again, replicating itself in wounds on the bodies and souls of the perpetrators. That means you and me, Danny. (*Pause.*) I'm going to write a book about it, mate, when I find the time, and I'm going to call it *In the Moment of Return*. Try and tie it all together, but keep that to yourself, will you?

Danny Of course.

Michael I can trust you, Danny, but you can't be too careful. It's a bit of a bombshell. What do you think of the title?

Danny It's great.

Michael No, it's not. It's a crock of shit. (*Slight pause.*) I know what you're thinking, Danny. You're thinking that I'm a cynical, two-faced bastard and that I don't give a flying fuck about Aboriginal Dreamtime. You might be right, why should I? I bet you've got a way with words.

Danny I don't know.

Michael Hey, you've had quite a day or two.

Danny I'm dead.

Michael Which reminds me. Sit down.

Michael indicates a small sofa. Danny obeys. Michael sits beside him.

Now, before we go any further, I'd like you to tell me *exactly* what happened.

Danny (*trying to sound enthusiastic*) Well, to be honest I was fucking nervous, I've never done anything like this before, I didn't know what was going to happen, and in my present state of mind, well . . . I just, um . . . didn't know what was going to happen. All these things running around in my head . . . and I'm trying to remember the order of things. It was getting dark. I felt pretty lonely out there . . .

Michael Out where?

Danny A stranger's door. The flickering light of the telly. The sound of voices, you know. Knock. Knock. I am an artist.

Michael I don't believe this, Danny . . . There's only one rule in this house and I call it rule number one. We never, *ever*, talk about work here. This is my *home*. I don't want to have to discuss this matter again, is that clear?

Danny Of course. I'm sorry.

Michael Don't apologize. I want to know what happened *in* there, not out there – I know what happened *out* there, you sold three bloody paintings, we've dealt with that. In there. Last night. With Lizzie.

Danny Oh God. Right.

Michael I mean, you tell me that by candle light, to the sound of John Lennon, you rape a woman called Lizzie, who's the girlfriend of an *extremely* close friend of your mother's. You unleash on her all that pent-up aggression and violence that you feel towards women.

Danny I didn't say that . . .

Michael . . . possibly even towards your mother . . .

Danny What?

Michael You savage her, you leave her for dead – and by the sound of what you told me this morning, it might be worse. Maybe it'll be all over the papers in the morning. Now, I want to help you, mate, because I like you and you need help, that's simple, but when I ask you about it, for more *detail*, which is fair enough – it's like it didn't happen. All you want to talk about is selling three fake landscapes to some half-brain in Gringegalgona. Which leaves me feeling pretty freaked out by you, Danny. Which leaves me feeling that either you're, A, a callous self-serving bastard or, B, a genuine one-hundred-per-cent psychopath. Either way, where would that leave me? (*Pause.*) So, which is it? A or B?

> *Pause. Danny is sitting with his head crunched in his hands. Michael starts to laugh.*

Only joking, mate. I want you to make a phone call.

Danny Who to?

Michael Guess.

Danny My mother?

Michael No, I want you to ring *her*. Lizzie.

Danny I can't.

Michael Course you can. Don't worry, mate. She's fine. I just want you to call her and . . .

Danny . . . how do you know she's fine?

Michael . . . and tell her you're OK. She'll be sick to death with worry about you, and so will the very close friend of your mother's – what's his name?

Danny Joshua.

Michael So will Josh. He'll be back from his business trip and he'll be shitting himself.

Danny She's not fine. I know she's not fine, really.

Michael Listen, mate, how old are you?

Danny Nearly nineteen.

Michael You're eighteen years old, you've had your first taste of a bit of rough-house rooting. It's nothing. It's normal, it happens all the time, believe me – ring her. Tell her you've met me, tell her my name, you know, and that we get on like a house on fire, etc., that I've given you a job in my gallery on the Toorac Road, and a place to stay. Tell her you've landed on your feet, you really appreciate all the hospitality they've shown you during your Australian trip, but that you've been offered opportunities which at your age you'd be a fool to pass over. Or something like that.

Danny How do you know?

Michael If I'd been lucky enough to meet me at your age, I'd be counting my lucky stars, matey.

Danny No, how do you know she's all right?

Michael Because I just do. Now I'm going to bury Robert and give the old one-eyed trouser snake a shake, and while I do so I want you to call her, so I'll see you later. Good luck. I'll keep my fingers crossed. (*He leaves. Pause. He comes back.*) Now if she isn't fine . . .

> *Pause. Michael exhales sharply and leaves. Danny is alone. He stares at the telephone for a few moments. He picks up the receiver. He puts it down again. He stands up. He returns to the phone. He picks up the receiver and dials. As it rings he mutters the lyrics to 'I am the walrus'.*

Danny Hi, Joshua, it's Danny . . . I know, I'm sorry . . . No, I'm fine . . . Did she? How is she . . . ? Is she . . . ? No, no, look I'm sorry I didn't call . . . I'm sure you were . . .

Michael returns.

No, I've really landed on my feet, I've got myself a job . . . He's called Michael . . . This morning . . . I know. I'm sorry. I really appreciate everything you've done for me . . . Sorry . . . ? In an art gallery, on the Toorac Road . . . I guess so . . . No, we get on like a house on fire . . . I don't think so . . . no, nothing like that . . . Yes, I'm at his place at the moment . . . Yes, he is . . . I'll call her . . . Of course I will, and I'll tell her how kind you've been . . . Yes, OK, I will . . . Does she? Send mine to her . . . OK. I will, bye . . . Bye.

Michael Told you so.

Danny (*standing*) I can't believe it. I cannot believe it. Fuck me!

Michael Did you tell him you'd be staying for a bit?

Danny Fuck me. I don't believe it. He said she's fine. She's absolutely fine.

Michael You're not going back then?

Danny No. If that's all right with you.

Michael It's more than all right, Danny. I'm delighted mate.

Danny Phew!

Michael You're looking pretty fucking pleased with yourself. You're like a rat with a gold tooth, Danny-boy.

Danny Would you mind missing out the 'boy' bit, you know, after what happened? Or what I thought happened. Fuck me. I do not believe it. I really thought . . .

23

Michael . . . that's exactly my point Danny-*boy*. You didn't kill her, but answer me this. Why do you think it is that you thought that you did?

Danny What?

Michael Why did you tell me that you did, when you didn't?

Danny I don't know. It must have been the grass.

Michael Ah! So you were *hallucinating*. That's one hell of a trip, Danny – but then, you know what I reckon? – I reckon there might be another reason, because you're not a liar, are you, Danny?

Danny I try not to be.

Michael Well, no more than the rest of us, eh? What I'm driving at, Danny, is that although you clearly didn't either rape *or* murder this woman Lizzie, who's the lover of Josh, who may well have fucked your mother – when would that have been?

Danny I don't think he did.

Michael We're dealing in ifs here, mate. If he did, when would he have done it?

Danny He didn't.

Michael He possibly did – and it would have before you were born. I leave you to draw your own conclusions. But, that's not my main point . . . My main point is that you *wanted*, somewhere in your deepest, darkest subconscious, you wanted to rape and murder this woman, who, whether you like it not, is indirectly linked with your mother.

Danny Michael, you hardly know me, but . . .

Michael We know each other pretty well, matey, and I'll

tell you why. I'm reading your mind now, you're wondering why there's no woman here. No flesh-and-blood Sheila. There's something I want to tell you, Danny, and it's not easy, mate. Come and sit down.

Danny I'm fine.

Michael No, you're not. Sit down.

Danny does so. Pause. Michael joins him.

It's like this, matey, whereas you thought you'd killed a woman, well, I really did.

Danny What?

Michael I killed a woman. So here we are.

Danny What do you mean, you killed a woman? How?

Michael How did I kill her? I thought you'd want the details. (*Pause.*) I loved her, Danny . . . She was, without doubt, the most beautiful woman you ever saw. Danny, she was fucking gorgeous, mate, and you know what I did to her?

Danny No.

Michael She was . . . (*He trails off.*)

Danny You don't have to tell me.

Michael No, I really want to, Danny. (*Pause.*) By the time I'd finished with her . . . she'd been . . . hacked to pieces, mate.

Danny Was she? How . . . ? Sorry.

Michael No, it's fair enough. You want to know how. We were up Alice way. I fell asleep at the wheel . . .

Danny . . . It was an accident . . .

Michael We went off the road, straight into a telegraph

pole. The car was a write-off and she was completely mutilated. What do you mean by accident, Danny?

Danny She died in a car crash, you happened to be driving, but you mustn't feel . . . You mustn't blame yourself . . .

Michael I don't believe in accidents, Danny. (*Pause. He suddenly stands up.*) Now I'm dying to show you round, mate. Look around you. What do you see?

Danny Sculptures.

Michael In various degrees of abstraction, the female form. Sheilas by Sheilas. They saved my life, mate, I don't mind telling you that, because, believe me, Danny, I'd fallen clean off the swing, mate. What do you think of them?

Danny They're great, lovely . . . I'm exhausted.

Michael They're more than great, they're fucking world class. They'll be worth a load, I mean a load of bucks in a few years, and I was here at the beginning. Trish Carter, Libby Meyer, Trilby Trynan – the Auguste Rodins of tomorrow.

Danny Libby who?

Michael Libby Meyer. That's hers. Quite something, eh?

Danny Wait a minute. Libby Meyer?

Michael Oh, you've already heard of Libby, have you?

Danny I don't know. What's she look like?

Michael Oh, she's gorgeous, Danny – about thirty, long dark hair, great arse, tits like . . .

Danny (*interrupting*) Long dark hair. I do know her, well, I used to know her. Do you know where she is?

Michael I should do, I've commissioned a new piece out of her – a lot of dough – and she's a bit fucking late to say the least. Before long I'll be round there to chase it up. Fucks me off. I even told her about the death of Tania, to give her inspiration. I mean, you try and help people. So, how do you know her?

Danny It was years ago. I don't believe this. Libby! I didn't know she was an artist.

Michael Without me, she wouldn't be. Sounds like it was something pretty special.

Danny Her mother and mine go way back.

Michael So, she's another extremely close friend of your mother. I see. I bet you're absolutely dying to see her again, aren't you?

Danny I am.

Michael Well, I'll tell you what, take the evening off (*whispering*) work tomorrow and pop round. She's not on the phone, but I'll give you the address.

Danny Thanks, I will.

Michael And, when you see her, you can tell her from me to pull her index finger out. No, don't tell her that. Just tell her I'm *really*, *really* looking forward to hearing from her. Hey, you're looking buggered, mate. Come with me.

Michael leads Danny across the room.

Your room's in here, bathroom's there. You'll find everything you need. What else? (*Pause.*) See you tomorrow. It's great to have you here, Danny.

Danny Thanks.

Michael You're more than welcome. See you tomorrow.

27

Danny Goodnight.

Michael Sweet dreams, Danny-boy.

SCENE FOUR

Becky's *and* **Libby**'s *place.* *Danny is at the door.*

Danny My name's Luke . . . Danny Rule. I'm looking for Libby Meyer . . . Am I in the right place?

Becky How do you know Libby?

Danny I'm a close friend.

Becky Well, any friend of Libby's is a – what did you say your name was . . . ?

Danny Danny Rule.

Becky . . . friend of mine, Danny. Come in. She'll be back soon. Take a seat.

Danny Thanks.

Danny does so. Silence.

Becky Comfy?

Danny Thanks.

Becky (*lights a stick of incense*) Libby hasn't mentioned you.

Danny No? Any idea when she might get back?

Becky Presently. She's on her way back from Kalgoorlie.

Danny Aaah!

Becky You've been there?

Danny Briefly.

Becky So, that's where you met her?

Danny No, no, I knew her in England.

Becky 'Seventy-six?

Danny That's right.

Becky A very hot summer in England.

Danny That's right. How do you know that?

Becky Libby told me. She said it was like being in Australia. Funny that.

Danny What?

Becky That she should mention the weather, but not an extremely close friend who calls himself Danny Rule. It's a bit odd, if you ask me.

Danny Well, it's certainly surprising.

Becky So what did you think of Kalgoorlie? Did you go to the brothel?

Danny No. No. Actually I was staying in a place quite near Kalgoorlie, called . . . Kookynie. I loved it. It's an old ghost town. Really atmospheric. You know there are old cars, just sitting in the sand, untouched since the . . .

Becky . . . sand? You mean *earth*? We don't call it sand.

Danny Anyway, they really struck me. A kind of monument to the pioneering men of Australia.

Becky What about the women? What about the pioneering women of Australia?

Danny Men and women, that's what I meant to say.

Becky I don't think you did. I don't think it occurred to you to say 'women'. How do you think your omission leaves me feeling?

Danny I didn't mean to offend you.

Becky It leaves me feeling pretty fucking excluded, Danny. (*She lights a joint.*)

Danny I'm sorry.

Becky What did you say you were doing in Kalgoorlie?

Danny Just having a look. Part of my trip.

Becky It's a pretty funny place to go for a holiday.

Danny Well, I had my sketchbook with me.

Becky You're an artist? Libby won't like that.

Danny No, I wouldn't say I was an artist.

Becky You just said you were in Kalgoorlie with a sketchbook. When was this?

Danny Oh, a few weeks ago.

Becky Libby was there then.

Danny I wish I'd known that.

Becky Were you alone?

Danny Yeah, I was feeling pretty down. My girlfriend had just dumped me.

Becky Good for her. You won't find many women choosing to be in Kalgoorlie. I expect you feel at home with all that maleness – brothels – Two up – miners – machinery. I expect you get off on what men have done to this country.

Danny Oh, no, quite the reverse. I think it's tragic. They've raped it.

Becky I hate it when men use that word. Here, do you want a smoke?

Danny No, thanks, not for me.

Becky Go on. Be a devil. You might get more interesting.

Danny No, really. I ought to get going. Would you mind telling Libby that I called . . . ?

Becky (*interrupting*) She'll be back soon – any minute. Please don't go. I'm a bit lonely actually.

> *Becky smokes the joint, then passes it to Danny. Becky goes over to a tape-deck. Danny sits down on a sofa. Becky selects a tape and puts it on. It's a John Lennon compilation. Long Pause.*

Danny So what was Libby doing in Kalgoorlie?

Becky Fuck off, smart arse. (*Pause.*) I'm sorry. I'm really sorry, Danny. I didn't mean that. I miss her, that's all.

Danny Don't mention it.

Becky How did you know to come here?

Danny I'm staying with a close friend of hers. He gave me the address.

Becky He?

Danny Michael.

Becky Michael?

Danny Yeah, do you know him?

Becky I know Michael all right. I hate that man.

Danny Oh.

Becky He's a fucking jumped-up parasite. The art world's full of them.

Danny That's interesting.

Becky Why is it interesting?

Danny I don't know.

Becky I hate small talk.

Danny I'm sorry.

Becky Don't apologize.

   Pause.

Danny So, what do you do?

Becky I'm old money. What about you?

Danny I'm a bit broke, actually.

Becky Oh, dear! Bad luck. I'm also a writer, and I look after Libby.

Danny What are you writing?

Becky A book.

Danny Oh.

   Pause.

Becky It's about art and it's about women. I can't tell you any more.

Danny Sounds interesting, anyway.

Becky I may call it *Conflicting Messages*. What do you think of the title?

Danny How do you feel about it?

Becky That's the right answer, Danny-boy. So, tell me more about you and Libby. In *England*.

   Becky sits on the arm of the sofa, facing Danny.

Danny Oh, she was great. She taught me such a lot.

Becky What about?

Danny Everything, everything. She was great.

Becky How old were you?

Danny Fourteen.

Becky And what exactly did she teach you? Do you think I'm attractive?

Danny Very much so.

Becky Why?

Danny Well, you've got . . . um . . .

Becky Do you know how much I weighed when I was fourteen? Five stone. And there wasn't any Libby in my life, I can tell you. But, I'm all right now. Look. (*She caresses herself.*) Don't you think?

Danny You're lovely.

Becky I hate my father. So?

Danny So?

Becky I asked you what happened between you and Libby, in the summer of '76.

Danny It sounds stupid now, but she changed my life.

Becky There's something you ought to know about Libby, Danny.

Danny Is there?

Becky About that time. In England.

Danny What?

Becky It was a bad time for her.

Danny I thought she had a really nice time. She was staying with my family.

Becky Well, she didn't. It was a terrible time, which is why she's wiped most of it. I thought you ought to know.

Danny Thanks . . . I didn't catch your name.

Becky I'm Libby's flat-mate. That'll do. Do you like John Lennon?

Danny I love him.

Becky Terrible to die like that. Two of the bullets went straight through him. He must have looked a real mess. The worst part was the policeman who drove him to the hospital. Do you know what he asked him?

Danny No.

Becky 'Are you John Lennon?' John Lennon said he was, then he died. I mean, fuck me. Poor Yoko . . . Oh, I see, you love John Lennon, but you hate Yoko Ono.

Danny I didn't say that.

Becky All men hate Yoko.

Danny I think that's a bit of a generalization.

Becky (*overlapping Danny*) Because she's a strong woman, because she's an artist and because she isn't white.

Danny (*overlapping Becky*) Sure, if you call 'A hole to look at the sky through' art, I'll go along with you.

Becky Can you see my knickers?

Danny That's strong grass. (*He puts the joint out.*)

Becky It's Moroccan hash. Can you?

Danny Yes.

Becky Do you like what you see? Pretty erotic, isn't it? Looking up a strange woman's skirt. You're all eyes.

Danny It must be the hash.

Becky I'm a strong woman, Danny, but I'm being a very naughty girl, don't you think? Have you got a hard-on?

From where Becky is sitting on the arm of the sofa, she very deliberately stretches one leg out and kicks him.

Ooo! Sorry, my foot slipped.

Danny Hey!

Becky I think Danny-boy's a bit out of his depth.

Danny You're really freaking me out.

Becky Great. (*She stands up.*) Wait a minute. Don't go away.

Becky turns the music up. She starts to dance, very provocatively. She dances closer and closer to Danny, eventually moving behind him. As she does so she suddenly hits him on the head.

Danny Don't hit me.

Becky Why not?

Danny It's fucking irritating.

Becky Getting angry, eh? Makes you want to hit me back, eh? Go on, then, give it a go, if you dare.

Becky jumps on top of him, lunging at him sexually and hitting him wildly.

Danny Please stop. Please. This is really freaking me out.

Danny escapes. Becky is up like a flash and stands in front of him, blocking his way.

Becky I know.

Danny How do you know?

Becky Because I can see things.

She pushes him back on to the sofa and kisses him violently.

Where are you going, Danny-boy?

Danny I'm going.

Becky Please don't go, Danny, I can't stand it. People are always going.

Danny struggles. Becky locks her legs around him. Confusion: she is thrusting herself against him. Her hands around his throat. As Danny attempts to enter her she starts to strangle him. He can't breath. He panics – attempting to pull her hands away from his throat. He succeeds, but their bodies are locked together – out of control. Becky seems to go into some kind of spasm. It is a few moments before Danny realizes that she isn't moving. Her hands limply around her own throat. Danny gets up slowly. He leaves as the John Lennon track swells.

SCENE FIVE

Michael's place. Michael is naked, meditating in an upside-down, double-lotus position. Danny rushes in.

Danny Michael, I am so pleased to see you.

Pause.

Sorry.

Pause.

Sorry.

Danny picks up Nietzsche's Thus Spoke Zarathustra.

He sits down and desperately tries to concentrate on reading.

Michael (*upside-down*) So, I gather Libby wasn't there?

Danny How do you know?

Michael Steady on, matey. A little birdy told me. (*He sits up and collects himself for a few seconds.*) How ya going, mate?

Danny I'm all right.

Michael You don't look all right. Do you know what this is?

Danny A tape-recorder?

Michael No. It's a telephone answer-machine. Give it a couple of years and it'll be all the rage. Listen.

Michael plays the answer-machine. A John Lennon song. Danny drops the book and holds his hands over his ears.

Danny Aaah!

Michael roars with laughter.

Michael I thought you'd like that. No, no, listen. (*He replaces the message tape.*)

Libby (*voice*) Hi, it's Libby here. I understand that Daniel Rule was here today. Hello, Michael, how are you? This is a message for Danny. Danny, sorry I missed you, but I'm back and it would be very nice to see you again. If you can make it tomorrow, I'll be in the Botanical Gardens in South Yarra, Leopold Street entrance, at three o'clock. I hope you can make it. Bye.

Michael Don't worry. I'll tell you how to get there. What's the matter, Danny?

Danny I'm fine. I'm so pleased to see you.

Michael Nice of you to say so, mate, but you look a bit *strange*, Danny.

Danny I'm exhausted.

Michael You're *always* fucking exhausted, Danny. No, I reckon you look a bit freaked out, mate. Still if you don't want to tell me, that's fair enough. I don't like secrets very much, Danny. I thought we were mates.

Danny We are mates and, as I said, I'm really pleased to be here, but I just want to go to bed.

Michael Fair enough. Come with me.

Michael leads him to a sink. He slowly washes Danny's hands and then dries them.

You've got three guesses. What did that mean?

Pause.

Danny You thought my hands needed washing?

Michael Yes, but no. Second guess?

Danny I've done something I need to um . . . wash my hands of?

Michael I'm sure you have, Danny-boy. But, no. Guess number three?

Danny Something religious?

Michael God is dead, Danny, according to Nietzsche. (*He makes a gesture towards the discarded book on the floor.*) And I go along with him. You've had your three guesses. I'll tell you. It was just to let you know that I'm here, mate.

Danny Thanks, Michael.

Michael Now you get some sleep, and I'll see you tomorrow.

Danny Right. Goodnight.

Michael is watching as Danny crosses the room. Danny stops for a moment to pick up the book and leaves, reading.

Michael (*as Danny leaves*) Sweet dreams, Danny-boy.

SCENE SIX

Botanical Gardens. **Libby** *is alone. She is looking up at a branch which overhangs the stage.*

Danny (*approaching*) Libby . . . ?

She looks at him.

Libby.

Libby Danny.

Danny hugs her.

Danny I'm so pleased to see you. I can't tell you. How are you?

Libby I'm fine.

Danny God, am I pleased to see you.

Libby Is Michael coming?

Danny I don't think so, but he said he's really, really, looking forward to seeing you. He asked me to tell you that.

Libby I didn't know you were a friend of Michael's.

Danny I know. It's incredible, isn't it? How are you?

Libby I'm fine. (*She spreads out a plastic sheet on the ground and sits down.*) Come and sit down.

Danny Thanks. (*He does so.*)

Libby Becky said . . .

Danny Becky?

Libby My flat-mate. She said you were in Kalgoorlie.

Danny Not really, I was just passing through. I was on my way to Kookynie. I wanted to see the gold country.

Libby How long were you there for?

Danny In Kookynie?

Libby No, Kalgoorlie.

Danny Oh, no time at all, really. A couple of days, at the most. What *else* did Becky say?

Libby What do you mean?

Danny Well, we had a pretty *weird* evening. Me and Becky.

Libby Weird? In what way weird?

Danny She didn't tell you?

Libby She didn't say it was weird. You think Becky's weird? In what way?

Danny No, no, no . . .

Libby (*interrupting*) She said that she thought you were very charming, and that you were staying with Michael, I don't know what else, and that you'd been in Kalgoorlie.

Danny Oh well, anyway. No, I liked her. Libby, there's so much I want to tell you.

Libby So, when were you in Kalgoorlie?

Danny Um, about three weeks ago.

Libby What was the exact date?

Danny It was the beginning of the week, Monday or Tuesday, I think.

Libby So it was the ninth?

Danny It may've been.

Libby Try and remember. You might be able to help me. Were you there the day John Lennon died?

Danny Yes, I was. That's right.

Libby This is incredible. I arrived on the twelfth. Where were you staying?

Danny You know the main street?

Libby Yes.

Danny Well, it was just off the main street.

Libby The Grand Hotel?

Danny No, it was a small one.

Libby Did it have a pool table?

Danny Yes.

Libby I could definitely hear the sound of pool. Do you play pool?

Danny Sometimes, but not in Kalgoorlie.

Libby Was there a telephone near the pool table?

Danny I can't remember.

Libby Do you remember a tall man, with long dark hair? Scruffy-looking. Loves pool.

Danny I'm not sure.

Libby He sometimes wears an old bush hat. Wait a minute – do that again.

Danny What?

Libby You looked away just then. Do it again.

Danny looks away.

That's it. If you were ten years older and grew your hair down to here, you'd look a lot like him . . .

Danny . . . Libby, I've got to tell you something. I've got to come clean. I wasn't, and never have been . . .

Libby (*interrupting*) You weren't what? You seem pretty nervous, Danny. What's the matter?

Danny I *am* nervous, I'm seeing you again. I can't believe it. Dear old Libby. You were wonderful with me.

Libby Was I?

Danny You know you were.

Libby In what way?

Danny All the things we used to talk about. You taught me such a lot. You must remember.

Libby Of course I remember. Tell me how you remember it.

Danny Well, it was that really hot summer.

Libby Nineteen seventy-six, I remember.

Danny I was feeling pretty lost, the house was full of arguments, then you came along.

Libby How was I wonderful?

Danny In every way.

Libby I was perfect?

Danny (*laughs*) Well, to me you were.

Libby Describe me.

Danny I'm sorry?

Libby Describe me as you remember me in the summer of '76.

Danny You haven't really changed.

Libby I haven't changed? So, I'm still perfect?

Danny Well . . . If you put it like that.

Libby In your mind, I haven't changed, in your eyes I'm perfect.

Danny Libby – are you all right?

Libby I'm fine. Why?

Danny You seem a bit distant.

Libby That's what everyone says.

Danny I thought it was me.

Libby No, it's me, I sometimes find it hard to take part, but I'm lots better. How long have you been staying with Michael?

Danny A couple of weeks.

Libby How did you meet him?

Danny In a bar.

Libby I see.

Danny No, no. I didn't have anywhere to stay, so he offered, you know?

Libby Are you working for him?

Danny I'm going to help out in his gallery on the Toorac Road. But I haven't started yet.

Libby I see. You must have seen my work, then.

Danny Yes, I have.

Libby Which pieces?

Danny It was a woman – sort of cut off from the knee and, um, across her . . .

Libby Tits?

Danny (*laughs*) Yes. I liked it.

Libby I cast it from my own body.

Danny Did you? No wonder then.

Libby Why did you like it?

Danny I thought it was lovely.

Libby It's about self-mutilation.

Danny Is it? It was just the shape . . .

Libby I ripped it out of me, like a . . . (*Pause.*) It's not communicating. What's the point? It's meant to *shock*.

Danny It does shock. It does . . . Oh, dear, look, please, you mustn't listen to me.

Libby Why not?

Danny Because I'm not really not an expert.

Libby What do you mean by expert?

Danny I meant that I know nothing, *nothing*, about modern art. So don't listen to me.

Libby What do you mean by modern art?

Danny Forget I said that. I suppose I don't really know

what I like.

Libby But you liked my piece?

Danny I did.

Libby Because you thought it was lovely.

Danny Can you imagine my surprise when Michael told me it was yours? He loves it.

Libby I know. I hate him, I hate him. No, I don't. Don't tell him I said that. I like him a lot. He's been wonderful. I don't want to talk about Michael.

Danny Fine, it's just that when I knew you in England you didn't say anything about being an artist.

Libby (*interrupting*) I didn't know what I wanted. So, what did we use to talk about?

Danny Everything. Everything.

Libby Try and be specific.

Danny Well, sex, I suppose. Mainly sex.

Libby Sex. How long was I there for?

Danny It must have been a few months.

Libby And what happened?

Danny You know what happened, Libby.

Libby I want you to tell me.

Danny Tell you what?

Libby Exactly what happened, as you remember it.

Danny I remember everything.

Libby There must be some things you remember more than others, there must be some key incidents in your memory. I'm not saying I don't remember. I just want you to tell me what *you* remember. I'd really like that.

Danny Key incidents?

Libby Or incident. The key incident as you remember it.

Danny OK, then. One night you came into my room. It was late. It was dark, but not so dark that you couldn't see. You opened the door really quietly and whispered my name. You came and sat on the edge of my bed, and told me you couldn't sleep. I said I couldn't either. You asked me why. I told you it was because I was thinking about you. You put your hand out and touched my head. Really gently. I was so nervous. You told me not to be. You told me that you loved me and that everything was going to be all right. You pulled back the sheet. 'I want to hold you,' you said, and you lay beside me. And, you know . . .

Libby What happened then?

Danny We . . . you know.

Libby You entered me.

Danny Yes.

Libby You entered my body. You see that branch? (*She points to the overhanging branch*.) That one there? Next to the one which is broken off.

Danny Yes.

Libby Can you reach it?

Danny I don't know.

Libby Would you mind trying?

Danny What for?

Libby Please. It's important.

Danny OK.

Danny tries to reach the branch and fails.

Libby Jump.

Danny jumps. He fails to reach the branch.

Nearly. Try again.

He does so. He gets a handful of leaves.

Well done. Give them to me.

Danny does so.

Thanks.

Danny sits down.

Do you think you'll remember doing that?

Danny I suppose so.

Libby I'll always remember it.

Danny That's good.

Libby And it actually happened. You really did it. Why are you here? What do you want with me?

Danny Nothing. I just wanted to see you again.

Libby You expect me to believe that you track down a woman you think is perfect, and that it hadn't occurred to you that you might get to have sex with her? If you want to have sex with me, just say so, and I'll give you a straight answer. Who else have you told that story to?

Danny No one. Libby, it's not a story.

Libby Have you told Michael?

Danny No, really.

Libby Well? (*Pause.*) Do you?

47

Danny (*looking around*) What, *here*?

Libby Don't be silly. Danny?

Danny Yes?

Libby Listen, why don't you come over to my place and I'll make you supper? What do you say?

Danny Will Becky be there?

Libby Of course not, she'll be away. I'd really like you to, Danny. So what do you say? How about Wednesday the week after next?

Danny Fine. Thanks.

Libby Great.

> *She stands up and having folded up the plastic sheet, she leans forward and kisses him with surprising passion – breaking away suddenly.*

Tell Michael the new piece is very nearly finished. Very, very nearly. I'll be delivering very, very soon and it's really, really exciting.

Danny I'll tell him.

Libby The day after tomorrow then. My place. Just you and me, Danny. It's so good to see you again. See you later, alligator. (*She turns to leave.*)

Danny In a while, crocodile.

Act Two

SCENE ONE

Becky's and Libby's place. Danny is at the door.

Becky Danny! I want to hear you say, 'I am not a vegetarian.'

Danny I am not a vegetarian.

Becky I am so pleased to hear you say that. I've got you a lovely side of beef.

Danny Where's Libby?

Becky She's just popped out, she'll be back in a tick. Make yourself at home, you know your way round. Open the wine and help yourself. Oh, and happy '81, Danny. May all your dreams come true.

Becky leaves for a position upstage. With one hand she makes cooking noises while changing into a flimsy black outfit. Meanwhile Danny opens the bottle of wine and pours himself a glass, which he smells first, then drinks.

(*Calling through*) It's a bummer, Danny. I have completely fucked up the timing. It's going to be *quite* a wait.

Danny Don't worry. Where did you say Libby was?

Becky I'm not sure. Look on the table, can you see a carving knife?

Danny Yes.

Becky Sharpen it for me, will you?

Danny looks for the knife, finds it. Next to it is a steel.

Danny OK.

Becky You know what she's like, always going walkabout. Sometimes she's such a difficult person to love, don't you find that?

Danny picks up the knife and the steel and begins to sharpen the knife, but stops as Becky speaks. Becky continues to change her clothes.

'I've invited Danny to dinner,' she announces, so guess who ends up doing the fucking cooking? I've really fucked up here. I've been like this ever since Libby got back. Can you blame me? Out the blue she just walks out the door, saying she's going to Kalgoorlie, just because that *man* calls up, and when she's in Kalgoorlie she doesn't once think of calling *me*, and then, to top it all, when she gets back, she rips the phone out and we have a *total ban* on phones in the place. I mean it's my place, Danny. It makes me sick, the way some women give it all away for men. They're all just running around looking for a daddy to believe in. Except it never is daddy, it's just one more side of beef after another. 'Because I love him', well I say fuck that. The last time a man said to me 'I love you', do you know what I said to him, Danny? I said, 'Fuck off with your *cage*.' Of course the tragedy with me and Libby is that we can't have children together. That's our great sadness. Do you want children, Danny?

Danny What?

Becky What I'm asking you is, do you want to be a father?

Danny I haven't given it much thought.

Becky Well, maybe you should. It's a pretty big subject, don't you think?

Pause. Danny sharpens the knife. Becky returns. She is

carrying a glass bowl of cherries. Danny doesn't see her until she speaks.

So, what do you think of this little number?

Danny stops sharpening the knife.

Danny I thought you were cooking.

Becky I like doing two things at the same time, it can make life more interesting. Well? (*She slowly twirls around.*) What do you think?

Pause. Danny is staring at her.

Danny Um . . . I really like it.

Becky Do you? It's Libby's. She hates it when I wear her clothes. But, fuck her, eh? God, she can be selfish. So, you thought I was in the kitchen cooking you a side of beef? Because Libby told me to. Well, just maybe I wasn't. Maybe I was in the kitchen putting your precious side of beef straight in the rubbish bin. Maybe I'm on strike. (*She eats a cherry and wiggles suggestively.*) What do you think of that?

Pause. Danny is lost for words.

Only kidding. I like to get a reaction – it goes way back.

She joins him at the table.

Danny Does it. Ha! Ha!

Becky I hate sarcasm. Smells delish, don't you think?

Danny (*sniffs*) I can't smell anything.

Becky Can't you? I can. I can smell you. You smell lovely. What is it?

Danny I don't know.

Becky Don't you? That's a bit strange. God, this outfit

makes me feel so attractive. Do you want a cherry? Go on, it'll keep the wolf from the door while you wait for the beef. I hate meat. I only eat it when I'm really, really hungry. I'd like to give it up altogether. Do you reckon that knife's sharp by now?

Danny has been holding it in his lap.

Danny Yes.

Danny puts the knife on the table. Becky gives him a cherry, which he eats. Becky picks up the knife and tests the blade with her finger.

Be careful.

Becky Oh, Danny, I didn't know you cared. (*She puts the knife down.*) Do you feel attractive?

Danny I feel fine. I'd feel even better if Libby was here.

Becky Don't keep on about it. It's not *my* fault. I think you look lovely. Is that a new shirt?

Danny Yes, it is as a matter of fact.

Becky Aaah! You bought it specially to impress Libby. How sweet. Pity she isn't here to be impressed, but don't worry, she'll be back really, really soon. Do you like the wine?

Danny It's very nice, thank you. Lovely.

Becky It's a native. From Mildura.

Danny Aaah! I mean, oh, is it?

Becky So, you've been to *Mildura* as well as Kalgoorlie, you've been *everywhere*, Danny.

Danny Yes, I worked the grapes. I had a terrible time. I was stuck in cabin with a bunch of no-hopers from the city. I used to head up-river to a place called Gol Gol. I'd sit beneath the river gums and found peace and inspiration from the width of the sky, the green of the leaves, the branches of the trees – distorted liked twisted human limbs – but in the centre of it all the river, the great and beautiful Murray river, flowing, flowing, like life itself.

Becky You can be so poetic, Danny.

Danny I'm also a bit of a philosopher. I've been studying Nietzsche's (*'Nee-chee's'*) theory of Eternal Return, whereby he suggests that it's our destiny to be forever returned to those moments in our lives which have most marked us. Or, to put it another way, they return to us, for Nietzsche it's the same thing. So, our future is in our past, in the mass of constantly returning moments. It's a pretty disturbing concept, isn't it, Becky?

Becky Nietzsche (*'Nee-chee'*)? Don't you mean Nietzsche (*'Nee-cha'*)?

Danny Nietzsche (*'Nee-cha'*), Nietzsche (*'Nee-chee'*), same thing.

Becky Oh, Danny, you're such a sweetie-pie. I think you'll find it's Nietzsche (*'Nee-cha'*), but I think you're lovely all the same. Nietzsche was a woman-hater. Did you know that?

Danny No.

Becky Which reminds me. Libby mustn't know about the other night.

Danny What about it?

Becky Danny, I thought you'd never ask. I really enjoyed it. I mean *really* enjoyed it.

Danny You did?

Becky I thought it was wonderful. You were wonderful

and I haven't been with a man for quite a while I can tell you. So, when I say it was wonderful you can take it as read.

Danny Wonderful?

Becky Don't put yourself down. Just bask in the compliment.

Danny Why?

Becky You really opened me up, Danny, and I've been pretty fucking closed for quite a while.

Danny Opened you up, but all we did was . . .

Becky (*interrupting*) Don't spoil it, Danny, and promise me not to breathe a word to Libby. She can get ever so, ever so, jealous, you know. Do you want a smoke?

Danny No, thanks.

Becky Suit yourself.

She lights a joint and sucks on a cherry. Danny is staring at her. She blows smoke in his face. Pause.

Danny Becky, you're quite something.

Becky I could eat you . . .

Danny Please don't . . .

Becky (*offering him the joint again*) Oh, go on, have a smoke. It'll help push the time along while you're waiting for Libby and your side of beef.

Danny All right, then.

He takes the joint. Becky watches him smoke a couple of drags, then she stands up while Danny continues to smoke. She hesitates by the cassette-player. She puts a John Lennon compilation on. Volume up.

No, no, no, no. No. Right, that's it. I'm off.

He stands up. Becky has already picked up the knife. She stands in front of the door, blocking his way, the knife outstretched in her hand.

Becky Oh, no, you're not, Danny, you're not going anywhere.

Pause.

Danny Becky, listen to me. Now listen. Why don't you put the knife down? Give me the knife.

Becky Leaving are you, Danny-boy?

Danny Becky, listen to me. I'm not leaving.

He moves slowly towards her, one step at a time. Becky stares at him dispassionately.

I think you're lovely, Becky. I think you're really attractive. Just now, I could hardly keep my hands off you. I mean when you were standing there looking so dead sexy in that outfit – and then when you ate that cherry like that. Now, how about giving me the knife? That's it.

His hand is very close to the knife, inching closer. As he is about to touch it, Becky flinches – flicking the knife at him dangerously. Danny recoils.

Ooow!

Becky So you want the knife? Here you go. I'm sorry, Danny.

Pause. Danny looks at her for a moment. He approaches her again – very cautiously.

Danny Thanks.

He reaches out for the knife. Becky slashes out with it, cutting his ear. Danny screams.

Aaaah! Look what you've done. My ear. Look. It's bleeding. I'm bleeding. My *ear* is *bleeding*.

Becky I thought you said you were an artist, well now you look just like Vincent van Gogh. It suits you, Danny-boy. How dare you humiliate me? How dare you?

Danny (*interrupting*) Right.

He lunges at her. There is a terrible struggle. He grabs hold of the hand she's holding the knife with. They seem dangerously out of control as he forces her to the ground. Danny slowly releases his grip on her wrists. As he does so she remains immobile – the knife still gripped in her hand. Danny slowly stands up, watching her all the time. She doesn't move, simply staring ahead of her. Danny takes a couple of steps away from her.

Are you all right? (*Pause.*) Um, I'll be off then . . . (*He leaves.*)

SCENE TWO

Michael's place. Danny enters. Michael and Libby are sitting together on a rug, having finished a meal. Becky remains outstretched on the stage with the knife. Michael and Libby are smoking a joint. Michael is wearing a long wig and flowery waistcoat. Libby is wearing exactly the same type of black dress that Becky was wearing in the previous scene, with necklaces of beads. John Lennon/ Beatles tracks are playing quietly on the sound system. Danny is dumbstruck.

Michael Danny. *Man!*

Danny Libby?

Libby Danny.

Michael Leave this to me, darl. I'll explain. No sooner had I dropped you off at Libby's pad – who should I see but Libby.

Danny My ear is bleeding.

Michael What happened, mate, did you fall off the tram?

Michael and Libby convulse with laughter.

Danny (*to Libby*) Where were you? We had an arrangement. (*To Michael*) What happened to your hair?

Michael We'll come to that. So, there she was, and you know what I did? I brought her back here and cooked her coq au vin and talked about where her new piece is coming from. Then, on the spur of the moment – and it was a fab moment, Danny – I had this brainwave, man, I said, 'Why don't we have a little sixties revival?' Libby really dug it, but I've got you to thank, Danny, because you put me in mind of it, what with your birthday coming up. So, we've got you to thank for this evening, because we were your age in 1967, mate. I really like that. We're all eighteen years old together, aren't we, Libby?

Libby We are.

Michael Right here and now, Danny – it's 1967, we're eighteen, and we have you to thank . . . But, in the process of *returning*, we've got ourselves very, very stoned. Haven't we, Libs?

Libby We have.

Michael And also in the process, you know what happened, Danny? Libby forgot all about her arrangement with little old you, you know what with digging out all the old John Lennon LPs, there was a lot to remember, and you, Danny, just disappeared, man. I mean, there you go. Never mind, eh?

Danny (*to Libby*) Libby, is this the truth?

Libby I'm sorry, Danny. We can have another arrangement another time.

Michael 'Truth', what do you mean by 'truth', Danny? Danny, man, *mellow out*. I see a shadow, Danny. I see a shadow over your head.

He stands up and goes up close to Danny.

It's the shadow of my youth, Danny-boy. It's the shadow of my youth. And, I can hear music. I can hear the voice of Johnny-baby Lennon, he's singing to us all, the poet of my youth, and Libby's too – and you know what, Danny? I pity you – because me, Libby and John, we've already been everywhere you could ever possibly want to go. Some joker might have killed him, but no one's ever going to bury him see? It's a fucking long shadow, mate. (*He sits down again.*) Can you see it, Libs?

Libby I think so. Yes. I can. I can see it.

Danny Libby? I don't understand. You were meant to meet me, but you met Michael instead and you forgot about me.

Libby That's right.

Danny I see. So, what else have you been doing, Michael? Apart from getting stoned and making a fool of yourself? Telling Libby here to pull her index finger out.

Pause. Michael takes the wig off.

Michael Have you been using my Eau Sauvage?

Danny Yes.

Michael Well, don't you think you could have asked first? Do you know how much that set me back?

Danny No, I have no idea.

Michael I'll tell you. A lot of dough.

Danny Really, well I'm sure you can afford it, Michael. I just thought Libby might like it. Besides, you told me that there's only one rule in this house. You know, rule number one. 'I never want to have to discuss matter again.'

Libby What's the matter?

Michael She does like it, don't you, Libs?

Libby Not really.

Michael Don't you, darl?

Danny But instead of spending the evening with Libby, as arranged, I ended up spending the evening with Becky. (*To Libby*) Have you got two dresses like that?

Libby How do you know that, Danny?

Danny A little birdy told me. So, to pass the time, while I was waiting for Libby here to turn up, I told Becky all about my painting expedition to Gol Gol, Michael. You know, Gol Gol, grapes, no-hopers, width of sky, life itself.

Michael Steady on, matey.

Libby I didn't know you were a painter, Danny.

Danny I'm not, I worked the grapes. Then Becky pulled a knife on me and cut my ear.

Michael Wait a minute. I think I've heard this story before. Don't tell me, then you savaged her and hacked her to pieces.

Libby What do you mean, 'hacked her to pieces'? Danny, what happened?

Michael Don't worry, darl, she's fine. Old Danny-boy

here's got a very vivid imagination – specially when it comes to his *sexual* activities.

Libby Actually, you have a bit, Danny. You've got to admit it.

Michael Oh, so you've noticed it too, have you, Libby?

Danny I'm going. I'm leaving. I'm going. Now. Right now.

Michael (*laughs*) Oh, you're going are you? And where exactly are you going *to*, matey? I'll tell you. Nowhere. Because you've got nowhere to go.

Libby Don't go, Danny.

Danny leaves the room and quickly grabs his sleeping-bag, rucksack and guitar. When he comes back, Michael is blocking his way.

Michael What are you doing, Danny?

Danny I told you. I'm going.

Michael Doesn't look like you're going. Looks like you're standing in my front room confronted by me. So, where does that leave you? I reckon it leaves you going to bed and waking up in the morning, matey. I can't let you go, Danny. I can't let you just walk out on to the street, in the middle of the night. I wouldn't be able to live with myself, mate. I mean it's pretty fucking dangerous out there, you never know who you might run into. So, off you go to bed. You're not thinking straight, old chap. Put your things back and go to bed.

Libby Michael's right, Danny.

Danny puts his guitar down.

Michael That's it.

Danny rushes for the door, trying to pass Michael.

Suddenly Michael has him on the floor. Danny struggles, but Michael is much too strong.

Danny (*shouting*) Let me go. Let me go.

Libby Don't hurt him, Michael.

Michael ties Danny's hands to the back of his rucksack, which is heavy enough to immobilize him. Then binds his legs, leaving him face down.

Michael Now, Danny-boy. I'm going to bed, me old mate. So, I'll see you in the morning. Libby, I'm sorry the evening had to turn out this way, but there you go. Would you like me to drive you home, darl?

Libby No, thanks, Michael. I'll get a taxi.

Michael Let me give you the money, presh. Here. (*He gives her the money.*)

Libby Thanks, Michael.

Michael and Libby kiss.

I'll sit with Danny for a bit.

Michael Suit yourself, darl, but if you ask me, I reckon we should just leave him there to chill out on his own.

Libby No, I'd like to. I'll let myself out.

Michael As I say. Suit yourself. Come here.

Michael and Libby kiss again.

I can't wait for the new piece, darls.

Libby It'll be finished next week. I promise.

Michael Not before fucking time, possum. I mean, if you ask me, it's high time you pulled your index finger out.

Libby I know.

Michael See ya. (*He bends over and looks at Danny.*) Goodnight, Danny, I'll see you in the morning, mate.

Michael moves upstage. Pause. Libby finds some cottonwool and a glass of water.

Libby Now, let's have a look at that ear. What did you say happened?

Danny I'm not sure. I don't think Becky is fine.

Libby If you're fine she'll be fine. Believe me. Come here.

She washes and bandages his ear. She stretches the bandage around his head. He sits in silence while she does so.

I'm going to untie you now, Danny. And then you're going to go to bed, all right?

Danny All right.

She does so. Danny is free to go. He just sits on the floor.

Libby Come on.

She leads him upstage to a bed. She helps him undress. She is kneeling before him, removing his jeans, while he takes off his shirt. For a moment she holds him close to her. Danny responds sexually. Libby stands up, facing him.

Now, go and clean your teeth, Danny.

Danny does so. As he cleans his teeth, Libby sits on the edge of the bed, lost in thought. Danny gets into bed.

Danny Libby?

Libby Danny?

Danny Why are you so sad?

Libby Go to sleep, Danny.

Danny Tell me.

Libby I'd like to . . . but, it's a long story.

Danny So?

Libby And, it hasn't ended.

Libby kisses Danny. As she does so, Becky, who is now standing by the table, blows a candle out. Becky and Libby move away from Danny and stand together, gently rocking with eyes closed – as if asleep. Having watched them go, Danny closes his eyes. After a few moments Michael enters. He picks up Danny's scattered belongings and puts them neatly away. He turns the music off. He blows a candle out and picks up a plate of food. He stands next to the sleeping Danny for a few moments.

Michael Danny? (*Pause.*) Are you asleep, mate?

Danny Yes.

Michael tentatively sits on the edge of the bed.

Michael You know what?

Danny What?

Michael You look just like Kirk Douglas as Vincent van Gogh. Should go down a treat tomorrow at work, eh?

Danny (*smiles*) Work?

Michael That's the first time I've seen you smile all night, mate. It suits you, Danny . . . Have you eaten?

Danny Yes, thanks, I had a cherry earlier on.

Michael Here, I've brought you some Sao bickies, Coonawarra Camembert and some grapes. Yum yum.

Danny sits up and starts to eat.

Do you know why I didn't let you go?

Danny No.

Michael (*unsentimentally*) Because I've got a funny way of showing it, but I really like you, mate. I think you're a special bastard, and when I meet special bastards, I look after them.

Danny Thanks, Michael.

Pause.

Michael There's something I want to say to you, Danny. I want you to feel free to use my Eau Sauvage whenever you want. I want you to help yourself.

Danny Thanks, but I don't think it really suits me.

Michael Fair enough. Anyway, that wasn't what I really wanted to tell you. I know I talk a lot, but mostly it's bluster and I don't always mean what I say, because I'm a bit of lying bastard, mate, to tell the truth. But, there you go, and I'm not saying I like myself for it, Danny. But, I reckon you can see through me, just like I can see through you, in a way. And you know what?

Danny What?

Michael I like what I see.

Danny Do you?

Michael I do, and I like having you here, mate. I know you won't be here for ever, you won't even be here for very long, but while you are here I feel a bit special as well. That's all I want to say.

Silence. Very gently, Michael touches Danny's head. Danny moves his head with the caress. Michael falls asleep beside him, head to foot.

THE PRESENT

SCENE THREE

Dawn. Danny gets up quietly and gets dressed, leaving Michael sleeping. Becky and Libby are standing separately with eyes closed. Danny picks up the portfolio and faces the audience. His ear is still bandaged.

Danny (*monologue*) Good evening. My name is Luke Murray. I'm an artist from England. I'm in Australia on a scholarship from the Royal College of Art in London. I've spent the last few months exploring your Outback and attempting to convey its mysteries in my landscapes. I was wondering whether you might be able to spare me a few minutes to show you my work. (*He moves forward and spreads the paintings out on the floor.*) This one? I had a feeling you'd like that one. It's a ghost town called Kookynie in WA. It's my favourite too. There's a bit of story behind it, actually. I was in Kalgoorlie, low on cash and inspiration. I used to play pool at a run-down hotel in Hay Street. There was a man there that I'll never forget. He played pool all day, he had long hair, he was scruffy-looking and wore an old bush hat. I never caught his name. There was something about him. I don't know, he didn't say a lot, but he seemed to be carrying this great sadness inside him. We shot pool for an afternoon, and again the following day – but we still hadn't exchanged a word. Suddenly, he broke off from the game and made a phone call. I heard him say, 'Libby. It's me. Don't hang up, Libby. I'm in Kalgoorlie, I can't live without you . . .' Down went the phone. He phoned again, but the line was dead. He slumped down in the corner and beckoned to me. I sat down on the floor with him and he told me the story. It's an old, old story, but he told it with such feeling that he made it new. He told me about this woman back in Melbourne. How she'd loved him to the point of madness and how he'd treated her badly. You know, the whole lot:

65

violence, lies, other women, and something about a lost child. But, however badly he treated her, she kept returning. It went on for years, until one day, she woke up and realized that he was killing her. So she left him. It was only then, he told me, when she wasn't there any more, that he was really able to *see* her. But it was too late, because she'd gone and he'd lost her. He liked me. He asked me to go north with him. He reckoned we'd find gold in the old fields. I went with him some of the way, but I stopped here, in Kookynie. If you look carefully you can see his footprints in the red earth as he left me, without a wave, on foot, in boots which were full of holes. Off he trudged into the desert. Just like some prospector of old. Maybe he thought that he'd win her back with his crock of gold. He's probably still out there. But my journey stopped here, in Kookynie, with the old broken-down Holden. Later, I looked up the woman in Melbourne and, I think, understood his love. She'd moved on, of course, in the way people do. But, maybe somewhere she still loved the lonely stranger in a bush hat. I don't know, but I thought I recognized his sadness in her eyes. Anyway, that's the story. It's a painting about lost love and the end of a journey . . . What? Well, I'm sure you'll agree that given the fact that it's so important to me, I'm sure you'll understand that I can't really ask for less than . . . one hundred and twenty dollars . . .

Michael and Libby lay the table behind him. Becky stands up.

One hundred . . . ? Let's call it ninety-five – it means a lot to me, you're killing me here . . . OK, ninety . . . eighty-five, I can't go a cent lower . . . For you, madam, yes. Eighty. Eighty bucks. We have a deal . . . (*With a seductive smile.*) Thank you. (*He removes the bandage.*)

SCENE FOUR

*Michael's place. On the table a cake with nineteen
candles, which Libby is lighting. As Michael starts to
speak he pops a bottle of champagne. Becky gives Danny
the knife.*

Michael Happy birthday, Danny me old mate, or should I
say, 'Many Happy Returns.' I've got a present for you to
unwrap.

> *Danny moves over to the table, blows out the candles,
> cuts the cake, then sits down. Becky is sitting next to
> Libby. Michael is at the head of the table.*

Danny You didn't have to.

Michael I know. But I did. But you can't have it, do you
know why, Danny?

Danny You tell me why, Michael.

Michael I will. Because, before you can see what I've got
for you, Libby's going to show me what she's got for me.
So, on your birthday, I get a present as well. I like that. So?
What d'you say, Libs?

Libby All right. (*She goes to a covered sculpture. She is
about to uncover it. Pause.*) I can't.

Becky Go on, Libby.

Michael Go for it, Libby. We're going to love it, and you
know why? Because it's come straight out of you, darl.

Becky Michael?

Michael Becky?

Becky Can you do me a really big favour?

Michael That all depends, sweetheart.

Becky Can you shut your horrible big fat jumped-up mouth? Just for two seconds. I'd really appreciate that.

Michael Becky? You're right. You're dead right, girl. Please excuse me. Put it down to nerves. Over to you, Libs presh. My lips are sealed.

Libby OK. I hope you like it. (*She takes the cover off. Pause.*) It's called *Disconnected Telephone with Leaves.*

Libby returns to the table and sits down. Pause. Michael is staring at Libby's piece.

Michael (*puzzled*) I'm lost for words, darl. (*Long pause – then he is suddenly delighted.*) It's a fucking winner, girl.

Becky (*whispering*) It's your way of saying sorry, isn't it?

Libby nods and smiles.

I love you.

Becky and Libby kiss.

Michael I love you too, kid, and the words are coming . . . I can feel them coming . . . It's the past and it's the future, and you've said it with economy and you've said it with wit.

Libby Thanks, Michael.

Danny Thank *you*. So, Danny?

Danny Yes.

Michael It's your turn, mate. Here.

He gives him a boomerang wrapped tightly in psychedelic paper.

You've got three guesses.

Danny A boomerang.

Michael No.

Danny It must be.

Michael Guess number two?

Danny It's a boomerang.

Michael You're on to your third guess, matey.

Danny It must be a boomerang.

Michael I reckon you'd better open it, Danny-boy.

Danny opens the present.

Danny It is a boomerang . . . Isn't it?

Michael Not quite. (*He takes it back and examines it above his head.*) It's a *returning* boomerang. It's an original, mate, found in 1962 in the Western Australian desert. The year of your birth. Probably been sitting there for hundreds of years. Quite something, eh?

Danny Are you sure, Michael?

Michael No.

He gives it back to Danny.

I want you to have it, mate. I'm delighted that you clearly appreciate it.

Becky (*cuddling up to Libby*) I haven't got you a present I'm afraid, Danny. Does that mean I don't get any cake?

Michael Of course you do, Becks, me old darl. And I'll tell you what, baby, just so's the boomerang doesn't get lonely, I'm going to throw in another present for Danny, and he can pretend it's from you. Just so you don't feel bad. Here you go, your very own copy of Nietzsche's (*'Nee-chee's'*) *Zarathustra*.

Becky Don't you mean Nietzsche (*'Nee-cha'*)?

Michael No, Becky, I don't. I mean Nietzsche. You prefer the English pronunciation, I opt for the American. Where do you come from?

Becky North Melbourne, actually.

Michael I'm from Blacktown in Sydney. Not much of a place. My dad installed fibreglass swimming pools and my mum was from Italy. Now, I'm not saying you have to like me, you might even hate my jumped-up guts, but you and me, Becky, we're both Australians, and I reckon we should say the old bugger's name exactly the way we want to, don't you?

Becky Michael. You're right. I'm sorry.

Michael Don't mention it. I want to add one thing, Becky darl, you're looking absolutely fucking *divine*, this evening. Put some music on, Danny, I'm going to give old Becks here a squeeze or two, even if she does think I'm a bit of a rough-necked bastard.

Becky Michael? You know what?

Michael You tell me, Becks.

Becky You're fucked up.

Michael Well, I'm absolutely delighted to hear that we have so much in common, darl.

Becky smiles.

Now that's what I call a gorgeous fucking smile.

Danny has put on a John Lennon song.

I love it, Libby. It's going to be really big. Well worth the wait. Now I'm going to steal Becks from you for a few mins, if you don't mind. Come on, Becks.

He leads Becky by the hand and they start to dance,

which they continue to do as Libby and Danny speak.
Danny is still holding the boomerang.

Libby Danny?

Danny Yes?

Libby I want you to tell me what you think.

Danny Do you?

Libby Of course I do.

Danny I think it's lovely.

Libby I'm so pleased. I couldn't have done it without you
. . . Danny? I want you to come away with me.

Danny Where to?

Libby Kalgoorlie.

Danny I've already been there.

Libby You liked it, didn't you? Will you come with me?
You can show me Koo – ?

Danny Kookynie.

Libby Kookynie. You made it sound so wonderful.

Danny Libby. I haven't been there – I've never been to
Kalgoorlie or Kookynie. I'm a liar. I'm a lying bastard. (*He
is suddenly very upset.*)

Libby Come here.

She kisses him.

It doesn't matter. Look at those two.

*They look at Michael and Becky, dancing closely with
eyes closed.*

I really want you to come with me.

Danny When?

Libby Tomorrow. I've got the tickets. Please, Danny. Don't say no. Please come with me. We can have long talks, like we used to in the summer of '76.

Danny What happens if you find him, Libby?

Libby I don't want to find him . . . (*She smiles.*) But I have to keep looking. Please don't make me go alone. You never know, we might strike gold. Please say yes. Come with me.

Danny OK.

> *Danny puts down the boomerang and picks up his guitar. Meanwhile Libby digs some red sand out of a bucket and puts it on the floor. She gestures for Danny to stand on the sand. Becky and Michael leave. The music fades. Danny starts to play the guitar and sing the Beatles' 'A day in the life'. As he sings Libby makes a perfect circle of sand around him. When she has finished she takes the boomerang and sticks it into the sand in front of Danny. She sits down in the circle with him. Danny stops singing and puts the guitar down.*

SCENE FIVE

The Western Australian desert, near Kookynie. Libby and Danny make love, then lie still as the red light of dusk fades.

Libby There's no wind. Let's light a candle. (*She sticks a candle in the sand, next to the boomerang. She lights the candle. Silence.*) Listen . . . Did you hear that?

Danny I can't hear anything.

Libby There's someone out there.

They both listen. Libby facing one direction, Danny another. Pause. Libby turns to Danny. She reaches out her hand and touches his head. He closes his eyes. She gently leans him back, until he is lying on his back in the sand and kisses him. Pause.

Everything's going to be all right.

Danny I know.

Libby gets up slowly. She stands. She looks in the direction that she thought she heard something. She walks off into the darkness. Pause. Danny remains lying on his back.

(*monologue*) My name is Danny Rule. I'm lying in a dry river bed, north of Kookynie in Western Australia. It's exactly as I imagined it. The sun has disappeared beyond the ghost gums, and I am perfectly alone. But, as Luke Murray used to say, 'This is no place for a white man.' I think he might be right. Tomorrow, I'm heading north – up to the old gold fields. What else? I'm nineteen years old . . . and I'm getting cold.

He leans over and blows the candle out.

APART FROM GEORGE

For
Gee

CHARACTERS

Pam Sutton Mid-thirties.

Linda Sutton Fifteen.

George Sutton Early forties.

Arthur Loveless Mid-sixties.

John Grey Late fifties/early sixties.

SETTING

The Fens of East Anglia.

TIME

The present day.

DESIGN

The play should be performed with the minimum of props,
furniture and settings to allow for smooth transitions
between the scenes and locations. Lighting should be used
to locate and define the different scenes.

SOUND/MUSIC

In the original production the music/sound score, composed and performed by Richard Heacock, was highly integrated into the overall texture of the play. It is impossible to notate exactly the effects achieved so I have indicated in simple terms how the action might be enhanced by the use of sound and music. It will depend on the individual director and composer how this aspect of the production is developed.

ACCENTS

All the characters, apart from John Grey and Arthur Loveless, should speak with East Anglian accents although the script is not written in dialect.

Apart from George was first staged in four private performances on 19 and 20 March 1987 at the National Theatre Studio, with the following cast:

George Sutton Matthew Scurfield
Pam Sutton Amelda Brown
Linda Sutton Katrin Cartlidge
John Grey Michael Turner
Arthur Loveless Michael Turner

Directed by Nick Ward
Music Richard Heacock
Designed by Fred Pilbrow

The play subsequently opened at the Traverse Theatre for the Edinburgh Festival 1987 prior to a national tour and production at the Royal Court Theatre Upstairs in November 1987 with the same cast.

Act One

The sound of the wind. As the lights fade up **Pam, Linda, George** *and* **Arthur** *enter slowly. They take up positions in isolation from each other. A distant melody – which will be developed into the theme of 'A Moment's Time', the song Linda sings – is heard. Arthur moves to an extreme upstage position – standing still. The Sutton family move together slowly – they stand posed as if for a photograph. Pam smiling, Linda looking away, George positioned behind Linda, looking to camera.*

Pam *(moving downstage)*
A moment's time, a moment's space
Shall waft you to the 'eavenly grace
Or shut you up in Hell . . .

> *Linda begins to intone the same very quietly.*

My Gran said that to me mum and her brothers and sisters, and her grandmother – me gran's that is – said it to all her children – boys and girls. I don't believe in that stuff no more, but it were frightening, well, it is really . . . Still I told it Linda when she were little, all the same . . .

Linda *(louder)*
A moment's time, a moment's space
Shall waft you to that 'eavenly grace
Or shut you up in Hell.

> *Linda moves downstage, away from George. Faster, half singing.*

A moment's time, a moment's space
Shall waft you to that 'eavenly grace

Or shut you up in Hell.

Pam It's not right what he's done . . .

Linda (*moving agitatedly*)
A moment's time, a moment's space
Will shut you in that 'eavenly place
A moment's time, a moment's space
Will shut you up in Hell.

Pam It's not right what he's done . . .

    George sinks to the floor.

Linda
A moment's time will shut you up.
A moment's space will shut you up . . .

I used to believe in him but he never once gave me nothing
what I wanted . . . Nor changed nothing . . . So I
stopped . . .

Pam It's not right what he's done, what he does . . . (*Pam exits.*)

Linda You're meant to love your dad – but I don't – don't
want to be shut up any place . . .

    Linda exits, leaving George lying on stage.

SCENE TWO

*Arthur Loveless, who has been standing still in an extreme
upstage position, turns slowly to the audience. George
remains outstretched before him. Sound/music (optional) –
a distant melody – possibly a Bach fugue combined with
the sound of the wind.*

Arthur (*to audience*) My name is Arthur Loveless.
Ordained. Ordained many years ago . . . and you know,

I'm a pretty useless fellow . . . yes, when it matters, when anything really matters, I'm a pretty useless fellow. Didn't used to be. Am now. Certainly in the face of this. (*Indicates outstretched body of George.*) What is this? I will try to explain to you what this represents. But I must confess that in the face of it I'm no good, no good at all . . . Welcome to the Fens . . . We used to talk of our little flock . . . My flock is now so small it's hardly a flock at all . . . I am an educated man, you know, but nobody listens to me. Why should they? But there was a time when I commanded a little respect amongst these people and their ways. Not any more. I'm a lonely man. A very lonely man . . . Let's talk congregations. Not so many years ago this fine old church could command a congregation worthy of the name . . . Not all the pews would be occupied, except on special days of course, but there would be a gathering of some thirty souls . . . They were my flock. Where have they gone? Where has my flock gone? I've done my bit. Thirty years, but I've lost my flock . . . I've lost my sheep . . . Are you not surprised that I am a little, shall we say, bitter? Yes, bitter. I'm a lonely man. People are different now . . . Need, true need, suffering. (*Indicates George again.*) This represents these things. A lonely land. There is loneliness on this landscape. In my old age, I am given to metaphysical meditations, you must forgive me. But the reality (*indicates George*), ah, that is far more difficult to comprehend. Real need. True need. Need blows like screams in the wind across this landscape. Who hears the screams? Silent screams on a landscape of loneliness. I hear them, but I cannot reply. No more. Christ on the cross – he screamed, silently – 'Why hast thou forsaken me' . . . His hour of need . . . His supreme utterance – true need – and what was the reply? Silence . . . A man, George Sutton, unknown to Church, is found by me, in position prostrate upon my aisle . . . There he lay – I see him still – his image is etched upon my brain. A long-forgotten need, which once I could have answered. But now, I could see only the man, legs, arms, body, hair, eyes – outstretched upon my aisle . . . Rather than address the need I saw only the man . . . Before he went I begged him to return.

Arthur exits. Pause. George gets up and walks downstage to 'domestic' area.

SCENE THREE

Pam and Linda enter. They both carry chairs. Pam places a chair behind George.

Pam (*to audience*) It hurts his pride, me being the bread winner, hurts it something mean.

George sits.

It's not that I'm working so much, as who I'm working for. Unless you're going to move away, Mr Grey is the only man around here with any jobs at all. Always been the case . . . He owns the land.

Linda (*to audience*) I hate it here. Hate everything about it . . . I want to go away, somewhere else . . . Soon as I can, I'll be off, where he can't find me . . . You're meant to love your dad, but I don't, why should I . . . ? Look at him slumped there. He'll look at anything on that old TV, anything at all . . . I hate him.

Pam (*to audience*) We only got Linda – that sets us apart from other folks. Me mum had ten. But then me and George weren't meant to have any at all, really. Me mum told me that – on account of something not known about who George's dad were. Probably nothing. I think me mum knew what was what, but she never said nothing. George never knew nothing, nor no one else. We don't talk about such things. Best not to. Linda's all right though.

Linda (*to audience*) They hate each other an' all, but they're not meant to, so they hide it, but not from me they can't . . . They could never hide nothing from me. I can see it. I got ears an' all. Things they said. Things they done. I don't forget things see, like they do . . . There's things he done I won't forget, to her and me – her mostly – but she likes to forget, but I don't forget. Not never. One day I'm going away. I shan't be coming back.

She sits on the floor near George.

Pam (*to audience*) Course I've always worked for John Grey . . . Seasonal . . . Always . . . Well, you have to, to make ends meet. 'Tatoes mostly, and carrots . . . But it's different now that I'm charring – never thought I would – not in John Grey's house, nor nobody's. But there you are – he gave it me, the very next day after he laid George off . . . See, I blew me top at him – nothing would have stopped me – not when George come home and told me what happened – not John Grey nor nobody. Wouldn't care who they was. Nobody would have stopped me. I was angry, and I don't care what the reason was – 'cause it were wrong to lay off a man if he's worked for you all his life. Good work and all, and if he needs the work, and there's no other work to be had . . . That's got to be wrong whatever way of looking. Anyway, I told him he couldn't do it. What was George to do? I says to him. He says to me that he had to do, 'cause times was hard for him and all. Hard to believe when you look inside that house I got to clean. Makes you wonder what he wants. Times were hard for him, now the subsidies was gone, he said . . . Didn't cool me down none though, I can tell you – so he offered me this job. I felt bought. But I'd have been a fool to have said no. George won't ever like it. No, never. But where'd he be without it? He says he'd rather starve – but I was only doing good by George – telling John Grey he couldn't do such a thing – when George should have spoke up for himself rather than taking all folks tell him with his mouth shut – when he's not at home or down the pub . . . Anyway John Grey's all right . . .

George leaves domestic area and takes up position upstage.

. . . although I'd never thought to hear myself say it.

SCENE FOUR

During this scene Pam and Linda remain in domestic area. John and George can move anywhere on stage except the domestic area. The sound of the wind.

John George.

George Yup, Mr Grey.

John Terrible chill. East wind.

George It's cold.

John Can I walk with you, George?

George Course you can.

John Which way are you heading?

George Just knocking off, so I'm off home.

John Bit early to knock off, isn't it?

George Gone four-thirty, Mr Grey. Always knock off at four-thirty. Always have done . . .

John Of course you have, George. I wasn't suggesting

anything . . . I'm just surprised it's so late already. Spring must be on its way . . .

They walk around the stage in silence.

George.

George Yup, Mr Grey.

John (*stops walking*) How long has it been, George?

George What's that, Mr Grey?

John Long time, eh, George?

George Yup.

Pause. John absent-mindedly surveys the landscape. George looks awkward.

John You know, George, I know every inch of this land.

George Yup.

John I know this land almost as well as you, I should say, George.

George Thank you very much.

Pause.

John Do you ever look about you, George . . . ? No, of course you do. (*Pause.*) Do you ever look carefully at this land of mine and think to yourself that we shouldn't really, by rights, be here?

Pause.

George Is it something in particular you were wanting to talk with me for? I shall have to be getting on home soon.

Pause. John is not listening to George. John moves away from George. Leaves George standing, waiting.

John (*to himself*) More difficult than I thought . . .

Sometimes I imagine I'm looking down from a great height
. . . It wouldn't take long for this land of mine to return to
the marsh and bog it was before Vermuyden drained away
the water. Not long at all. A nothing land, the Fenland.
Not long at all. A nothing land which God would soon
return to nature if it were not for the simple water pumps
. . . Yes, we are perched, George and I, on a land snatched
from nature and waiting its return.

George I'll be getting along now, Mr Grey, if that'll be all.

John Of course, George. I was lost in thought. I'll walk a
little further with you.

  They walk, pause.

So what would you do, George, if the land returned to its
natural state?

George Don't think that way.

  Pause.

Is there anything else you were wanting, Mr Grey?

John Things are changing still, you see, George . . .
Richest land in Europe, the Black Fen – but things are
getting hard even here.

George Things don't change that easy in my eyes.

John Anyway, George . . . Goodnight.

George Goodnight, Mr Grey.

  They separate.

John George?

George Mr Grey?

John What job are you actually on at the moment?

George Clearing Twelve Foot Drain.

John I see . . . Goodnight.

George Goodnight to you.

Exit John. George returns to domestic area joining Pam and Linda.

SCENE FIVE

Pam, Linda and George.

Pam (*to audience*) I knew John Grey knew he were doing wrong, otherwise he would have said it straight out to George – not played him up for a day or two – not really saying what he meant . . . That's his trouble though, really, he thinks he got too much to lose if he changes his mind when he's set to something. Too much pride and too much money, I call it. Made me angry. Three days it were before he said it. George knew it though – well it were obvious probably . . . But we all suffered . . . (*to George*) What's wrong with you, George? You've not said a word all night. Not a word since you come home . . . Not a word . . .

Pause.

Well . . . ? What is it? Sitting there looking like I don't know what . . . Well?

Linda Don't start.

Pam George. I'm speaking to you. What is it with you, sitting there like you've got no ears . . . ? (*to Linda*) and you shut up, girl.

Linda leaves domestic area. She stands just outside domestic area – as if listening from another room. Pause.

George John Grey's up to something.

Pam So what's different? John Grey's always up to something – always has been . . . What's he been up to, George?

George Don't know what John Grey's been up to . . . Don't know.

Pam Well, what's he said?

George Shouldn't talk to Linda like that. Shouldn't.

Pam What's he said?

George Nothing – he's said nothing – it's the way he said it.

Pam What's got into you, George Sutton? Talking in riddles. What are you? Going soft or something?

George (*suddenly very angry*) I'm not fucking soft in the head – you fucking ask me, I fucking tell you. You shouldn't talk to Linda like that. I don't like it, right . . . ?

Pam Don't shout at me.

George I'll fucking shout . . . I do what I fucking like . . . (*Violent*) I want to fucking shout . . . I fucking shout . . . I'll fucking shout if I want to fucking shout . . .

    George and Pam separate.

John Grey's up to something . . . (*Pause.*) I fear it.

    George leaves the domestic area and takes up position as in the previous scene with John Grey in the field.

Pam (*to herself*) I don't care . . . I don't . . . Not at all . . . Not any more. It's not right, not right what you do. It's not, not right, George.

    Linda returns to domestic area. Pam and Linda stay in position during Scene Six.

SCENE SIX

John and George outside domestic area. The sound of the wind.

John George?

George Yup, Mr Grey.

Pause.

John When do you think you'll be finished with the Twelve Foot Drain?

George Another hour in the morning, Mr Grey.

John I see.

Pause.

George Anything else you'd like doing?

John No, but I'll have a word with you in the morning.

Exit John. George returns to domestic area.

SCENE SEVEN

Pam, Linda, George. Long pause.

George (*muttering*) Don't know what he wants . . . Don't.

Linda What's he said then?

Pam Don't start him. Right? Leave him be . . . He'll only . . .

Pam and Linda leave domestic area – taking chairs, leaving acting space empty.

George (*moving downstage*) Always done Twelve Foot. Time of year. Good job an' all.

SCENE EIGHT

John and George at extreme ends of the stage. George facing away from John. The sound of wind.

John (*calling out, as if a great distance separates them*) George . . . ! George . . . !

   George turns slowly. John moves towards George, but maintains distance between them.

George . . . I've been looking for you.

George You have, Mr Grey?

John How are you today, George?

   George nods.

I'm going to have to lay you off, George.

George Yup.

John It's not an easy thing to do, George. You've been here a long time. This is not easy for me. Not easy for me at all.

George There's nothing else for me.

John (*interrupting*) It's hard for me, George, you understand that, don't you . . . ? Surplus . . . You understand, don't you, George . . . ?

George Nothing I can do . . . What about . . . ?

John Can you come and see me tomorrow? At the house. We'll talk about things then.

George Tomorrow?

John Yes, come and we'll talk tomorrow.

   Pause.

Things have changed for all of us, George.

John leaves stage. George is left standing alone. He moves upstage, to the same position as for the beginning of the play. Linda enters.

SCENE NINE

George remains standing upstage.

Linda (*monologue*) Burning bugs. Used to. Magnifying glass didn't cost much, when I were little . . . Burnt 'em up – couldn't see 'em no more. Feel the heat . . . See 'em scurry. Sun heat. Scurry. Scurry. Get away. Hot sun. Bright light. Nasty. Get away. Try . . . Woodlice, under stones . . . They were best . . . Felt bad if I burnt a ladybird. Pretty. Burn real quick. Did though . . . Sometimes. Green underneath . . . Woodlice and ants. Do me for ages. White light. Hot light. Burnt 'em. Ants get away. Move real quick. Make me cross. Get hundreds with me foot. Killed 'em. A moment's space will shut you up.

George sinks to the floor – the same movement as at the beginning of the play.

Mum said I shouldn't kill any living thing. Felt bad. Still did though . . . More sometimes . . . Don't know when I stopped. It were sudden. One day did. Next day didn't. I were in charge . . . Move real quick. Smoke. Lie still, then nothing at all. I liked to see the smoke coming off their backs. Don't do it no more.

Exit Linda. Enter Arthur.

SCENE TEN

George outstretched on the 'aisle'. In the same position as for the beginning of the play. Arthur approaches him slowly from an upstage position. Church sound/music (optional).

Arthur George Sutton? George Sutton, isn't it?

George I don't want to go home.

Arthur Stay here.

George Thank you, sir.

Arthur Do you need to talk to someone?

George Don't need nothing – go home now.

   George stands.

Arthur Perhaps I can help you?

George Excuse me, sir. I'll be on my way now . . . Thank you for your trouble.

Arthur Nothing is any trouble, George.

George (*leaving*) Yes, thank you for your trouble and I'll be on my way now, won't be stopping any longer. Thank you.

Arthur George?

   George stops.

George Yes, sir.

Arthur George . . . Come back here soon.

George Come back?

Arthur Yes, you must come back soon.

   Pause.

Will you come back soon, George?

George Right you are . . . Very nice to see and I'll be off home now.

Exit George followed by Arthur.

SCENE ELEVEN

Pam and Linda sitting separately.

Linda Mum?

Pam What is it?

Linda Where's Dad?

Pam Not here.

Linda Don't try and be funny.

Pam Well – what you think I am? Psychic?

Pause.

Linda I want me food.

Pam What are you in such a hurry for?

Linda Nothing.

Pam Well then, shut your noise.

Pause.

Linda He might not come home, like before.

Pause.

What's the time anyhow?

Pam Half past six.

SCENE TWELVE

Pam and Linda. Linda watching television. Pam standing.
They have both changed positions to suggest time passing.
The television should be simply represented by the sound
of loud music.

Linda Mum?

Pam What is it?

Linda Give us me dinner.

Pam You can have it.

Linda What's the time anyway?

Pam Half past seven.

Pause.

SCENE THIRTEEN

Pam and Linda watching television. Sitting separately.
Volume of television has increased. Pause.

Pam Load of old rubbish.

Pause.

Linda Shut up, I'm trying to watch it.

Pause.

Pam Rubbish, that's what it is.

Pause.

Linda What's the time?

Pam Eight o'clock.

SCENE FOURTEEN

Pam and Linda watching television as in previous scene. George enters domestic area. Loud music from television.

Pam And where you think you been . . . ? Hope you're not hungry 'cause dinner's ruined. Could have come home first before going off . . . George . . . ?

Linda Shut up. I'm trying to watch.

Pam George? Are you all right . . . ? What's the matter, George? What is it?

George Been laid off, ain't I.

Pam You what?

George walks slowly downstage and mimes turning off the television. Silence.

George Been laid off.

Exit George and Linda. Pam moves to an upstage position. John enters domestic area.

SCENE FIFTEEN

Pam and John. Pam upstage facing audience. The sound of the wind.

John Ah, Mrs Sutton.

Pam You can't do this to us, Mr Grey.

John I was expecting George.

Pam Well, you got me.

Pause.

John Indeed.

Pam You can't do this to us.

John Come in, Mrs Sutton.

Pam I will not, Mr Grey . . . You can't do this to us, you can't . . .

John Will you please come inside . . . ?

Pam I don't want to come inside . . . I don't want to . . . Don't have to go indoors to say what I've come to . . . Why you do this to us, Mr Grey? You can't do it . . . Why?

John Mrs Sutton, now listen to me, please . . . I refuse to discuss . . .

Pam (*interrupting*) Give George his job . . . What's he to do? Tell me that?

John Please come inside, Mrs Sutton.

Pam What are we to do . . . ? Tell me that . . . I don't need to come inside for you to tell me that . . . You can't do this to us, you can't.

John I'll try and explain things as best I can, Mrs Sutton, but you must come inside . . .

Pam You'll explain things 'as best you can' . . . You will, and no mistake . . . I'm not soft in the head, Mr Grey . . . You can explain things just as they are . . . Just as they are . . . and I'll not be going till you do . . .

John I am not used to this kind of thing, Mrs Sutton . . .

Pam You're not used to it . . . ?

John Are you going to come inside?

Pam I've told you what . . .

John (*interrupting*) I am shutting the door, Mrs Sutton . . .

Pam You shut the door, Mr Grey, and . . .

John shuts the door, suggested by turning away from Pam.

(*shouting*) You shut the door, Mr Grey, but you won't get rid of me that easy. You can answer my questions, Mr Grey – you can't . . .

Long pause.

I haven't gone, Mr Grey – I'm still here – and I'm not going. I'm stopping here till you tell me what I asked. It's not right, Mr Grey – it's not . . . Mr Grey! Mr Grey! You'll come out here and answer my question.

SCENE SIXTEEN

Pam and John.

Pam (*to audience*) I weren't going away . . . I would have stood outside John Grey's house all night if I'd 'ave 'ad to. I went in.

Pam enters domestic area. She sits opposite John. Sound of a clock ticking.

Then I 'ad to sit through all John Grey's justifications. He had all the phrases, I couldn't get a word in edgeways . . .

John You have to understand, Mrs Sutton, that George's redundancy is not a personal issue, it is an unfortunate commercial necessity.

Pam It ain't right to take away a man's job when he's worked for you all his life . . . Good work, too . . . I don't know about your commercial necessity, but I do know that . . . (*to audience*) I told him that. He could see he weren't going to get rid of me that easy. He could see that I were in the right and he were in the wrong, no matter what he said. I weren't going to budge see. Not at all . . . He could see that an' all . . .

John I was wondering, Mrs Sutton, whether you would feel able to come and help me out with the cleaning, here in the house – on a regular basis, of course . . . Is that something you might feel able to do . . . ? It would certainly be a great help to me.

John starts to leave domestic area. He stops as Pam speaks.

Pam (*to audience*) His wife's dead, see, and it's a big old house. I said I would.

Exit John.

Didn't have no choice really . . . Well, what could I do? George very near killed me when I told him . . . Don't know how it's going to end out.

As she speaks she moves upstage. George approaches from opposite side of stage. As they come together they freeze. Linda appears through the gap between them.

SCENE SEVENTEEN

Linda (*monologue*) Dreaming of screaming . . . Head tight, inside and out. Half awake . . . What's he done? Dreaming screaming – wake me up. Listen tight, listen close. Here he comes – 'bout time . . . Where's he been? What's he done? Home time . . . Goodnight, sleep tight, mind the little bugs don't bite, if they do, get a shoe, break their little heads in two . . . Scream dream, red and black . . . On the floor . . . Long way off. Eyes open, go away – dots don't go, fall over. Hush. Hush. Where's he been? This time of night? What's he done . . . ? Want to sleep now. Shut the dots. Rushing close. Scream dream. Smell him, just smell him . . . What *is* the time? Please don't go . . . No, don't go . . . Fuck off, woman, fuck you. Come here now. Don't you touch me . . . Scream dream. Come here. Fuck you . . . Where you been? Door slam dream. Scream again. Never stopping, dots are coming. Crashing, smashing, water running . . . Never stopping . . . Glass dreams. Sharp gleams. Stop the dots. Dots . . . Dots . . . Dots . . . Dots? Smell him now, even here, only him . . . Let me sleep. Don't wake . . . Dream . . . Dream – get away . . . Let me go . . . What's he want? What's he need? Not nothing really . . . Scream dream . . . Sleep please . . . Dream away. Away.

Blackout.

Act Two

SCENE ONE

Arthur alone on stage. Pause. Enter George. Church sound/music (optional).

George Afternoon, sir.

Arthur George. Come in, do.

George Thank you.

Arthur Yes, do come in. (*Arthur collects two chairs.*) I'm glad to see you looking a little more, shall we say, upright.

Pause.

Anyway, I'm so pleased you felt able to come back . . . Fine spot of weather we're having and would you care for a drop of tea?

George Yup, thank you.

Arthur Oh, right.

George No . . . No, thank you . . . No tea today, thank you.

Arthur Are you sure . . . ? It's no trouble. I've a kettle in the vestry. Just boiled.

George No tea, thank you. Didn't mean to say yes in the first place. Wasn't thinking.

Arthur Well, if you're quite sure.

Pause. Arthur sits. George remains standing.

I bumped into John Grey yesterday.

George You did?

Arthur Yes. I see him often . . . He told me . . .

George What'd 'e tell you?

Arthur We often speak, George, we often speak . . .

George What did you tell him? 'Cause that were not why I was here.

Arthur He's a church-going man, George . . . It was chance that we met and talked . . . But anyway he told me that you had been made redundant.

George Didn't come here about that.

Arthur It's understandable, George. It is. To be severely shaken. Your livelihood taken away . . . Family to support . . . I know there isn't much alternative employment in the region, if working the land is what you've been bred to do.

George Bred? What I've been bred to do . . . ? That's not it . . . No, that's not it at all . . . You see . . .

Arthur sits George down.

Arthur No, George, listen, it's nothing to be ashamed of, really it isn't . . . You know, he's not a bad man, times are hard for him as well – maybe not as hard as they are for the rest of us, but things are not easy for him, no, he's not a bad man, not at all. You know, George, I can always rely on John Grey to support my little fundraising activities, yes indeed . . . Does that surprise you?

Pause.

Of course, he *can* afford it.

Pause.

So you see, George . . .

George I didn't come here to be told all that I knew before, all that about John Grey and being laid off, which I knew, and family to support and fundraising and weather and cups of tea and upright and that, I wouldn't have come, that weren't it, that weren't it at all . . . (*George almost breaking down. Long pause.*)

Arthur Forgive me, George.

George That weren't it.

Arthur Forgive me, I've been insensitive.

George Not at all, not what I meant by it.

Pause.

Arthur Forgive me . . . I talk too much . . . I'll listen, George. (*Pause.*) You talk . . . You tell me. (*Pause.*) It gave me a shock, you see, a grave shock, to find you like that . . . (*Pause.*) You talk, George . . . I'll listen.

George Can't talk no more.

Arthur Why?

George Not today anyhow.

Pause.

Arthur I see.

Pause.

George Sorry for . . . I'm not . . . Before . . .

Arthur It's *I* who should apologize.

George (*stands, starts to leave*) I'll be off now . . . Thank you very much.

Arthur No, please stay.

George No, thank you. I'll be off now. Must be.

Arthur Will you come back?

George What for?

Arthur When you feel like talking again – will you come back? – and I promise I will listen, won't say a word.

George I'll want you to, sir. No point otherwise, is there?

Arthur Of course . . . So you will come back? Good.

George Thank you, sir. I'll be on my way home now.

Exit George, followed by Arthur.

SCENE TWO

George and Pam. Pam on hands and knees washing the floor with a cloth and bucket. George sitting. Long silence.

Pam Don't just sit there, George.

George What?

Pam I said don't just sit there, you heard . . . Haven't you got anything better to do with yourself? (*Pause. Pam cleans.*) I'm talking to you, George . . . Go and buy a paper . . . Look for a job . . . There are jobs, if you look . . . We can't go on like this and that's the truth.

Pause.

George Has Linda gone?

Pam Course she has . . . Look at the time . . . Move your feet . . . George! Move your feet, I've got to finish off here . . . Got to go soon . . . You don't help me, do you . . . ? Don't help at all . . . Move your feet.

George moves to another chair. Pause . . . Pam cleaning.

Could always sign on, you know, George, for the time being.

George Not signing on.

Pam Well, you ought to . . . We need the money, George . . . It's been two weeks now – and what have you done . . . ? Well, what have you done . . . ? George?

George What?

Pam I said, what have you done?

George Nothing. I ain't done nothing. (*Pause.*) So, what do you do?

Pam What?

George So what do you do in the house of John Grey's?

Pam What you think I do?

George I don't know what you do. If I knew, I wouldn't be asking, would I?

Pam Well, use your head . . . I do the same as I do here . . . George, move yourself, will you?

George It's my bloody house, you know.

Pam It's not your house – it's John Grey's house . . . and lucky for us, John Grey's letting us stop.

George Shut up, woman.

Pam Don't talk like that . . . I'm trying to clean up . . . Two houses ain't easy, you know.

George picks up rubbish bin and begins to empty it on to the floor.

George Clean that up then, and that, clean up that fucking lot . . .

Pam Clean that up . . . This instant, George . . . Clean it up . . .

George Shut your face.

Pam Clean it up, clean it up . . .

George Shut your face.

Pam Clean it up . . . Who d'you think you are?

George You bloody clean it up. You clean it up. You can clean up my rubbish as well as John Grey's.

Pam Clean it up, George . . .

George Give me money an' all . . . You don't give me any money . . .

Pam Right, it can stop there . . . 'cause I'm not clearing it up . . .

George Give me money . . . Give me ten pound . . . Give it me . . .

He grabs Pam's purse.

Pam What are you doing? George, what are you doing? I haven't any money to give you, George . . . I haven't enough . . .

George takes a ten-pound note.

George Plenty more you can get like that. Plenty more where that come from.

George leaves. Pam is left alone looking at the rubbish on the floor. Pause. She begins to pick up the rubbish – slowly at first, then angrily. After she has cleared up all the rubbish, Pam leaves carrying bucket and dustbin. John enters domestic area.

SCENE THREE

John and Pam. John sitting. Pam enters, carrying a bucket. Sound of clock ticking.

Pam Sorry, Mr Grey, excuse me. I didn't know you was sitting in here.

John I often sit in here, Mrs Sutton . . . Warmest part of any house, the kitchen . . . Don't you find that?

Pam It *is* warm.

John Nothing I like better, you know, than sitting in here after I've been out in the morning.

Pam I'll come back if you like.

John Come back?

Pam Well, you did say that you wanted me to give the kitchen floor a going over, but I can come back . . . Only I've finished off elsewhere and I can't stop long.

John Go ahead – don't mind me.

Pam Well, if you're sure.

Pam starts to wash the floor with a cloth and bucket, on her hands and knees, as in the previous scene. Long pause while Pam washes floor. John watches her.

John Everything all right with you, Mrs Sutton?

Pam Sorry?

John Everything all right?

Pam Not used to bricks – we got lino.

John Looks fine to me. It's been a long time since they looked like that.

Pam I'll get 'em looking all right.

*Pam continues cleaning. Long pause. John watches
Pam intently. As she gets close to where he is sitting he
lifts his feet from the floor and sits hunched up on the
chair.*

John How's George?

Pam Can't complain.

Pause.

John (*half to himself*) Weather's looking up anyway . . .
Yes, spring is on its way . . . Smell things grow – my father
used to say that he could hear things growing in the
springtime . . . 'I would I had some flowers of the spring'
. . . Something like that.

Pam (*who doesn't seem to have been listening*) I don't like
it when it's hot. (*Pause.*) So, who else you laid off, apart
from George?

John George is the first, but there will have to be others
. . . (*Stands.*) Well, I shall have to be getting along . . .
Thank you for your help . . . Your money is in an
envelope in the hall . . . I'll see you tomorrow.

Pam Right you are.

Exit John followed by Pam.

SCENE FOUR

*George and Linda sitting separately. Linda is reading/
doing school work. Silence. George keeps looking at her.
Tension between them. Long pause.*

Linda What are you staring for?

George Nothing . . . Can look at you, can't I?

Linda What for?

George Nothing.

Action continues in silence. George keeps staring at Linda. Long pause.

Linda What are you staring for?

George Nothing. (*Pause.*) What's that you're doing?

Linda Nothing.

George Can't be nothing. (*Pause.*) Come here. Show it me.

Linda It's nothing . . . School stuff.

George What is it?

Linda Told you, school stuff. Nothing you'd understand.

George No need for that. (*Pause.*) Interesting, is it?

Linda It's nothing, right . . . Got to do it . . . Shut up. (*Pause.*) Stop staring.

George Don't have to stop here, do you?

Pause. Enter Pam.

SCENE FOUR

George and Linda as at end of previous scene. Pam enters. She has just finished work. Sits down exhausted. Pause.

Linda (*monologue*) Talking? Don't talk – they don't . . . Don't talk, nor nothing. So quiet, you can hear it. Like a buzzing getting loud . . . I can hear it – feel it coming – in his looks, in her look. Just a look getting stronger. Nasty. Trouble. Nothing but trouble. Hate trouble. He hit her, sometimes, often. White fist. Bloody face. Then I hear laughing. Inside my head, deep inside . . . Feel like crying.

Don't though . . . That's not all he done. (*Linda winces at the memory.*)

Pam (*to Linda*) What's got into you?

George What?

Linda (*monologue*) She hit me, sometimes, once or twice. I ain't hit no one. Got no one to hit.

Pam Linda?

George Shut up.

Linda (*monologue*) Hate trouble. See it. Feel it coming. Don't talk, no, nothing – leave me out of it – right? Get away. (*Linda stands and makes to leave.*)

Pam Linda, I'm talking to you . . . (*to George*) You, keep out of it. (*to Linda*) Well, what's got into you? Can't you talk . . . ? Lost your tongue, have you? Can't you even talk to your mum . . . ? Where you going so soon? Can't you even say hello nor nothing? And there's jobs to be done, you know. Where you going so soon?

Linda Going up . . . Got to do my reading . . . (*Linda leaves domestic area. But remains visible just outside it. Listening.*)

Pam I don't know . . . I don't . . . What's got into that girl, George . . . ? George? I'm talking to you . . . George?

George What?

Pam Can't you answer me an' all?

George What?

Pam What's got into her?

George Don't look at me.

Pam Well, she's been funny since you got laid off, and that's a fact.

George Shut up, woman.

Pam Well, have you even looked . . . ?

George Shut up.

Pam Did you look in the paper . . . ? Did you? Did you even buy a paper . . . ? Did you . . . ?

George Shut your fucking face . . . You're all fucking right. 'Did you look in the paper?' . . . (*Shouting. Moves towards her aggressively.*) All right for you, ain't it . . . ? Just shut your face, right . . . ?

Pam (*calmly*) There's no need for that talk, George.

George slowly retreats. Sits down. Pause.

George Come here, love.

Pam You shouldn't use that language, George . . . There's no need.

George Come here.

Pam What do you want?

George Come here.

Pam What is it, George? What you want?

Pause.

George What you think? Remember when we were courting . . . ? Remember where we did it . . . ? Do you remember, love? We did it in the living room at your mum and dad's . . . By the fire . . . Nowhere else to do it, were there? Did it by the fire, remember? It were nice, weren't it? You liked it, didn't you?

Pam You know I did . . . Wouldn't have done it

otherwise, would I . . . ? It were nice. What's got into you, George?

George They could have come in any time . . . Just walked right in . . . Never did mind, and seen us there doing it on the carpet, with the bits of coal that got every place you didn't want 'em.

Pam What's made you think of that, George?

George I liked it, you liked it. You with your arse in the air.

Pam Course I liked it, George – what you thinking of? What's got into you?

George I want it now.

Pam Don't be soft, George.

George I want it right now . . . Here right, like then.

Pam Linda's still . . .

George Come here, I want to smell you.

Pam What are you, soft in the head?

George Come here, that's real exciting that is, with Linda coming in any time . . . Come here.

Exit Linda.

Pam Don't be so damned soft, George.

George Come here. (*Pause.*) Fuck off then . . . Fuck off, fuck off, fuck off.

Exit George followed by Pam.

SCENE SIX

John, sitting. Pam enters. Sound of a clock ticking.

Pam Do you want the kitchen floor doing again, Mr Grey?

John Thank you . . . Go ahead . . . Don't mind me.

Pam prepares to start cleaning the floor.

Before you start, Mrs Sutton, can I have a word . . . ? Sit down.

Pam If you like. (*Pam sits.*)

John How are things?

Pam Mustn't complain.

John How are you managing?

Pam Well, you know, Mr Grey, can't complain – times is hard – you know that – making ends meet and that since George was laid off . . . He won't sign on, see. Won't do it . . . So things is difficult really – and that's the truth . . . Only mustn't complain mind.

John Mrs Sutton, there's something I want to ask you.

Pam Oh yes, Mr Grey?

John Yes. (*John stands. Pause. He moves downstage. Half to himself:*) This is difficult (*Pause.*) Mrs Sutton. (*John moves towards her.*)

Pam Mr Grey?

John Now the other day I noticed that a ten-pound note went missing from the sideboard.

Pam I put it back . . . I did . . . Next day, after you paid me . . . I put it back, swear I did . . . Needed it quick though.

John I know you put it back . . . It just seemed strange to me that you didn't feel able to ask me for an advance.

Pam Didn't know how to say that . . . I'm sorry I did it. I am . . . Never do it again . . . That's for sure . . . Only when you're living day to day, you can just run out sometimes. We never saved nor nothing. Sometimes you just run out, specially now, see, through no fault of your own . . . I put it back as soon as I was able, next day . . . And I won't do it again . . . Only I saw it there and I borrowed it – just for the day . . . Felt dreadful though, afterwards, and that's the truth . . . Never taken anything in my life. (*Pam is close to tears.*)

John You're an honest woman, I know that . . . You're a good woman . . . So, next time, all you have to do is ask . . . You're already a great help to me, Mrs Sutton.

Pam That's good.

John I'm beginning to wonder how I ever managed without you . . . So next time you have a shortfall, Mrs Sutton, all you have to do is ask . . . (*Pause.*) I'm a fair man, Mrs Sutton.

Pam It won't happen again. Thank you very much . . . And now I must be getting on.

Exit Pam followed by John.

SCENE SEVEN

George sitting. Linda enters domestic area (from school). Sits down. Starts doing homework. Ignores George. Pause.

George Linda?

Linda What?

George What time is your mum getting in?

Linda How should I know?

Pause.

George I've been thinking about you today . . .
Linda . . . ?

Linda What?

George What do you want to do?

Linda What?

George What d'you want to do when you've finished
school . . . ? What d'you want to be?

Linda How should I know . . . ? Not getting married.

George Why?

Linda Shut up. (*Pause. Quietly:*) Hairdresser.

George What?

Linda Hairdresser. I'm going away when I can . . . Soon
as I can, I'm going away . . . Get away from you.

George Linda, there's no need for that . . . No need at all
. . . Was only asking . . . (*Pause.*) Didn't know that . . .
Didn't know you wanted to be a hairdresser.

Linda Course you didn't . . . Shut up, will you?

Pause.

George What do you want to be a hairdresser for?

Linda Just do . . . Not here though.

George Where then?

Linda I don't know, do I . . . ? Ely . . . Newmarket . . .
London . . . They always need hairdressers in London.

George No more than round here, they don't . . .
Wouldn't go there . . . London.

Linda Shut up . . .

George There's no need for that talk, Linda . . . I'm only
being interested.

Linda Yeah, well, don't . . . I've got to get on anyhow – so
shut up.

Pause.

George Just talking.

Linda What for . . . ?

George Just being interested.

Linda Yeah, well, don't be, right, 'cause I've got to get on.

Pause.

George What is it?

Linda Nothing.

George Can't be nothing.

Linda What you think it is?

George School work, ain't it?

Linda Right, so shut up . . . Don't want to talk, specially
not with you, right, so shut up.

George You don't have to stop here.

Pause.

What you want to go away for . . . ? Linda? What you
want to go away for?

Linda Others don't, but I do . . . Shut up, will you?

Pause.

119

George Don't know what you want to go elsewhere for
. . . Things are no different . . . Folks are no different
elsewhere, you know . . . Well, you've seen London on the
telly . . . Don't know what you want to go there for . . .
Things are the same . . . No different. Everywhere . . .
Only worse, probably.

Long pause.

Do mine if you want.

Linda What?

George Do my hair if you want.

Linda Don't be daft.

George Well, you can if you want.

Linda Don't be daft . . . Look at it.

George What d'you mean . . . ? If you want to be a
hairdresser, you could start with mine . . . Practise . . .
Could do with a trim.

Linda You 'aven't got any . . . Shut up, will you . . . ? Just
shut up. (*Pause.*) Just smell your feet.

George What d'you mean?

Linda Put your shoes on, will you?

George Don't smell.

Linda Do . . . It's disgusting.

George tries to smell his feet.

Can't you wash 'em or nothing?

*George takes off his socks. Starts washing his feet in the
bucket. Long silence.*

Not in there . . . That's for the floor.

George continues to wash his feet. Long pause. Having washed his feet. George moves towards Linda. He is barefoot. Linda does not look at him.

George That's better, eh?

George puts his arm around Linda.

Linda Get off. Get off me.

George tries to touch her head. Linda pushes him away.

Get off me . . . Leave me be . . . Lay off.

George I . . .

Linda (*shouting*) Fuck off, right fuck off. Leave me be.

George I'm going out.

Linda Good.

George puts his shoes on. Stands. Puts his coat on. Pause.

George I'm going out then.

Linda Good.

George leaves domestic area. Linda sits alone, relieved he has gone. Pause. Exit Linda.

SCENE EIGHT

George and Arthur. Church sound/music as for previous church scenes (optional).

Arthur George. Welcome. My good man. I'm so pleased to see you again. Well. Well. You came back. I'm so pleased you came back.

George Well, you said to come back.

Arthur Indeed, and you have come . . . Well, well. Do come in. Let's not stand on ceremony, George. How good it is to see you. Come in, come in.

Arthur leads George across the stage. He leaves George standing while he collects two chairs, which he places close together. Arthur sits. George immediately feels very awkward and remains standing.

How good of you to come, George . . . Let's have a good talk shall we . . . ? A chat . . . Oh, I'm so pleased.

George That pleases me that you're pleased, Mr Loveless, it does . . . I wasn't sure you see.

Arthur No. No. I'm absolutely delighted, George. Made my day.

George Well, that's good, Mr Loveless . . . Thing is, there's a thing or two I would like to discuss with you, if you've got the time, and that's the truth.

Arthur Made my week, George. So good to see you. Do sit down.

George sits. Pause.

Well. What is it, George . . . ? I'm pleased you came. Really pleased.

Pause.

George Shouldn't have . . . Shouldn't have come really.

Arthur But I'm pleased you came . . . I am really.

Pause.

George Shouldn't have . . . Wish I hadn't now . . . Don't know what it was made me really . . .

Arthur You came because I invited you to come, George . . . That's why you came.

Pause.

George (*speaking slowly*) When I'm buried, I don't want no 'eadstone over my 'ead. Not at all . . . Is it wrong to . . . ? If you have nothing . . . Is it wrong . . . ? If you have nothing . . . Not nothing at all . . . Is it wrong? Is it, Mr Loveless? I'm not a good man, Mr Loveless, that's the truth . . . I don't want no stone when I'm gone . . . I don't. It's only folks who die young should have an 'eadstone . . . When I'm buried I don't want no 'eadstone, right . . . ? Will you see to it? The love you leave behind should be your memorial – not 'eadstone – I've used up my love now – used it all up . . . What you got, Mr Loveless, if you've used up all the love you were give . . . ? Tell me that.

Arthur Is it wrong? You asked me whether I thought it was wrong – wrong to what? George, wrong to what?

Pause.

George What I meant . . . What I want to know, Mr Loveless . . .

Pause.

What I got to live for . . . ? Tell me that . . . What I got?

Arthur What have you got to live for?

George Yup.

Arthur To live for?

George Yup . . . Tell me that . . . What I got to live for?

Arthur Big question that, George . . . You have your good wife and lovely daughter . . . I'm sure you'll find another job, in time . . . But that's not really it, is it, George . . . ? That's not really what you're getting at.

George has stopped listening.

When I was young man, perhaps I could have answered your question . . . With conviction . . . You know, George, it is a very cruel world . . . Why do any of us want to live? Good question.

George What I got to live for?

Arthur It's a question not everybody asks, George . . . and you know more people should . . . What have I to live for? Why do I live?

Pause.

George I don't want no memorial . . . I don't want one, Mr Loveless. Not never . . . Will you see to it, Mr Loveless? Will you? I can't make things fit no more, see?

Pause.

Arthur You know, George . . . I'm so pleased you came . . . We're alike, you know . . . You and I . . . You know what it is – we think too much . . . A glimmer of the void . . . A glimpse, and everything falls away, doesn't it? Falls away. Life, death, faith, doubt, need, eh, George? All one . . . I'm a pretty useless fellow really, you can see that, can't you, George?

George I don't want no memorial . . . No 'eadstone . . . I want to be forgotten . . . Will you see to it, Mr Loveless? (*George stands.*) I must be going now, if you'll excuse me. (*Exit George.*)

Arthur Come back soon, George – I do enjoy our little chats. (*Arthur sits alone. Pause. He leaves slowly.*)

Act Three

SCENE ONE

Enter Pam.

Pam (*to audience*) It's taken me this long . . . He's gone a very funny colour . . . Hanging from a pipe . . . Water pipe in the kitchen, as if to say he meant it . . . I had to take him down. Weren't half heavy . . . I laid him on the floor, till they took him away . . . This is what I've been thinking . . . Can't help what I think, can I? Anyway can't undo it . . . I don't know . . . I don't . . . There was so many things straight after, like who to call, what to do, who to turn to, what to say . . . Then there was the funeral, with the family and everyone watching . . . Is it any wonder I haven't known what to think? Not to myself. Not at all . . . 'Why'd 'e do it Pam? Why'd 'e do it?' . . . Family were the worst, then there's the neighbours, they can't let you alone with it, which is what you want . . . With all the business of it and not being left alone, I haven't had time to think.

> *Enter Linda. Linda moves around acting space as she speaks. Pam remains standing. Linda and Pam are unaware of each other.*

Linda (*to audience*) I'm glad he's fucking dead . . . Won't tell no one though . . . Not her neither . . . Don't have to tell no one now . . . Won't happen no more . . . Like the times before. Could never say nothing and I don't have to 'cause it were wrong, always knew that. Could never tell her. I'm glad he's dead . . . No more . . . What if he would never go away? What if he were to haunt me . . . ? Maybe if I don't think no more, he'll be dead in my head an' all . . . I want him to fuck off out me head . . .

Pam (*to audience*) I couldn't weep, couldn't grieve . . .
Couldn't do it . . . The waste . . . What we done . . .
Things we done . . . I can't grieve . . . Can't. Me sisters
could. Family could. Even old Reverend Loveless, I
thought he were going to fall right in on top o' George, he
were so overcome . . . He's never really been right in the
head . . . I couldn't cry, and I haven't had time to think
. . . Don't want to really . . . I'll be lonely. Real lonely.
That'll be the worst of it . . . I'll put flowers on his grave
. . . But however lonely I get, if it were right – and we all
got to go sometime – if it were right, I'm not sorry he done
it.

SCENE TWO

Pam and Linda.

Pam Linda?

Linda What?

Pause.

Pam We'll get by, eh?

Linda nods. Pause.

Linda I'm going away soon, all right?

Pam nods.

SCENE THREE

Linda (*to audience*) Screaming stops . . . Not a sound . . .
No noise now . . . Breathing, all inside . . . Heart sound,
inside – not a sound outside . . . after screams, nothing
just outside me . . . Where they gone . . . ? No door

sound, no slam . . . Breathing tight, inside, not out . . .
Dots have gone, turned to shapes, very dark . . . heart
sounds, thump, thump, thump . . . Not a word – nothing
heard . . . Wide awake, in the ground . . . Lying still . . .
Where's he gone . . . ? Sleep time . . . Creaking stair,
turning right or turning left? Thump, thump. Where's she
gone? Not a sound . . . And I'm lying there praying,
'Please God, don't let him come' . . . Flash of light from
the road, someone else, other folk . . . Shapes come back
. . . Ghosts are people that was unhappy when they died
. . . What if he would never go away? Keep coming back?
He were unhappy, else he wouldn't have done it.

THE STRANGENESS
OF OTHERS

For
Soph

Characters

Edward Goodchild Early/mid-seventies.

James Goodchild Mid-fifties. Edward Goodchild's son.

William Goodchild Early fifties. Edward Goodchild's son.

Dorothy (Dot) Late forties/early fifties. Married to
William.

Greg Early twenties. William and Dot's son.

Sarah Seventeen/eighteen. Greg's sister.

Amanda Eighteen/nineteen. Originally from London, now
lives alone.

Jim Fifties. Southern Irish, homeless in London.

Ed Late sixties/early seventies. Homeless in London,
sounds aristocratic.

Nancy Black Forties. Londoner.

Stuart Black Late twenties. Nancy's son.

Carl Early twenties. From a town in the industrial
north-west.

Katy Eighteen. Arrives in London with Carl.

Corinna Late fifties/early sixties. Homeless in London,
mid-European gypsy origin.

Kim Mid-twenties. From Northern Ireland.

Bill Late fifties/early sixties. Londoner.

Charlie Early/mid-thirties. Bill's son.

Josh Seventeen/eighteen. From a small village in East Anglia.

Marie Early twenties. Arrives in London with Josh.

STAGING

The transition between the scenes must be instantaneous. Often characters from one scene remain on stage during the following scene. Overlapping action and double-, sometimes triple-, focus staging is therefore a necessity.

DESIGN/LIGHTING

Nothing in the design should inhibit the smoothness of transitions between scenes. Props, settings, furniture should therefore be kept to a minimum. Lighting and sound/music should be the primary means of locating the different scenes and locations.

MUSIC

Although the script does not include any specific musical/sound directions, I hope that *The Strangeness of Others* in production will provide an opportunity for the development of a complex music/sound score which is integrated into the overall texture of the piece. Exactly how this aspect of the production is developed will depend on the individual director and composer.

The following notes are suggestions only. Music should be played live. Musicians should be visible or partly visible to the audience. No distinction in terms of 'sound' and 'music' should be made, rather the sound of traffic, wind, crowds, etc., should be combined with more specifically musical effects in the creation of the sound score. Recorded effects, whether they be sound effects or musical arrangements should be kept to a minimum. Music should not be used simply to disguise scene transitions. Use of naturalistic sound loops should be avoided in favour of a more imaginative and overtly theatrical treatment. A starting point for the development of the musical style might be the 'street' world of Jim. Literally using the idea of the street musician as a way towards a more subtle and wide-ranging treatment. The music/sound should work to create and define the different environments of the play. The themes of the play can be united through music, making connections between seemingly different characters and scenes.

SETTING

London.

ACCENTS

The play is not written in dialect, although many of the characters speak with a regional accent.

CASTING

The optimum cast is indicated above. The play can be performed with a minimum cast of eight, doubling as follows:

1   Sarah
    Katy
    Marie

2   Amanda
    Kim

3   Nancy
    Corinna
    Dot

4   Carl
    Josh
    Charlie

5   Stuart
    Greg

6   Jim
    James

7   William
    Bill

8   Edward Goodchild
    Ed

If cast in this way, the production should attempt to maximize the theatricality of the transformations – the actors should be *seen* to switch between characters.

An earlier version of *The Strangeness of Others* was first performed on 21 June 1988 in the Cottesloe auditorium of the National Theatre, London, with the following cast:

Edward Goodchild Michael Turner
James Goodchild Philip Voss
William Goodchild David Burke
Dorothy Goodchild Rosemary Martin
Greg Goodchild Jonathan Cullen
Sarah Goodchild Katrin Cartlidge
Amanda Rachel Joyce
Jim Dermot Crowley
Ed Michael Turner
Nancy Black Sandra Voe
Stuart Black Peter-Hugo Daly
Carl John Lynch
Katy Cheryl Maiker
Corinna Rosemary Martin
Kim Hilary Reynolds
Bill Trevor Peacock
Charlie David Bamber
Josh Jonathan Cullen
Marie Katrin Cartlidge

Directed by Nick Ward
Set design and lighting by Fred Pilbrow
Music by Richard Heacock
Musicians Richard Heacock, Rory Allam

This version of the play was first performed on 18 October 1989 at the Central School of Speech and Drama, London, with the following cast:

Edward Angus Wright
James Mark Jenkinson
William Mark Heal
Dorothy Sarah Ball
Greg Joseph Bennett
Sarah Lucy Scott
Amanda Julia Halliwell
Jim Philip Glenister
Ed Angus Wright
Nancy Victoria Alcock
Stuart Joseph Bennett
Carl David MacCreedy
Katy Indra Ové
Corinna Sarah Ball
Kim Zara Turner
Bill Mark Heal
Charlie David MacCreedy
Josh David MacCreedy
Marie Julia Halliwell

Directed by Mark Wing-Davey
Designed by David Taylor

Act One

SCENE ONE

Tight spotlight fades up slowly on **Jim** *who is lying still on the floor, covered by a blanket. Spotlight gradually widens. Jim starts to move very slowly. He lifts himself to a sitting position.*

Jim (*monologue*) Time was . . . Time was when I was . . . City sleeps, Jim awake . . . I have lived . . . Done that . . . Once. Before; then . . . Before these lights hurt my eyes in the dark. Long before. City lights. Bright lights . . . Even under our bridge.

> **Carl** *and* **Katy** *enter to an extreme upstage position. They carry luggage. They stand still – not seeing Jim. They are lit in a separate pool of light.*

Lights they don't switch off. They? It's safer for others. Others? They who fear the dark – well, I suppose it is . . . But, it's not the dark; if only it were! It's not the dark which gets inside your brain. No, light is far worse than dark when it's soothing night you crave . . . I can't even see the stars; with the lights they don't switch off.

> **Kim** *enters – taking up a position separate from Jim and Carl/Katy. She is lit separately. She warms herself against the cold. She remains in this position throughout the following scene. She remains separate from the action.*

Light pricks, like something in my brain I can't switch off . . . Memories? Lived? Oh yes. Done that . . . Rumble. Rumble. Traffic thunder . . . Listen! Rumble, rumble. The belly of the beast . . . But, has the beast a heart? Welcome!

> *Jim moves to another part of the stage. He watches the*

action. As he starts to move away Carl and Katy begin to speak.

SCENE TWO

Katy and Carl move forward at the beginning of the scene. Katy then sits on the floor with the luggage.

Carl Here we are.

Katy Here we are. (*Pause.*) Sit down here a minute.

Carl What for? We've got to find somewhere to stay.

Katy Sit down here.

Carl (*looking around*) Busy, isn't it?

Katy Don't be daft. Course it is. It's London.

Carl I know that. I was just saying.

Katy Sit down, Carl.

She caresses his leg.

Carl Not here. What you doing?

Katy Sit down. I want to tell you something.

Carl sits beside her.

I bloody love you. I love you. You know that, don't you?

Carl I love you too.

Katy I love you.

Carl I love you.

Katy Love you.

Carl Love you.

Katy We did it –

Carl Ay. Here we are . . . Love you.

He kisses her passionately.

Katy How much money have we got?

Carl (*counting the money*) Four hundred and sixty-two quid.

Katy We had five hundred.

Carl Well, we spent it . . . We've enough . . . For the time being, anyway –

Katy Where's it gone, Carl?

Carl I said we've enough . . . Anyway, we've got to find somewhere to stay . . . We can't hang round here.

Katy kisses him again.

Not here, love. There's time for that.

Katy Who's watching us?

They kiss.

No one's watching.

Carl (*stands*) Right. We're off.

They pick up their bags. Start to leave.

Here. Stop a minute.

Katy What for?

Carl I want a photo of you. You look so beautiful.

Katy Get away. I look shit.

Carl Shut up. Sit there. Like you were. Just like you were a minute ago.

Katy sits down with the baggage again. Carl takes his time lining up his shot although his camera is unsophisticated.

Katy Get on with it. I know I look shit anyway.

Carl There's snapshots and there's photographs. Me – I'm a photographer, right. So sit still. (*Pause.*) Look natural like.

Katy I look shit, Carl.

Carl You look beautiful. Think of something.

Katy What?

Carl Me.

Katy OK.

Carl That's it. Beautiful. (*Takes photo.*) Come on then.

They start to leave again.

Katy (*stops*) Hey, Carl.

Carl What?

Katy (*laughing*) Do you think they noticed?

Carl What?

Katy That we've gone?

Carl Don't give a shit. We're here, that's all I care about. Fucking London. Come on.

They leave.

SCENE THREE

Night. The stage is empty except for Jim who is still sitting separately and Kim, who is standing. **William** *enters. He walks briskly across the stage.*

Kim Looking for love?

*William pauses for a moment. He leaves. **Ed** has entered and started to speak before William has left.*

SCENE FOUR

By a circular route Ed makes his way downstage.

Ed Loss – a terrible thing . . . To lose something without even the chance of giving it away . . . To have something taken . . .

Stuart *enters in police uniform, he paces up and down for a while. Kim sees him and moves to another part of the stage. Stuart doesn't notice her. He rubs and blows his hands to keep warm. Ed continues to speak without interruption.*

. . . without even the choice . . . If you've lost everything all you can reasonably expect is the odd surprise.

He sees Stuart and approaches him.

(*to Stuart*) Have you seen my blanket . . . ?

Stuart ignores him.

Crabbed age and youth should not live together . . . I'm nobody's fool, and sometimes still I think . . . (*to Stuart*) have you seen my blanket? I won't ask you again . . . I do think.

Stuart Come on – on your way.

*Stuart looks at his watch and moves to an extreme upstage position. He stands still with his back to the audience – until scene with **Nancy**. Stuart's departure has not interrupted Ed's speech.*

143

Ed . . . And I've a warm heart . . . Only it's a trifle cold. Keeping warm in a cold world is the least one can do. (*He leaves.*)

SCENE FIVE

William and Kim. William has returned.

Kim Is it love you're looking for?

William stops. He follows her to another part of the stage. They leave. Kim following William.

SCENE SIX

Greg *and* **Amanda.** *Greg is standing. Waiting. Amanda appears.*

Amanda Greg.

Greg I love you.

Amanda Greg, what are you doing?

Greg Waiting.

Amanda (*interrupting*) Why . . . ?

Greg (*interrupting*) For you . . . Sarah told me about the new job.

Pause. Amanda looks down. Then at her watch. Then at Greg. Greg is looking away.

How is it then?

Amanda What?

Greg The new job?

Amanda Yeah. (*Pause.*) It's OK. (*Pause.*) Look, Greg.

Greg (*interrupting*) What?

Amanda I really can't . . .

Greg I thought you . . .

Amanda Look, whatever it was . . . Finished. Please leave me alone.

  Pause.

Greg You enjoyed it, didn't you . . . ? I mean. Did you enjoy it?

Amanda What?

Greg It . . . ? You smell great.

Amanda I had a great time.

Greg It was a surprise; it's not like it was; anyway. Please. Please . . . It's just, you know – different.

Amanda Please.

Greg I love you.

Amanda (*interrupting*) Rubbish.

Greg You said.

Amanda Look, Greg, I've got to go; all right?

  Greg stretches out his hand to touch Amanda's face.

Just don't touch me.

Greg Why? You said.

  Greg touches her.

Amanda (*pulling away*) Leave me alone. (*Pause.*) Why did you come here?

Greg Will you see me?

Amanda I am seeing you, Greg – and I'm telling you that I don't want to see you.

Greg I mean can we talk at least . . . I feel so; you see?

Amanda Greg, please; I'm sorry . . . It just shouldn't matter.

Greg Why?

Amanda Please go away. Look I've got to go anyway. All right?

Greg Drink?

Amanda You're not David.

Greg I know I'm not David, I'm Greg.

Amanda And that, Greg, is the problem.

Greg Let's have a drink anyway.

Amanda Go away . . . Bye.

They both move to another part of the stage – standing separately.

SCENE SEVEN

Stuart remains in an extreme upstage position.

Jim (*monologue*) I know your love, you lovers . . . 'Give me money; buy me time . . . Find me love,' you say.

Amanda moves downstage and sits separately. She does not notice Jim.

I know you. I've seen you all a thousand times. I know what you do for need of love and love of money . . . Give me twenty pence and I'll tell you a secret.

Sarah *enters and stands separately watching Amanda from a distance.*

'Need me . . . Want me . . . Love me,' you scream . . . Love screams from a thousand desperate faces. Listen carefully! You can hear them too.

As Jim leaves **Corinna** *enters.*

SCENE EIGHT

Sarah, Amanda, Corinna. Greg leaves. Corinna listens to the following:

Sarah Hi.

Amanda Hi.

Sarah All right?

Amanda Yeah.

Sarah So what happened?

Amanda David just left me.

Sarah Just like that.

Amanda Just like that; well, not just like that.

Sarah I'm pleased you rang . . . Haven't seen you for ages.

Amanda Do you understand?

Sarah I think so. (*Pause.*) Am I still your best friend?

Amanda Of course.

Sarah I missed you . . . I never liked David.

Amanda You didn't know him, Sarah.

Pause.

Sarah What's the job like?

Amanda OK. (*Pause.*) So what are you up to?

Sarah Studying.

Amanda You're looking too thin.

Sarah Why didn't you phone me earlier?

Amanda What about *you* . . . (*Laughing*) Have you got a lover?

Sarah I thought you didn't want to see me . . . I miss you.

Amanda I've been in love, Sarah.

Pause.

Sarah Why didn't you want to see me?

Amanda It's your family.

Sarah What?

Amanda Your brother.

Sarah What about my brother.

Pause.

Amanda He kissed; we – well, we kissed. Goodnight. Since then he won't leave me alone.

Sarah Who?

Amanda Greg.

Sarah My brother Greg?

Amanda Well *more* than just kissed . . . (*Laughing*) A *lot* more than just kissed; but it was nothing.

Sarah Greg?

Amanda We slept together.

Sarah You're joking.

Amanda I'm not joking, Sarah . . . I slept with your brother . . . I wanted to tell you.

Sarah Greg?

Amanda I was missing David. You know what it's like when you miss someone.

Sarah Yes.

Amanda You don't.

Sarah I do.

Amanda No, you don't – I mean, to be on your own, live on your own – it makes a big difference, Sarah.

Sarah I don't choose to live at home.

Amanda It doesn't matter.

Pause.

Sarah So what was it like?

Amanda What?

Sarah What was it like?

Amanda Fine . . . Look it's not a big deal.

Sarah I won't forgive you for this.

Corinna coughs as if she is about to speak. They look at her briefly.

Amanda Don't be stupid.

Sarah (*interrupting*) Don't call *me* stupid.

Amanda What is your problem . . . ?

Sarah I hate you. I'm going . . . Bye. (*Sarah leaves.*)

Amanda Listen.

Corinna (*to Amanda*) Don't love another if another isn't loved, that's worse than all . . . I loved one.

Corinna offers her the flowers. Amanda leaves. Corinna calls.

Don't trust 'em. Men, never trust 'em. (*Corinna leaves.*)

SCENE NINE

Kim enters, she walks across the stage. **Bill** *and* **Charlie** *also enter – taking up positions for next scene – separate from Kim. Kim is looking at William's wallet.*

Kim (*monologue*) William Goodchild MP . . . There's a bit.

She continues to look through the contents of the wallet throughout the exchange between Charlie and Bill. Bill lying. Charlie pacing restlessly.

Bill I don't know where she is – don't know . . . If I knew I'd tell you honest, Charlie.

Charlie Well, what did she say?

Bill Nothing, she said nothing. Not to me.

Charlie What did she say?

Bill Don't hit me, Charlie.

Kim (*monologue from separate position*) William Goodchild . . . William Goodchild MP.

SCENE TEN

Bill and Charlie.

Bill (*monologue*) 'Put 'im in a home.' Easy . . . Only; he won't go. No, he won't . . . He wants to stay at home. His home . . . 'If you don't do this' . . . 'If you do do that' . . . 'If you don't behave, you're going into the home.' It were very sudden. Last winter. Holborn. Blacked out. Slipped on the bleeding ice. Fit? Me . . . ? I was. Charlie's a bad boy . . . Revenge he calls it. If it weren't for young Kimmy I'd have no comfort at all. Old girl's been gone a long while . . . He's chucked me out of me own bleeding room. So I have to stop out here. Out here for Christ's sake . . . It's not bleeding right.

Charlie (*monologue*) Old Fart.

Kim (*monologue from a different part of the stage*) It's cold now; but I'm not going home; not for the moment, anyway; not going back there . . . Sometimes a rest from home, which is a name for it, is what you need.

*Bill, Charlie and Kim exit. As they leave **Nancy** enters. Stuart turns towards the audience.*

SCENE ELEVEN

Katy and Carl enter to an extreme upstage position. Nancy and Stuart establish a domestic area downstage.

Carl It must be down here some place.

Katy We've been walking around for hours.

Nancy Stuart?

Stuart What?

Nancy You do look cross. Let me give your back a little rub, you like that don't you?

Nancy helps Stuart off with his shirt. She begins to rub his back.

Stuart There's that couple coming about the room.

Nancy Come on, Stuey . . . You are in a mood.

Stuart Scum.

Nancy Language.

Stuart Scratch! Scratch! That's it, Mum . . . Lovely.

Nancy All right?

Stuart Bit lower . . . That's it.

Carl and Katy have moved downstage.

Katy (*Looking at outside of Nancy's house*) This can't be it.

Carl It must be . . . It's all right. What d'you expect?

Pause.

Stuart That'll be them.

Nancy I'll go.

Stuart No, you stay here . . . I'll see to it.

Katy It's shit.

Carl It's going to be fine.

Carl and Katy kiss as Stuart interrupts them.

SCENE TWELVE

Carl, Katy, Stuart, Nancy. Carl and Katy are standing outside Nancy's boarding house.

Stuart (*intimidating*) Yes?

Carl (*nervous*) I phoned you earlier about the room.

Stuart Oh, yes.

Carl Phoned earlier.

Stuart Both of you?

Carl No, it was me.

Katy and Stuart speak at the same time.

Katy Carl.

Stuart You trying to be funny?

Carl (*to Katy*) What do you want?

Katy He means, do we both want the room?

Carl Course we bloody do.

Stuart No need for that language. (*Pause.*) Wait here.

Stuart leaves them, moving upstage to Nancy.

Katy I don't like him.

Carl Course you bloody don't. What d'you expect?

Pause.

Katy Let's fuck off.

Carl Shut up.

Nancy appears.

Nancy Yes?

Katy We've come about the room.

Nancy What, both of you?

Carl Ay.

Nancy It's only a single you know. Clean though. Eighty pounds.

Katy Eighty quid.

Carl Is that eighty quid a week?

Nancy Course it is. Where have you been? You don't have to stay here. There's plenty others who will . . . You don't look like brother and sister.

Katy That's 'cause we're not.

Nancy I thought you said you were. You working?

Carl Not yet, but I will be.

Nancy You're not working.

Katy He said not yet. I'm not working yet either.

Nancy You can't stop here, you know.

Carl We want to stop here.

Katy Carl.

Nancy Not since the new regulations came in. Not if you're signing on, and you've got to pay the rent . . . My son's a policeman – so you'll not be stopping if you don't pay the rent. Right?

Carl Ay.

Nancy And there's the deposit – and one month in advance. That's three hundred and twenty plus one hundred deposit. That's four hundred and twenty.

Carl No problem.

Katy Carl.

Carl (*to Nancy*) We got money, you know.

Nancy Well, that's all right then. (*Pause.*) Do you want to see it then?

Katy Course we do.

Carl If you don't mind.

Nancy Follow me.

Nancy leads Carl and Katy to an area upstage. Carl and Katy remain on stage throughout following scene. They establish their room. Remaining separate from Kim and Jim.

SCENE THIRTEEN

Jim and Kim. Middle of the night. Illuminated by the light from street lamps. Kim is moving about looking for Jim.

Kim Jimmy, are you there? Jimmy? Jimmy?

Jim Kim, my little love . . . What are you doing so late?

Kim I'm cold tonight.

Jim I've only the one blanket, Kimmy love. Only the one.

Kim I'm cold, Jimmy.

She pulls the blanket partly off him.

Jim There's only the one blanket, Kimmy my little love. Not really made for sharing.

She lies down beside Jim. She wraps the blanket around her. Jim is left partly exposed.

You have to go home now, Kimmy – can't stay here.

Kim Don't want to go back.

Jim Bed time, Kimmy . . . The blanket isn't for sharing.

Kim Don't want to go to bed . . . Want to sleep now . . . (*Pause.*) . . . Blanket smells anyway.

Jim Course it smells, Kimmy my love; of course it smells.

Kim Smells of your shit, Jimmy.

Jim It's not my shit.

Kim (*shouting*) Your filthy fucking shit.

Jim (*moving away*) There is no need at all for that language . . . I happened to find that blanket . . . The blanket smelt like that when I found it.

Pause.

Kim You nicked it.

Jim Someone left it; it was spare.

Kim Where?

Jim Over there somewhere.

Kim You stole it . . . (*Pause. Change of tone, conciliatory.*) I smell.

Jim We all smell, Kimmy . . . More or less.

Kim You know what I smell of, Jimmy?

Jim I know what you smell of.

Kim . . . Look what I got off him.

Jim What's that?

Kim Wallet. Nicked it. William Goodchild MP's, that's whose it is.

Jim You keep it, Kimmy.

Pause. Kim seems to have gone to sleep.

Now I'm cold, Kim . . . You've taken my blanket. I didn't say you could have it.

Kim You stole it . . . Want to sleep now, please.

SCENE FOURTEEN

Katy, Carl, Nancy. Nancy is listening to them – as if from behind a closed door.

Carl It *is* shit.

Katy Come here.

Carl You come here.

Katy Come here and shut up.

Carl goes to her. They sit on the floor.

We're here. That's what counts.

Carl (*shouting*) I love you.

They start to undress each other. Nancy enters. Carl and Katy separate.

Nancy There's not many rules to staying in my house and keeping on my right side without trouble . . . I only have respectable people – no one who'll be distressing the others and not paying the rent . . . Understood?

Katy Would you mind knocking?

Nancy You can have your privacy – but I won't have you disturbing . . . Now my son Stuart, he's a policeman, any trouble and that's that . . . Goodnight to you. (*She leaves.*)

Carl Do you hear?

They laugh and embrace.

SCENE FIFTEEN

Ed, Jim, Kim. Jim and Kim as at the end of the previous scene.

Ed (*appearing from upstage, shouting*) I warned you.

Jim Leave me alone.

Ed Irish thief.

Jim Leave me alone.

Ed kicks Jim. Jim falls over and lies still.

Ed (*to Kim*) Excuse me please . . . I wish to reclaim what is mine.

Ed starts to take the blanket. Kim holds on.

Kim Get off.

Ed falls on top of Kim.

Get off me. Fuck off.

Ed Are you my daughter? Ingratitude! All the love I showed you.

Kim Fuck off.

Ed Are you my daughter? You look rather like her.

Kim I said fuck off. I know your fucking game. Fuck off. I'm fucking sick.

Ed snatches the blanket and moves away. He stands upstage, within hearing range.

Jimmy . . . Jimmy, are you dead?

Ed comes back.

Ed Excuse me – may I lie with you – may we share the blanket perhaps?

Kim I said piss off. I don't want your blanket. There's more important things in life, you know.

Ed Ah, but that is where you are wrong . . . Nothing in life is more important than a little warmth – except for love – and a little love is extremely hard to find.

Kim I'm not listening to you – so just piss off.

Ed The thing is that there are enough blankets to go round – but not enough love . . . You see – a blanket's a blanket – shouldn't disappear, unlike love which always goes away or turns into the other thing – only sometimes the blanket does go away, then you're left with nothing. Goodnight to you. (*Ed moves away.*)

Kim Jimmy. Jimmy. He kicked you. Are you dead? (*Pause.*) Jimmy?

Jim (*moving slowly*) If a man kicks you always pretend to be dead then he won't kill you – now you know.

Kim I'm cold, Jimmy.

Jim Off you go, Kimmy my love.

   Pause.

Kim Jimmy?

Jim What?

Kim Get me drink – here's money.

   She gives him the wallet.

Jim Too late for drink.

Kim Get me drink, Jimmy – get me drink and fags, I want fags.

Jim Too late, Kimmy – off you go now . . . Let Jimmy find a blanket. Bedtime, Kimmy.

Kim (*screaming*) Get me drink . . . Get me booze and fags . . . Get me them. Now . . . I gave you money . . . Do it, Jimmy . . . Fucking do it.

Pause. Jimmy moves off a little way, leaving Kim alone.

Please, please, please, Jimmy – Poet Jim, please please please . . . I'm cold. I gave you my money.

Kim lies still.

Jim (*returning*) Here.

He places the wallet beneath Kim's head.

Don't know where you got it, but I don't want it; no, not at all . . . Not at all. (*He leaves.*)

SCENE SIXTEEN

James *and Greg. James is carrying camera equipment. Greg walking. The stage is bare.*

James Well, if it isn't Gregory Goodchild.

Greg Uncle James.

James Well, well . . . (*Pause.*) Greg – you look ridiculous; why are you wearing such absurd clothing?

Greg I'm an anarchist.

James (*laughing*) I see . . . Haven't seen you for ages; years, must be . . . What are you doing?

Greg Nothing much.

James Still at home?

Greg nods.

Your Dad's in the news . . . The shame of it, eh? God, the things he says . . . Good to see you, Greg.

Greg I was just wandering about.

James How's Sarah?

Greg We don't talk much.

James She must be seventeen.

Greg Studies a lot . . . We don't get on.

James Going anywhere in particular?

Greg What?

James Direction?

Greg No.

James Oh, Greg, you do look ridiculous – what must your father say?

Greg Are you laughing at me?

James No, no.

Greg I'm leaving home soon, anyway . . . Don't give a shit.

James Good, good . . . Do you mind if I walk with you for a bit?

Greg Fine.

James Catch up on a few things, eh?

Greg Sure.

They leave.

SCENE SEVENTEEN

Charlie and Bill.

Charlie (*very angry*) Where the fuck is she? (*Shouting.*) She's been out all fucking night. (*Pause. Shouting.*) Dad . . . (*Shouting very close. Pushes him.*) Dad, where the fuck is she?

Bill Don't hit me.

Charlie I said, 'Where the fuck is she?'

Bill I heard.

Charlie Well?

Bill Don't hit me, Charlie . . . Please.

Charlie It's very important that I know where she is, right? So where is she?

Pause.

Bill Important?

Charlie Yeah.

Slight pause.

Bill Why is it important?

Charlie Because I need to talk to her.

Bill What about?

Charlie Nothing – shut up. (*Pause.*) You don't know nothing. Nothing about what it's like.

Bill What?

Charlie I don't have to fucking well explain myself to you.

Slight pause.

Bill What what's like?

Charlie Shut up.

Bill What, Charlie?

Charlie Missing someone . . . Needing someone – you know nothing – just go on and fucking on.

Bill You don't love her.

Charlie (*interrupting*) What do you know about it?

Bill (*interrupting*) Else you wouldn't treat her so bad – that I do know.

Charlie Love – you dare to use the word . . . Shut it . . . It's none of your business. I don't want to talk to you, understand? (*Pause.*) Where is she?

Bill Don't know.

Charlie You better not. (*Slight pause.*) *Love* – well, I love Kim and you're fucking well giving her ideas – oh, yes, you are – putting your fucking ideas in her head – 'You shouldn't let Charlie treat you like this, you shouldn't let Charlie treat you like that.' I'm sick of it. I'm sick of you.

Pause. Charlie threatens Bill.

Bill Don't.

Charlie 'Don't hit me, don't hit me . . .' What a poor sad, little old man.

Pause.

Bill I'm not old.

Charlie Where is she?

Bill Don't know.

Pause. Charlie sits down.

Charlie . . . ? Charlie?

Charlie What?

Bill While you're here, I've got something I want to ask you.

Charlie For fuck's sake.

Bill No, it's just that I . . .

Charlie (*with fake tenderness*) What's the matter, is there anything I can do for you?

Bill When can I go back in my own room, Charlie?

Charlie You want to go back into your own room . . . ? Well, I never would have guessed that's what it was . . . So full of surprises.

Bill Charlie.

Charlie Oh, for fuck's sake . . . How many times have I got to tell you . . . ? You stay in here . . . Right . . . ? Kimmie's got to use the other room, and there's not a lot the old cripple can do about it . . . Except go on and fucking on . . . (*Shouting.*) Where the fuck is she? (*To Bill*) You really choose your fucking moments, don't you? (*He walks slowly towards him.*)

Bill No, Charlie . . . No.

Charlie If I hear one more word about the other room. One. One more complaint out of you, you know where you're going, don't you?

Bill No, Charlie, no.

Charlie Shut your face, then.

Bill Don't hit me.

Charlie 'Don't hit me. Don't hit me' . . . (*He clips him.*)

Bill I want me room.

Charlie You stay put or fuck off right out of it . . . The room is for the girl.

Charlie sits down again. Pause.

When did you last see her?

Bill Couple of days.

Charlie When?

Bill Late at night. (*Pause.*) She said she were going out.

Charlie And?

Bill Wouldn't be coming back.

Charlie I'll fucking kill her . . . Wouldn't be coming back, eh?

Bill Wouldn't be coming back.

Charlie Shut up. (*Pause.*) I'll kill her . . . She'll come back . . . She's got to come back.

Exit Charlie and Bill.

SCENE EIGHTEEN

James and Greg, still walking as in previous scene.

James So the old man.

Greg . . . Old fart . . .

James . . . Now, now. Coming to stay. Retiring.

Greg Dad's after his money. He hates him.

James You *are* cynical, Greg. Well, a retired judge and an MP in one house – the Establishment closes ranks!

Greg I'm getting out.

James So you said.

Pause.

Greg You hate him as well, don't you?

James Who?

Greg Both of them.

James Yes and no . . . Your grandfather never forgives, you know that – he hates me more than I hate him – from his point of view he's probably got good reason. As for your father, well, he takes after your grandfather.

Greg His point of view – Christ.

James Everyone has their point of view. Some are more damaging than others . . . At least he's reasonably consistent . . . Have you got a point of view?

Greg What?

James Nothing.

Greg I'd better get going. (*Pause.*) James?

James What?

Greg You know I was told never to have anything to do with you. Never to speak to you. I was warned against you.

James Now that doesn't surprise me . . . So how is my dear brother?

Greg There's things I could tell you about *him*.

James Really, I wish you would.

Greg Things about his private life which might surprise you.

James Really.

Pause.

Greg James?

James What?

Greg Doesn't matter . . . I'll be off now.

James Right.

Greg starts to leave.

Greg . . . Hang on.

James takes a photo.

One day we'll both have a laugh. Come and visit me sometime – in the studio. I want to hear everything.

Greg Right.

James Soon?

Greg Right.

James Bye then.

Greg Bye.

They leave.

Act Two

SCENE ONE

Hard white spotlight. Like a television studio. William is sitting. He talks partly as if to a studio audience, and partly to camera.

William Yes, yes; I did hear your question. It is your question, which I heard first time, that I am trying to answer . . . Do you want to hear my answer to your question? (*Pause.*) Right. Yes, yes, of course we care . . . We care very, very much; and yes, of course we are aware of what you are saying . . . Of course we are aware of the hardship facing a minority in our inner cities . . . We are aware of the poor, we are aware of the homeless; the lonely – yes, yes, of course, we recognize the despair of these people . . . I have seen with my own eyes . . . I have heard with my own ears . . . Don't say I don't care . . . Don't say we don't care . . . (*Pause.*) But – and it's a big but – many, many, many people are doing well, are living better; some are doing very well . . . How many people now own their own homes . . . ? Many more . . . Building a secure future for their children . . . More can do well; more will do better, and we care about them too . . . For every ounce of unhappiness, every ounce of despair, there is a pound of happiness, of fulfilment, of achievement, of wealth . . . That is our achievement. (*Pause. He listens as if to an interruption.*) You may call it greed . . . We have a clear conscience and a vision of the future . . . There will always be the despair you speak of; always despair, always dissent; sometimes even hysterical dissent . . . But we are not hysterical onlookers, we are achievers; we are not critics, we are doers. (*William leaves.*)

Lighting crossfade to reveal Jim.

SCENE TWO

Jim (*monologue*) Somewhere still the lights go off; thousands of dark and loving places . . . Still and quiet and warm . . . Places not for then, but now . . . Not for me . . . No face to look at . . . To take the light off and kiss gently by the love light of the moon . . . No, no face now except my own . . . I have my friends though. Don't think I don't. Friends? Yes . . . I know your love, you lovers.

SCENE THREE

Charlie, Bill and Kim. Bill sitting. Charlie pacing, very agitated. Silence. Enter Kim. Charlie stops moving.

Bill Kim, Kimmy? Hello, Kim.

Kim is shaking.

Kim? You all right? You look . . .

Charlie (*interrupting*) Shut it. (*Pause.*) Where you been?

Charlie moves over to Kim. Kisses her roughly.

Kim I need . . .

Charlie Where have you been?

He threatens her.

Where have you been?

He threatens her.

Kim Please don't . . .

Charlie Where the fuck have you been?

Kim I need . . .

Charlie I know what you fucking well need.

He pushes her away. She sits.

Kim I need . . .

Charlie Well; I've got news for you.

Bill Don't.

Charlie (*to Bill*) What did you say?

Pause. He moves threateningly towards Bill.

Bill Don't hit her, Charlie.

Charlie suddenly leaves.

He's mad . . . Where you been, Kim?

Kim Out.

Bill You look bad, Kim.

Kim Look.

She shows Bill the wallet. She gives it to him.

Bill (*inspecting the wallet*) Goodchild . . . He's a bleeding MP. Hide it, Kim, you hide it; and there's money . . . Don't give it to Charlie.

Lights down on Kim and Bill. Kim moves away from Bill. She joins Jim who is sitting in an extreme upstage position. Bill leaves.

SCENE FOUR

Kim (*monologue*) Like being dead . . . Heavy . . . Nothing; nothing else matters . . . Not love nor nothing . . . (*Pause.*) Gave it up. God. I need it. Kills love . . . Kills

it stone fucking dead . . . If the smack gets you, love is
dead . . .

*She lies down with Jim. They remain on stage
throughout the following scenes.*

SCENE FIVE

James, Sarah, **Dot,** *William. James in separate pool of light
– a different part of the stage. Telephone conversation.*

Sarah Hello?

James Who's that?

Sarah Sarah . . . (*Pause.*) Hello?

James Hello, Sarah, is your father there?

Sarah Who is it?

James (*muttering*) Oh, I'm . . .

Sarah Sorry?

James We're old friends. I want to surprise him. Is he
there?

Sarah Hang on a minute, I'll get him.

Dot enters.

Dot Is it for me?

Sarah It's for Dad. Where is he?

Dot Upstairs. Who is it?

Sarah How should I know?

Dot Well, didn't you ask?

Sarah (*shouting*) Dad! . . . Dad! Telephone . . . Dad!

William (*calling out*) Who is it?

Sarah Don't know. (*She moves to a separate part of the stage.*)

Dot Sarah. Really. You should have asked. You know what he's like.

William enters.

William William Goodchild. (*Pause.*) Hello . . . ? Hello? (*Pause.*) Who is it?

James hangs up. He clutches his head.

Dot Who . . . ?

William Before you ask. I don't know who it was – and no, I'm not hiding anything, and yes, I do apologize for not saying hello when I got in, and no, I'm not very hungry, and yes, I've had a terrible day and I don't want to be disturbed.

Pause. William moves to a separate part of the stage. The following monologues by James and Dot should be delivered as single, uninterrupted trains of thought.

James (*to himself*) Fuck it . . .

Dot (*to herself*) Sometimes . . .

James (*to himself*) Damn.

Dot (*to herself*) Sometimes I could scream . . .

James (*to himself*) It's me. Me. Your brother . . .

Dot (*to herself*) Really scream . . .

James (*to himself*) Why didn't I say it . . . ?

Dot (*to herself*) A long, long scream . . .

James (*to himself*) Damn it . . . Coward.

Dot (*to herself*) A scream to empty me.

James (*to himself*) He's my fucking brother.

Dot (*to herself*) But I don't . . . Why . . . ? Don't . . . ?
Can't . . . ? Won't . . . ?

James (*to himself*) Ring him again.

Dot (*to herself*) Will I ever scream the pain away?

James (*to himself*) Right.

Dot (*to herself*) Bastard.

> *Dot holds her face in her hands. Pause while James
> dials. She is startled by the ringing. She answers.*

Yes?

> *James hangs up. Dot, William, Sarah, James leave.*

SCENE SIX

*Katy and Carl. Katy is alone. She has been crying. Enter
Carl.*

Carl Hey, Katy?

Katy What?

Carl (*speaking very fast, breathlessly*) I met this bloke,
today – I was just hanging around like and I met this bloke
– now he's a photographer, but professional. You know
. . . Anyway he says he wants an assistant – He said I got
to ring him for an interview and he'd give me – well, he
might – this job. Assistant photographer. He said he might,
but I think he will, you know.

Katy What do you mean, you were hanging around?

Carl What do you mean? Don't you think it's bloody great?

Katy Where?

Carl It's bloody great.

Katy I'm pissed off, Carl. I hate it here.

Carl Are you listening to me?

Katy Are you listening to me?

Carl Katy.

Katy I fucking hate her.

Carl Did you hear what I said? It's what I want. What I've been looking for.

Katy I want to get the fuck out of it, Carl. I hate her.

Carl Listen. You're not bloody listening – I'm going to be a photographer's assistant. I showed him that shot I took of you at the station. When we got here. Remember? He liked it. (*Pause.*) Katy . . . Katy? It's great.

Katy Ring then.

Carl What?

Katy You'd better ring then. Bloody ring him . . . Look I don't mean to be . . . It's great, love. I'm pleased for you. Really.

Carl I love you. You know that.

He kisses her.

Katy Yeah.

Carl Hey. You been crying?

Katy No . . . Ring him.

Carl You have been crying.

Katy I fucking haven't. I should know.

Carl I love you.

He kisses her.

Do you want to do it?

Katy Ring him, will you?

Carl Let's do it. Eh?

Katy Ring him, Carl. That's where your head is.

Carl (*laughs*) Right.

Carl leaves, followed by Katy. As Carl leaves, James enters. James watches him pass. James moves to an extreme downstage position – he stays there throughout the following scene – until the telephone conversation with William.

SCENE SEVEN

Edward, *Dot, Greg, William, Sarah. The family is together, having eaten.*

William Well, father . . . (*Raises his glass of brandy*.) . . . Here's to you . . . May your retirement be a long and happy one. Welcome.

Edward Well, let's all hope it isn't too long. Thank you, William . . . Thank you, Dorothy.

Pause.

William Where's Sarah?

Dot She said she wasn't hungry.

William What's got into that girl?

Greg She's working.

Edward So, Gregory, what are you going to do with your life? Follow in your illustrious father's footsteps?

Greg No.

William Greg.

Greg All right. All right.

Edward You must have some ambitions? When I was your age . . .

Dot (*interrupting*) . . . Of course you have ambitions, don't you, Greg?

Greg No.

Dot Greg.

William (*to Dot*) Please.

Sarah enters.

Sarah (*to William*) Phone call for you. (*She starts to go.*)

William Who is it?

Sarah Don't know.

William leaves. James, who is still visible, is waiting to talk to him.

Dot You should ask, Sarah.

Sarah moves to a separate upstage position.

Edward Dot, my dear, come and sit next to the old man.

Greg moves away from Dot and Edward. Dot moves to Edward. James and William are positioned on opposite sides of the stage, framing the scene.

SCENE EIGHT

William and James. Telephone conversation.

James William, it's me.

William Who?

James James.

William James?

James Your brother James. Don't hang up, please.

  Pause.

William What do you want?

James How's Dad? (*Pause.*) I hear he's come to stay.

William Who told you that?

James Your son.

William When? When did you see Greg?

  Sarah and Greg. They are unheard by Dot and Edward who are sitting together separately.

Greg Sarah?

Sarah What?

Greg I . . .

Sarah . . . Why didn't you tell me about Amanda?

Greg I didn't . . .

Sarah (*interrupting*) Why did I have to hear from her?

Greg What?

Sarah You heard . . . You're . . .

Greg You've seen her? What did she say?

Sarah She hates you and so do I . . . She's my friend, Greg.

Pause.

Greg What did she say?

Sarah Are you sure you want to hear this? She said you were terrible in bed.

She leaves. Greg sits alone.

SCENE NINE

Edward and Dorothy.

Edward Old age, Dorothy . . . ? Old age . . . Wanting to die quietly, is all I ask . . . I don't ask for love.

Dot You know we love you.

SCENE TEN

William and James. Telephone conversation continued.

James I want to see you.

William If it's money, you can forget it. Father's money too . . . I know your kind of trouble.

James No, I need to talk to you.

William Nothing changes . . . Nothing has changed.

James I need to talk to you.

William Talk away.

James In person – I need to see you; I must see you.

Pause.

William I can't help you. I won't see you . . . Don't ring me again.

James Right.

William Goodbye.

James leaves. William sits separately from Greg and Dot/Edward.

SCENE ELEVEN

Dot and Edward.

Edward A life of judging others; a dry, loveless old age is all I ask . . . A very peaceful death; a while in comfort before I die.

Dot Talk to me. I want you to talk to me. No one talks to me now. Not William. Not Sarah. Not Greg.

Edward I'll talk to you, Dorothy my dear, I'll talk to you – but maybe you won't like what I say . . . But I'll talk to you and you can talk to me – like two imprisoned birds, eh, Dot? (*Pause.*) Imprisoned.

Dot (*smiles*) Oh, Edward, you are so indulgent – (*slight pause*) – and so ungrateful, 'imprisoned birds'!

Edward Figure of speech, Dot, figure of speech.

They leave. William moves downstage.

William Greg?

Greg What?

William Why didn't you mention that you had seen your uncle?

Greg How did you know?

William It doesn't matter how I know . . . I asked you why you didn't tell me.

Greg What's it got to do with you?

William In our family there are certain rules, Greg. I am very angry. You have been told why our family has no contact with your uncle.

Greg Bullshit – you're just scared I'll tell him about you.

William What do you mean?

Greg You *know* what I mean.

William If I knew what I wouldn't be asking.

Pause.

Greg Your little excursions . . . You're frightened I'll tell wicked Uncle James about your little excursions.

William Greg, you promised never to mention that again.

Greg What?

William Greg, you are being very unfair, and breaking a *promise*. (*Slight pause.*) In the past, as I have explained, I had some – contact – of the kind you allude to. I also explained, although you can't have been listening, some of the reasons for that contact . . . I explained in great detail my relationship with your mother. In short, that the whole business was not as simple as you thought it was. I warned you that you might not understand . . . I apologized for upsetting you – for causing you pain . . . I explained that it would not happen again . . . I told you not to worry . . . That was two years ago – you had just left school – and now, here you are bringing that old episode to life . . . Here you still are, looking like a vagrant, treating my house like a hotel, because you haven't the guts to make anything of yourself . . . Here you are making contact with your Uncle James – well, I shall spell it out to you, Greg . . . While you continue to live under my roof you shall abide by my rules.

Greg I think I hate you.

William In a chaotic way, Greg, you are extremely hurtful. You will not see your uncle again. Is that understood?

Greg I see who I like . . . I'm leaving soon anyway.

William This is not a game . . . Did you say anything?

Greg About what?

William Did you say anything?

Greg To whom?

William Your uncle.

Greg None of your business.

Greg leaves, followed by William.

SCENE TWELVE

Kim and Jim. Jim is asleep.

Kim (*monologue*) Used to love . . . Charlie . . . With every fucking bit of me I loved . . . There was no one else, only London . . . No friend . . . Get so cold now.

Corinna enters.

SCENE THIRTEEN

Corinna and Kim. Kim ignores Corinna.

Corinna All right? (*Pause.*) Don't feel like talking?

(*Pause.*) Neither do I.

Corinna moves away a bit. She watches Kim.

(*part monologue and partly to Kim*) I don't come from
here and I'll come out when I've a mind to – but I was here
before you was born . . . You don't belong here either . . .
(*Pause.*) Don't trust 'em . . . (*to Kim*) Don't need to talk
. . . (*Pause.*) I understand that.

*Kim continues to ignore Corinna. Corinna approaches
Kim slowly, unnoticed by her.*

Kim (*monologue*) Doesn't rush – moves real slow . . .
Prick . . . Vein . . . No vein left. Black blood. Feels black,
not red . . . Black and slow . . . Brain is dead, it says.

Corinna Trust 'em . . . ? No.

Corinna sits with Kim, embraces her as she speaks.

Kim (*monologue*) My brain is black . . . Heavy . . . Heavy
like death . . . I'm cold. I'm sick – are you dead too, Jimmy
. . . Tell her to fuck off, Jim . . . Don't want to talk at all
. . . (*to Corinna*) Fuck off, you. (*Lays her hands against
the floor.*)

Concrete close . . . Hard and cold . . . Floating down . . .
Through concrete . . . Into what? Concrete grave – heavy
death – down in the ground . . . Floating down . . .
Floating? Falling. Falling . . . Don't give a fuck . . .

Pause.

Corinna Memory . . . (*Searching for the word.*) . . .
Consumes memory . . . He left me – don't trust them . . .

Sings.
'On her breast a turtle dove,
To signify she died of love . . .'

I'm a friend . . . Don't trust 'em.

Kim What?

Corinna Them (*Rhyming the word.*) . . . Men.

Kim Fuck off. (*Shouting.*) Fuck off, you.

Corinna leaves.

Corinna (*as she goes*) I'm a friend.

Kim (*monologue*) Don't give a fuck . . . No time for love
. . . Except the sort you sell . . . No time for love with
body dead and in the grave . . . Love is what you sell . . .
'Are you looking for a little love?' . . . I'm head dead,
Charlie . . . Dead head . . . Jimmy? Jimmy . . . ? He kicked
you, are you dead?

Jim groans as she tries to wake him.

Jim Who kicked me in the head?

Kim The man with the blanket.

Jim But that was ages ago, Kimmy.

Kim Ages ago?

Jim Ages.

Kim Ages ago; just now.

Jim Weeks ago.

SCENE FOURTEEN

James and Carl. James is showing Carl some photographs.

James So, Carl, what do you think?

Carl Great.

James They're all great? You don't like some more than
others?

Pause.

Carl No; I like the black-and-white ones best.

James They're old; ancient.

Carl This is brilliant.

James Vietnam . . . Strange really; can you believe that once I was fearless and feared.

Carl This is really great . . . This kid here, so frightened . . . Brilliant . . . Must have been a bugger to get it . . . How did you get it. You were *there* . . . Shit, I mean, shit.

Pause.

James Are you interested in politics?

Carl What?

James Politics.

Carl What do you mean?

James I wanted people to see what was going on . . . Seems such a long time ago . . . I was so *principled*. Committed. (*Laughing.*) We wanted to change the world . . . What about you?

Carl I want to be a photographer – that's it, really – to tell the truth. So I don't really know . . . I suppose so.

Pause.

James Mind you, I don't do interesting work any more. I am a boring photographer – advertising mainly . . . (*Pause.*) In fact it's not a creative job at all – photographer's assistant to a boring photographer like me is even more boring than being me, because you don't even get to take any photographs.

Carl I don't?

James No, and the money's terrible . . . But, Carl, I like you; I think we'll get on – so, the job, if you want it, is yours.

Carl Brilliant.

SCENE FIFTEEN

Bill, Kim and Charlie. Charlie enters, Kim moves away from Bill.

Charlie (*to Bill*) Here . . . (*Throws some money on to the floor.*) Don't say I don't look after you . . . (*to Kim*) Get something with it.

Bill Where's it from, Charlie?

Charlie Mind your own.

Bill Dirty money, ain't it?

Charlie Dirty money? Dirty money – all money's dirty money.

Kim True.

Bill (*to Kim*) Shut up.

Charlie It does . . . Dirty money? – maybe . . . Dirty money for a filthy old man . . . (*to Kim*) You owe me.

Kim I haven't got anything, Charlie.

Charlie moves towards Kim.

Charlie Liar.

Bill Charlie.

Charlie Shut it.

Charlie violently gags Bill with Kim's stocking.

Bill (*while being gagged*) Don't, don't. (*He is silenced.*)

Charlie Fucking leave it there.

Kim Leave him . . . Leave him alone, Charlie.

Charlie Oh, yes.

He hits her. Throws her to the floor. She lies still. Pause.

Charlie (*to Bill*) Leave it . . . Leave it – I'm sick of your voice.

He goes over to Kim.

(*to Bill*) You watching? Want to see me do it? Do you?

He starts to caress Kim. She seems to be unconscious.

Filthy old man.

Continues to caress Kim.

Maybe it's my turn . . . (*Pause.*) Could be dead . . . (*to Kim*) You listening to me? (*Pause.*) You owe me.

He hits her. She gives him William's wallet.

Kim It's all there.

Charlie (*looking at the wallet*) Now this, my little darling, is something.

Kim . . . I don't care.

Charlie leaves, followed by Bill and Kim.

SCENE SIXTEEN

Katy and Carl.

Katy What's it like then . . . ?

Carl All right.

Katy Only all right . . . ? (*Pause.*) What's 'e like . . . ?

Carl I don't care what 'e's like . . . What's that got to do with it? – I don't give a fuck what 'e's like.

Pause.

Katy What's got into you?

Carl What's all these bloody questions for?

Katy I want to know what it's like. (*Pause.*) Seeing as you don't want to ask what I do.

Carl I know what you do. You sit here.

Katy I meant what I *want* to do, Carl, not what I do do.

Carl Same difference . . .

Pause.

Katy Carl? (*Pause.*) Do you think we'll find somewhere better to stay?

Carl Here's all right.

Katy Here's all right? It's shit.

Carl All right, all right.

SCENE SEVENTEEN

Carl and James. Carl is cleaning the floor with a cloth and bucket. James is sitting.

James So, Carl . . . Where are you living?

Carl Not far . . . (*Points.*) That way.

Pause.

James Do you live with anyone?

187

Carl What?

James Do you share?

Carl No.

James I see . . . (*Pause.*) Who was the girl in the photograph?

Carl Just someone that I saw . . .

   Pause.

James Tell me about your family.

Carl I won't, if you don't mind.

   Slight pause.

James Don't you miss them?

Carl They're nothing to do with it . . . Of course I miss 'em. Not me dad. Me mum. I miss her . . . Sometimes . . . But she isn't going to make me into a photographer. So that's that; and that's why I'm here . . . (*Pause.*) Didn't tell 'em I was leaving.

James Really . . . Your poor mother . . . (*Pause.*) Carl, why don't you give her a ring? Tell her you're OK?

Carl I knew I shouldn't have told you. I don't want to. It's nothing to do with them.

James I was only . . .

Carl It's none of your business.

   Pause.

James I wish my feelings for my family were as simple as yours . . . I don't talk to my family either . . . (*Pause.*) Have you got a brother?

   Carl shakes his head.

You've probably seen my brother on TV – William Goodchild. Have you heard of him? The politician?

Carl Not sure . . . What you asking me all these questions for?

James No reason. Conversation . . . I'm interested.

Carl continues to clean the floor. Pause.

Or I should say my family doesn't talk to me.

SCENE EIGHTEEN

Kim and Bill. Kim is standing downstage. Bill sitting gagged. He is asleep. Kim slowly starts to move. Bill opens his eyes and looks at her.

Kim (*monologue*) I had a dream – the sea, the Irish sea . . . Deep . . . Cold . . . There were fish, and above the fish, a boat. Sailing boat. Sailing away . . . The sea was calm and still, very still . . . Like nothing here . . . It was a good dream. Just now. (*Pause. To Bill.*) Look at you. (*Laughs.*) It's an old, old story, Bill . . . Nothing new . . . My dad, he did worse than I've seen here . . . He hated me, so he said . . . So don't worry about me.

She moves over to him. She is in some pain.

Worry about you. I'll look after myself see.

She takes her stocking from around his neck.

Looks better on my leg, don't you think?

Bill You've got to look after yourself like you look after me.

Pause.

Kim I like you, Bill . . . (*Pause.*) You don't half smell . . .

You need a wash.

Bill I could do with one.

Kim I will if you behave.

Bill Go on then.

She fills a bowl of water and starts to wash him. Taking his shirt off first. She unbuttons his trousers.

(*smiling*) Still some feelings left.

Kim Dirty old sod.

Bill Sorry, love.

Pause.

Kim I want to go away . . . (*Pause.*) I want to go home . . . That's what I want.

Bill and Kim leave.

Act Three

SCENE ONE

Dot and Edward. Sarah listens to them unseen. Dot is staring ahead of her. Edward enters.

Edward You look so tired, my dear.

Dot Oh?

Edward Yes, so tired. (*He sits. Pause.*) Come and sit with me.

Dot sits next to him. Pause.

No; like we used to.

Dot (*smiling*) Oh, Edward.

She moves her chair closer: Edward puts his arm around her.

Edward (*coughs*) I'm not well, not well . . . Come on, come on.

Dot moves very close. She rests her head against him.

I'm not well. (*Pause.*) Do you remember . . . ? (*Pause.*) Dot?

Dot Of course.

Edward We never said anything, did we . . . ? Not really; eh?

Dot (*agitated*) I don't understand this. Are you all right?

Edward No. We never said anything.

Dot We couldn't.

Edward We kept so very quiet . . . Wicked, eh?

Dot (*suddenly laughing; slightly uncontrolled*) Did I fall in love with my father-in-law?

Edward Well, well. (*Pause.*) Are you pleased I've come to stay? Shall I be a frightful bore? Shall I? (*Pause.*) Well. I won't last long.

Dot moves away from him.

Dot It's so difficult.

Edward Difficult?

Dot And William is so difficult. (*She starts to cry.*)

Edward There, there; now. (*Edward coughs; shows pain.*) My life! (*Pause.*) I loved another once. A woman; a girl. So young you know . . . (*Moves towards her.*) Years ago, oh, before I married . . . And, you know, Dorothy, I thought I would never love another . . . (*Pause.*) I left her. Wonder why . . . Just left . . . (*Pause.*) I loved you. (*Pause.*) Dot?

He embraces her.

Dot Stop. Stop. (*Moving away from him.*) Leave me alone . . . Why are you here? No one wants you . . . This isn't happening . . . Where's William?

Edward (*coughing*) What?

Dot Where is he? What's happening to me? Tell me.

She leaves. Pause. Edward leaves. Sarah leaves.

SCENE TWO

Nancy and Katy. Katy is sitting alone. Nancy enters.
Pause.

Nancy You said you were getting a job.

Katy What?

Nancy Well, you're late with the rent . . . Where is he
anyway? Doesn't seem to be here much – you just sitting
here on your own . . . You ought to get out, earn a bit of
your own . . . You can't stay here, you know, if you don't
pay the rent . . . You're late with it, you know that? I'm
not a charity you know, you're a few days late actually . . .
Where is he then? (*Pause.*) I said, where is he?

Katy Working.

Nancy This time of night? What kind of work do you call
that . . . ? Hope he hasn't gone off and left you, because
then who'll pay the rent . . . You can tell him from me that
if he doesn't pay the rent he'll have Stuart to answer to;
then you'll be out on the street . . . I'm not being heartless,
love, but there are those who'd be pleased of the room and
can pay the rent . . . Things are not that easy for me . . .
Blame the government. New regulations . . . No, things
are not that easy. Since my Sid went . . . So, don't think I
enjoy all this – I don't, but I won't stand for it. (*She
leaves.*)

SCENE THREE

James and Carl. Carl is sitting on the floor. He is framing
photographic slides.

James Carl?

Carl looks up.

Nothing. (*Pause.*) You're doing well . . . Things are very difficult for me at the moment; and you're a great help.

Carl (*concentrating on his work*) Do me best.

Pause.

James I don't know what you're going to say, but; why don't you . . . ? Would you like to . . . ? To live . . .

Carl looks up.

. . . I mean, I've got the spare room – certainly save you on rent – You spend so many hours here as it is . . . Think about it anyway . . . I was just thinking that soon I'll be wanting you to do more of the real work . . . You're a very good photographer . . . Not just paperwork and cleaning . . . (*Pause.*) Think about it anyway.

Carl Do you really think so?

James What?

Carl I'm a good photographer?

James Of course . . . Let me know anyway.

Carl Right.

James Fine. (*He leaves.*)

SCENE FOUR

Ed alone on stage. He is looking for his blanket.

Ed Lost everything . . . Everything . . . Had a daughter, a child; where's she now . . . ? (*Lies down.*) . . . Who's stolen my blanket again? (*He is still.*)

Blackout.

SCENE FIVE

The lights come up slowly. The stage is bare except for Stuart, who is carefully laying a blanket over the dead body of Ed. Jim enters. Pause. Jim watches.

Jim Now, what earthly use is that to him now he's dead and cold . . . ?

Stuart Come on – push off.

Jim leaves. Stuart leaves. The lights fade on Ed beneath the blanket.

SCENE SIX

Carl and Katy. Carl is wearing new clothes.

Katy Carl.

Carl What?

Katy What's up?

Carl Nothing.

Katy There is.

Carl Nothing's up. Right. Nothing's up . . . What's up with you?

Pause.

Katy We need money.

Carl Earn it then.

Katy To pay the rent. (*Pause.*) Carl, are you listening to me. We need to pay the rent. Give me some money to pay the rent . . . She'll kick us out. She said she would.

Carl Great.

Katy What d'you mean?

Pause.

Carl I'm leaving. I'm getting out of it.

Katy What?

Carl I'm leaving you, I'm getting out.

Katy What?

Carl I'm getting out of it.

Katy What?

Carl Leaving you. Right?

Katy No.

Carl I'm going.

Katy No.

Carl Now.

He grabs a plastic bag, containing his old clothes. Katy tries to stop him. They struggle over the bag.

Katy No.

Carl Right now.

Katy What? What . . . ? No. No . . . What about the rent . . . ? What d'you mean . . . ?

Carl I'm going.

Pause.

Katy Carl – this isn't happening . . . No . . . What d'you mean . . . (*Shouting*) What the fuck is happening? What the fuck . . . (*Breaks down. Pause.*) You love me. Who?

Carl I've got to go. Right?

Katy Fucking who?

Carl You won't understand.

Katy Who?

Carl (*leaving*) I'll see you soon. Right? (*Carl leaves.*)

Katy Liar . . . This isn't happening. No. Fucking liar. (*Pause.*) Carl . . . ? Carl . . . ? Carl, don't go. No. You won't ever leave me will you? Carl? (*Exit Katy.*)

SCENE SEVEN

Charlie is positioned downstage. Dot and Edward positioned separately.

Charlie (*monologue*) I got his number out of the wallet what I got off Kim; his *home* number; and I rung him – so there I was on the phone to this fucking MP – and you know it's true what they says – nothing special – nothing at all special . . . He was scared. Frightened of me like anyone is who isn't an MP. 'You'll do what I says,' I says to him, threatened him with this and that . . . Newspapers . . . Making it up as I was going along . . . He was so fucking quiet – frightened.

Edward The truth is, Dot my dear, that nothing ever really touches us . . . Our hearts are untrue . . . We commit terrible crimes, detected by no one . . . The world crumbles, but doesn't touch us. (*Coughs. Pause.*) And we don't die as easily as we should.

Dot Could you ever forgive him?

Edward Who?

Dot James.

Edward Of course . . . Of course . . . But I could never tell him that I forgive him.

Charlie (*monologue*) I mean, I could have just found the fucking wallet. Lying around. He didn't think of that. He could have said fuck off to me; but he didn't, 'cause he was scared . . . You got to find the fear in people, then they do just what you want – learnt that in the army – and other things . . . Anything . . . Do anything . . . Give anything . . . Act stupid . . . It was dead easy. I was in charge . . . Made me laugh . . . 'You meet the girl – she gives you the wallet . . . Easy.' (*Slight pause.*) Easy. (*He leaves.*)

Greg enters in a hurry.

Greg (*shouting*) Mum! Mum! Where's Dad?

Dot Don't shout, Greg.

Greg Where is he?

Dot Upstairs – why? Do you?

Greg (*interrupting*) Great.

Dot What . . . ?

Greg has left. Sarah has entered unseen. She listens to Dot and Edward.

Edward What's got into that boy? Terribly ill-mannered.

Dot He's leaving home.

Edward Is he now? That's probably for the best.

Pause.

Dot I was married at his age.

Edward So young . . . We're all getting so much older, Dot . . . (*Pause.*) Yes, James . . . Maybe I should see James again.

Dot James?

Edward No, no . . . (*Pause.*) You love me, don't you, Dorothy?

Dot Of course I love you.

Edward You know me for what I am.

Dot I won't miss him – not really – he's been such hard work, and so difficult recently . . . Sometimes I look back and I think it all could have been different – my life could have been different – my life could have been other.

Edward Other?

Dot My life could have been different, quite different . . . I don't think I'm the person I was . . . The waste. The silence . . . But it's maybe all too late. I've been another person.

Edward Don't look back . . . What's past is past. (*Pause.*) Would you care to join me for a dance? Let's dance, Dot, a little waltz.

Dot Oh, Edward, you are ridiculous.

They dance a waltz.

Edward So you see, it's never too late.

Sarah is seen. They stop dancing and look embarrassed.

Sarah Sorry . . . No, I didn't mean sorry. (*Slight pause.*) I heard everything.

Dot Sarah, I . . .

Edward Now, Sarah my dear, let me explain.

Sarah (*interrupting*) Please stop talking . . . (*Pause.*) I don't hate you.

Edward Sorry?

Sarah I don't hate either of you, but I don't want to talk, because there's nothing to say . . . (*Slight pause.*) Mum?

Pause. Dot gestures for Edward to leave.

Edward I think I'll disappear. (*Edward moves away and stands separately.*)

Sarah I don't ever want to say the sad things I've heard you say.

Dot I don't want you to either.

Dot kisses Sarah and moves away to stand near Edward.

Sarah Ridiculous – selfish . . . Blind . . . I don't miss anything . . . In my memory, something still of love; the love goes cold – no words to express.

William enters and sits separately.

'What's got into that girl?' . . . 'You're looking too thin' . . . Looking me over, like someone else – I said I was fine . . . Alone. Alone. Dreams of out . . . No escape from within . . . Sometimes death is all I want . . . The old man, my grandfather – dancing with a woman – my mother – seen as if for the first time – but I felt so alone . . . How many like me in the moving world, not taking part while other people's stories move forward and fast and furious.

Greg enters and stands near William.

Blinded-hate stories in the name of love; and I stand still or move little by little inside and the further in I go the more I see and hear – the less I say.

Edward and Dot leave. Charlie and Kim enter and stand separately.

SCENE EIGHT

Greg, William. William is sitting.

William (*not looking up*) Not now, Greg, I'm extremely busy . . . (*Pause.*) Well? Can't this wait?

Pause. Greg staring at William. William still not looking up.

Don't just stand there, Greg . . . You are interrupting me . . . (*Looks up.*) Greg!

Pause.

Greg Have you lost your wallet? (*Long pause.*) Now, you see, I've just answered the telephone; hilarious really, but whoever it was thought I was you . . . The thing is, you're in big, big trouble.

They leave.

SCENE NINE

Charlie and Kim, both standing.

Charlie You'll *be* there all right . . . It's easy – meet him and he'll give you the money. You've got to fucking do it, Kim.

Kim I don't want to, Charlie – I don't want to – leave the poor fucker alone . . . I don't want to.

Charlie Kim – listen; you know I love you – you know that don't you? Kim?

Kim I don't love you.

Pause.

Charlie It'll all be different – like it was.

Kim Liar, Charlie.

Charlie You'll fucking meet this bastard if I have to fucking drag you.

Kim I don't care . . . I don't care – you'll do what you want.

They leave.

SCENE TEN

Stuart and Katy. Nancy is sitting alone on the other side of the stage throughout this scene. Katy sitting on the floor. Stuart enters. Pause. Stuart looks at her.

Katy What do you want?

Stuart Where is he then? Your boyfriend, where is he?

Katy Out.

Stuart Where?

Katy Out.

Pause.

Stuart Are you hungry?

Katy No.

Stuart You look hungry. (*Pause.*) Would you like an apple? (*He produces an apple.*)

Katy All right.

Stuart Wait.

He takes a bite, then gives her the apple. Stuart watches her eat the apple. She is very hungry and eats quickly. Long pause.

(*laughing*) And Eve ate.

Katy You're weird, you are. What are you doing in 'ere, anyway?

Stuart I came to give you an apple.

Katy Well now you can fuck off. Right?

Stuart Did you call me weird? (*Pause.*) Sorry . . . Did you call me weird? (*Pause.*) Well, did you?

Katy Get lost.

Stuart Oooh – I am not weird. OK? I said OK?

Katy Right.

Stuart Right. (*He starts to roll up his sleeve. Flexes his biceps.*) What do you think of that then? Not bad, eh? Bit more than you're used to, I'd say. (*Pause.*) Do you like this room?

Katy No.

Stuart It's a very nice room . . . Why don't you like it?

Katy' Cause you're in it.

Stuart We need the rent.

He sits and stares at her. Pause.

We need the rent . . . Rent . . . R – E – N – T. (*Pause.*) Unless of course . . .

He approaches her. He touches her.

Katy You touch me again . . .

Stuart (*half singing*) . . . And you'll call the police.

Katy (*shouting*) I'll fucking kill you . . . D'you think I'm scared of you, or something; fucking weird wanker. Just piss off.

Stuart I came for the rent, that's what I came for. (*He leaves.*)

SCENE ELEVEN

Stuart and Nancy. Nancy standing. Stuart enters. He sits. Pause. Nancy sits. Katy is still on stage – positioned separately.

Nancy Stuart? (*Pause.*) Stuart?

Stuart What?

Nancy Well?

Stuart What?

Nancy What did she say? Did you get it off her? The rent.

Stuart Yes.

Nancy Where is it?

Stuart No . . . No. I didn't get it, no.

Nancy Stuart, you either did or didn't.

Stuart I didn't.

   Pause.

Nancy You've been gone for a while. Thought you must have gone out or something – you said you were just popping to get the rent off her and I've been waiting and now you tell me you have and you haven't.

Stuart I said I haven't.

   Pause.

Nancy Was she there?

Stuart No.

Nancy (*interrupting*) I hope you're not lying to me, Stuart.

Stuart I meant not *really* there . . . I thought you meant is she all there. (*He points to his head.*)

Nancy Oh.

Stuart Because she's not. (*Slight pause.*) She's a bit weird actually.

Nancy How do you mean?

Stuart You know.

Nancy I thought so. (*Long pause.*) I do love you, Stuey, you know that, don't you . . . ? I love you more than anything else – you know that don't you?

Stuart Mum – course I do.

Nancy I just wanted to tell you – you're all I've got.

Stuart All right, all right.

Pause.

Nancy Am I all you've got too?

Stuart Course you are.

Pause. He holds her hand. Nancy is about to cry.

Nancy Only I wanted to tell you. I've got no one else to tell. Everyone else *is* weird – I sometimes think – well, not all – but most.

Stuart Come on, Mum . . . Put the telly on. You'll miss the news.

Pause.

Nancy She can't stay without paying the rent.

Stuart I know. I know. I'll tell her, right? Please, Mum.

Pause.

Nancy Stuart?

Stuart What?

Nancy What were you doing all that time, up there with her?

Stuart What?

Nancy What were you doing if you weren't getting the rent?

Stuart What *do* you mean?

Nancy Nothing.

Stuart I hope you don't.

Pause.

Nancy Stuart?

Stuart All right. I'll get rid of her.

Nancy Will you?

Stuart Course I will. She's no good.

Nancy Oh, I can relax now.

Stuart That's it.

They sit in silence for a while. They leave.

SCENE TWELVE

James and Greg. Carl is on stage – positioned separately in a different room, not hearing James and Greg.

Greg 'You meet the girl. Euston Station. She gives you the wallet. You give her the money. Easy . . .' That's how he put it.

James How extraordinary.

Greg Yeah, that's where he'll be – otherwise it's front-page time – I thought you'd be interested . . . I thought you'd like it.

James Interested! Greg, you are a master of understatement.

Greg Anyway . . . Yeah. (*Looking round.*) Great place.

James Thanks – stay for a bit.

Greg No, no . . . No . . . (*Pause.*) No, I'll be off . . . (*Pause.*) James? What went on between you two – you – Dad – whatever?

James We're brothers.

Greg I see . . . You see I can't really take it seriously – not really . . . But I do hate that bastard. (*Suddenly very upset.*)

James Greg – it's nothing . . . Really. Nothing to worry about. Really.

Greg I wish I hadn't told you, really – it's so . . .

James (*interrupting*) No, really. Don't worry . . . Please . . .

James puts his arm round Greg.

Greg I *do* hate him.

James No, you don't . . . Really you don't . . . You think you do but you don't.

Greg I don't know why you don't fucking hate him.

James I know.

Greg Look, I'll be off. (*He stands.*)

James No, stay.

Greg No, really. (*Starts to leave.*) Am I fucked up? You know, fucked up?

James We're all fucked up, Greg.

Greg Right.

Greg leaves. Pause. James alone.

James (*calling*) Carl.

Carl enters.

Carl So who was that?

James Just a friend . . . Kind of friend, anyway.

Carl Oh, aye – what's all the secrecy for?

James No reason.

Pause.

Carl To tell the truth I don't really appreciate it.

James What?

Carl You know, sitting next door while you . . .

James (*interrupting*) Carl, Carl.

Carl Well, I don't.

Pause. James looks distant.

Do you want me to carry on with this stuff?

James Yes.

Carl is cleaning a camera. Detailed work. Pause.

Oh, Carl – I do believe you're jealous.

Carl What d'you mean?

James 'What's all the secrecy for?' (*Laughs.*) If only you knew.

Carl No, I'm not – I don't give a toss about your friends to tell the truth – I'm just pissed off – that's all. (*Pause. Carl continues cleaning.*) I'm not here to . . .

James (*interrupting*) I want you to take a photo . . . It's a very difficult photo.

Carl Great.

James It's a photo of my brother.

Carl (*amused*) A photo of your brother? You hate your brother. What do you want me to take a photo of him for? I mean, it's a bit strange . . .

James It's a long story; but I want you to take a photo of him at a certain time, in a certain place . . . He mustn't know he is being photographed.

Carl You want to catch him out . . . You want me to spy on him. That it? What for?

James It's a long story.

Carl This is shit. You said if I moved in . . .

James You'll take photos when you're good enough to take photos.

Carl You're full of shit.

James (*angry*) Don't start, Carl . . . This is important.

Carl When?

James What?

Carl When will I take photos?

James Will you do it . . . ? Will you do it?

Pause.

Carl I don't give a fuck about your brother.

James If you don't you're out.

Carl You what?

James If you don't you're out.

Pause.

Carl Well, I'll have to bloody do it, won't I – but I tell you, this is shit.

James and Carl leave.

Act Four

SCENE ONE

Greg and Katy. Outside James's studio. Greg is knocking. Katy enters. She is carrying a bag.

Katy Where is he?

Greg Who?

Katy Do you live here?

Greg No, just visiting.

Katy Well, you can bloody well tell him I'm going.

Greg Who?

Katy Carl, who d'you think?

Greg I don't know him.

Katy He bloody lives here, doesn't he?

Greg Maybe.

Katy He's shit – if you see him tell him that from me . . .

Greg Who are you . . . ?

Katy Just tell him, right? He'll know who it is . . . Tell him I've gone, and he won't ever see me again . . . Will you tell him that?

Greg Where?

Katy What?

Greg Where should I say you've gone?

Katy Home – back home.

Pause.

Greg There's no one here at the moment . . . Before you go, have you time for a drink?

Katy No . . . You sure there's no one there?

Greg Pretty sure.

Katy What are you doing then, standing there . . . ?

Greg Don't know . . . Story of my life . . . (*Laughs.*) Are you sure you haven't time for a drink?

Katy Is he a friend of yours – James?

Greg Kind of.

Katy Well, tell him I hate him, for what he's done.

Greg What's he done?

Katy He's bloody turned him against me. That's what he's done.

Pause.

Greg Do you need somewhere to stay?

Katy Look, I know you're only being kind and whatnot, but I'd best be going.

Greg Look, I didn't mean.

Katy I know you didn't.

Greg It's just . . .

Katy Look . . .

Greg . . . It's funny the way you meet people . . . Strangers, and sometimes it doesn't matter.

Short pause.

Katy Could you do me a favour?

Greg What?

Katy It might sound a bit much, but could you lend me a bit of cash?

Greg You'll borrow money from me, a total stranger, but you won't go for a drink . . . Is that it?

Katy Look, friend, either you will or won't – if you don't want to, you just have to say so . . . I'm not in the mood to fuck about, all right?

Greg I like you.

Katy Great.

Greg What's your name?

Katy Katy.

Greg Katy, I'll tell you what . . . Have a drink with me and I'll lend you some money . . . OK . . . ?

Katy OK then.

Greg By the way, I'm Greg.

Katy Greg, right.

Greg Let's go then.

Katy Right.

They leave.

SCENE TWO

Stuart, Carl, Kim, Charlie, William, Jim. Stuart enters.

Stuart (*monologue*) I'm *not* weird . . .

He moves to an extreme upstage position. He stands with his back to the audience near to where Jim is sitting.

(*monologue*) I'm not weird . . .

Jim moves away from him. Jim watches the following scene with great interest. Carl enters with a camera. He takes up a position – as if hiding downstage. Kim and Charlie enter. Charlie leads her to a position centre stage. He then moves away and watches her from a distance. Pause. William enters briskly. He sees Kim. He approaches her. He gives her an envelope. She gives him his wallet. They freeze for a moment. Carl takes a photograph. William leaves. Carl leaves. Charlie snatches the envelope and leaves. Kim leaves. Stuart turns to the audience and walks downstage.

(*monologue*) I'm not weird . . .

He sees Katy and Greg enter. He leaves.

SCENE THREE

Greg and Katy. They are walking – night. Same evening as previous scene between them.

Katy I love him and I hate him, see . . . No . . . I just hate him; hate him. (*Pause.*) He just bloody left me . . . He's fucking well living with your uncle . . . I mean . . .

Greg (*interrupting*) Do you like me?

Katy What?

Greg Do you like me?

Katy You're all right . . . (*Pause.*) Have you got that money?

Greg Here.

He gives her some money.

214

Katy Thanks.

Greg I hardly see him; in fact I never see him.

Katy It's none of my business . . . (*Pause.*) Look, I'd better be going. Must be.

Greg Bye then.

Katy Bye.

Greg I like you.

He kisses her.

Katy Thanks. Bye then. Thanks.

Greg Bye . . . Hope you get back all right.

Katy (*defensively*) Look, I'm not giving up, you know that don't you?

Greg What do you mean?

Katy . . . But I hate this fucking place – London's shit . . . I'm better off where I was; and where I was is shit . . . I'll have no one saying I gave up . . . (*Short pause.*) Look, I've got to get going . . . What am I telling you for; what's it to do with you?

Greg (*trying to be reassuring*) Doesn't matter.

Katy You're right there, it doesn't.

Greg kisses her.

Greg Good luck, anyway.

Katy If you do see him tell him I love him . . . (*Short pause.*) Tell your uncle he's broken me heart . . . Will you tell him that?

Greg If I see him. I'll tell him.

Katy Tell Carl I think London's shit, and he's shit too –

and I love him and I'd never have him back – not in a million fucking years . . . Bye then, I've to rush if I'm to catch that coach.

Greg I'll come with you as far as the station if you like.

Katy I'd rather you didn't; thanks all the same. (*She starts to leave.*)

Greg Katy.

Katy What?

Katy stops.

Greg I lost someone too.

Katy Oh yeah . . . Bye then. Nice talking to you. Honest. Got to dash. Thanks.

Katy leaves. Pause. Greg leaves.

SCENE FOUR

William and James. James standing. William sitting. William is writing a cheque. Having written it he gives it to James. James gives William a photograph with the negative film. James moves away. William puts the photograph and negative in his pocket.

James What didn't surprise me, William, was the photo.

William (*interrupting*) How did you know?

James (*interrupting*) The photo itself – what the photo shows . . . Nor did it surprise me that you would be willing to pay so much to ensure its destruction – that didn't surprise me either.

Pause.

William Did Greg tell you?

James slowly rips up the cheque.

James What really surprised me was that you could ever have believed that I would have used it against you . . . *me.*

Pause. William staring at James.

So, you see, you still surprise me. (*Pause.*) Say something.

Long pause.

William So you're not in trouble?

James No.

Slight pause.

William You don't need money?

James No . . . Say something else.

Pause. William seems about to say something but doesn't.

(*ironic*) Trouble . . . ? Strange word . . . I mean, I am in trouble; the *world's* in trouble; but no, I'm not in the kind of trouble I was in when I came to you for help. All those years ago . . . No, I'm not in that kind of trouble . . . But, we are all in trouble. Even you, William, are in trouble; especially you.

Pause.

Say something else.

Pause. William laughs.

William You mean to say you went to all this trouble just to . . .

James (*interrupting*) . . . Shut up . . .

William . . . lecture me about . . .

James moves to behind William.

James (*interrupting*) Shut up.

James suddenly puts his hands around William's neck. William resists – attempting to release himself. James tightens his hold. For a few moments we should think that James is going to strangle him.

Sit still.

Pause. Silence. James starts to laugh. He releases William and moves away.

How absurd. This wouldn't be happening if you weren't my brother . . . I felt sorry for the girl; the girl in the photo . . . I wonder what her life is like . . . Now, I bet it wasn't her who made the phone call.

William Don't try and be clever, James, you *know* it wasn't her. Do you want to know the truth? Nothing happened with the girl . . . She stole my wallet . . . I didn't . . .

James (*interrupting*) Spare me the details, please.

William If you hate me so much, why did you come here?

James Hate you?

William Do you hate me?

Slight pause.

James Do you hate me?

William Yes. (*Pause.*) You disgust me . . . Do I disgust you?

James You don't disgust me. I don't find you disgusting. (*Slight pause.*) Do you really find me disgusting? (*Slight pause.*) Are you sure that's the right word?

William No, it's not necessarily the right word, the most accurate adjective.

James Hate? Are you sure that's the right word?

Pause.

William Why did you come here?

James How's Dot?

William Fine.

James Good. (*Slight pause.*) How's Sarah?

William Fine.

James Is she?

William Yes.

James Are you sure?

William She's fine.

Pause.

James Greg's fine. I know that. A little confused perhaps, but fine . . . I like Greg.

Slight pause.

William I do not want to discuss my family with you.

James Fine. (*Pause.*) Maybe Carl's right; maybe it all shouldn't matter.

Pause.

William James.

James Yes.

William What are you doing here?

James I don't know.

Pause.

William I will say something . . . Every opinion I hold, every conviction, everything I say, or rather everything you hate me for saying – I believe . . . Now, quite clearly that is more than can be said of you . . . Now quite apart from everything else, and even if you weren't my brother . . . I would therefore have reason to hate you . . . I have nothing more to say to you.

James We're brothers . . . There's so much I want to say to you – but you've heard it all . . . What Hell – your never-changing, never-seeing, never-listening self . . . What hope can there be? And you talk of 'the children', 'the future' . . . What's the point? (*Pause.*) It was the fear in your eyes, William, in that photo . . . The fear which, in the end, made me come here and which I shall never forget . . . (*Pause.*) One day people will see only that fear, the weakness . . . Nothingness . . . Maybe, one day people won't fear you . . . (*Pause.*) What's the point?

James leaves. William looks at his watch and leaves.

SCENE FIVE

Bill and Kim. Kim is sitting next to Bill. Pause. Kim is holding her feet.

Bill It int right . . . What he does; it just int right.

Pause.

Kim He'll be back – then it starts again . . . I don't want to live like this . . . No more . . . (*Slight pause.*) If I weren't here, who'd look after you?

Pause.

Bill Go if you want. (*Pause.*) Maybe you should, Kim,

maybe you should.

Pause.

Kim Where is he?

Bill Maybe you should.

Pause. Lights fade. Time passes.

SCENE SIX

Edward Goodchild and Corinna. Late at night. Edward walks slowly across the stage. Lost in thought. Corinna appears approaching from the opposite direction. Edward does not notice her. Corinna does not recognize him until they have passed each other. Corinna stops. Turns. Watches him go. Pause.

Corrina I saw him. Today. . . . Him . . . Only him. I'm sure. No. No. Him? Dream? No, no . . .

Put your hand in the creel
And draw an adder or an eel.
Goodbye, Goodnight, Goodnight.
Enough from me. Alone.

She leaves.

SCENE SEVEN

Bill and Kim. Bill watching Kim.

Bill Kim. (*Pause.*) Kim . . . ? (*Pause.*) I've got a little I could give you . . . (*Pause.*) I'd like to you see, Kimmy. Like to. Only, you've got to take it. Not say no . . . I want you to have it – not much. Few quid; well more than that – but I want you to take it – 'cause you've got to get out of it. Out of here – get away. You have to.

Kim moves. Pause.

Got to get away from Charlie. He'll kill you . . . I'd go if I could, but I can't – you can. (*Pause.*) If it's only money that's stopping you, you must . . . (*Pause.*) Here, you take it. (*He takes an old wallet from his pillow.*) Here it is . . . Saved it. All I got. More use to you; so you take it. You will, won't you. It's what I want. Kim?

Kim Bill . . .

Bill (*interrupting*) No arguments. It's a good deed. I'll feel good. It's what I saved, over a bit of time . . . No use to me, now . . . (*Pause.*) . . . And Charlie's not having it.

Pause. Kim moves to Bill. She sits close to him. Pause.

I'm not all bad.

Kim You're not bad.

Pause.

Bill He says I were just as bad . . . (*Pause.*) With his mum . . . (*Pause.*) There's truth in it . . . (*Pause.*) It's where he got it from, so you'd better take it – make me happy, see. I've not been a good man myself. (*Pause.*) So maybe I deserve it, but you don't. (*Pause.*) I'd be out in the cab some nights. Not come back. It weren't cabbing neither. (*Pause.*) He used to cry. Charlie. She said. Still, past is past.

Kim If I go, who'll look after you?

Bill He'll have to . . . Just have to. (*Pause.*) See, I don't want you staying, although you're my only comfort.

Kim What if I were to go back to it . . .? (*Pause.*) Won't. (*Pause.*) How much?

Bill You'd better look.

She looks. Counts money. There is a surprisingly large amount.

There's more than I thought there was, I remember that . . . There's enough . . . (*Pause.*) Off you go. Don't look back, love.

Kim kisses him. Pause. She starts to leave. She stops.

Kim What if Charlie don't come back?

Bill He'll come back . . . Always does.

Kim I won't fuck up.

Bill You won't . . . Fuck off now. Go on.

She kisses him.

Kim You'll be all right. Hey, Bill?

Bill What?

Kim Least you'll get your room back.

Bill True.

Bill nods. Kim leaves.

SCENE EIGHT

Carl and James. James is alone. Long pause. Enter Carl with a suitcase. James does not look at him. He puts the suitcase down and sits separately. Carl looks as if he is about to speak.

James Oh dear, Carl – teach me to be wise; and you once told me that you wanted to be like me . . . Like me!

Pause.

Carl I don't understand you. (*Pause.*) James.

James sees the suitcase.

James What's the matter . . . Carl? (*Pause.*) Carl?

Carl I'm leaving.

James What?

Carl Shut up and I'll tell you . . . I'm leaving . . . I really appreciate what you done . . . I really do, but I'm moving on.

James Appreciate?

Carl I've got another job, see; in a studio . . . They want me . . . So I'm going.

James You're leaving?

Carl You see, all that shit with your brother, making me take that photo . . . That's shit . . . I don't have to take that shit from no one . . . So, I'm going somewhere so as I can work . . . You had no right to make me do that.

James Just leave.

Carl I want some respect. I want to be a photographer . . . That's it . . .

James All right.

Pause.

Carl Right . . . (*Pause.*) Bye then . . . (*Short pause.*) I'm sorry for –

James (*interrupting*) Please . . . It's all right, I'm not saying anything. (*Pause.*) Go . . . Go.

Carl Right.

Carl picks up the suitcase and starts to leave. He stops. James watching him. Carl returns and embraces him. Carl leaves. James is left alone. Pause. James is very still.

A sudden flash of anger then he smiles.

James 'Say something! . . . Say something!' William, I just wanted to tell you a little about myself . . . I wanted you to tell me a little about yourself . . . To talk of love maybe . . . Impossible . . . I suppose what I wanted you to tell me was that you are not *really* what you seem . . . To find out that what you seem to be is simply an absurd conspiracy against yourself . . . I wanted to find out that you are not *real* – and then talk some more and maybe have a laugh . . . (*Pause.*) But you *are* real – and we must take you very seriously – so, no laughter; but, William, I'm not going to be ground down . . . Lonely, yes, but not ground down . . . (*Pause.*) Carl, good luck . . . I'll miss you very much . . . 'Appreciate . . .' (*Pause.*) Life goes on. (*He leaves.*)

SCENE NINE

Greg and Amanda enter separately. They meet. Greg is wearing a suit. He carries a briefcase in one hand, a large bunch of carnations in the other. He gives the flowers to Amanda. They are followed by Jim who listens to their conversation.

Amanda Greg, you look ridiculous.

Greg I don't look ridiculous . . . Got a job . . . Bank . . . Very boring . . . How are you? I left home, you know, I'm living on my own, like you, lonely, isn't it?

Amanda Quite, Greg.

Greg How much rent do you pay . . . ? I don't know how people manage; I really don't.

Amanda They don't – they have to do utterly boring jobs and become utterly boring people, Greg.

Greg I suppose they do – things *are* difficult, aren't they . . . ? Hey, it's a bit chilly out here, let's go for a drink . . . Love is more important when your life is utterly boring – I mean, the more boring you get, the more you need people.

Amanda The more boring *you* get.

Greg . . . The more boring I get the more obsessed I am by you. Do you like the flowers? Are you still obsessed by David? Do you think I am very conventional?

Amanda (*looking at the flowers*) I love them . . . You mean very little to me – but you make me laugh.

Greg (*pleased*) Do I? That's good. Isn't it?

Amanda Before you left home you looked homeless – now you look like you've never left.

Greg What do you mean?

Amanda You look more like your father every day. You *do* look comic.

Greg Do you earn a lot of money . . . ? I mean, you need so much money . . . Don't you find?

Amanda You do.

Greg Do you earn a lot?

Amanda I had to.

Greg Why?

Amanda To fall out of love – You know, I haven't read a book for nearly a year . . . I'm working for an employment agency.

Greg Really. Great.

Amanda It's very boring . . . How's Sarah?

Greg We don't talk.

Amanda I ought to see her, but I wouldn't know what to say.

Greg Do you think anyone will ever fall in love with Sarah? (*Pause.*) I can't imagine it.

Amanda Will she be all right?

Greg No – she's going to university . . . Tell me I've got a chance.

Amanda I'll only go for a drink with you if you don't tell me that you love me.

Greg Come on then.

They start to leave.

Have I got a chance, then?

Amanda Probably, Greg, probably; but I hope not.

They leave.

Act Five

Jim is alone on stage.

Jim (*monologue*) Stories . . . We all have stories . . . 'Cept I've heard most of the stories now . . . Love stories, hate stories, old stories, your stories . . . I've heard 'em all and lived a few myself; but you know – I'll tell you something I know – People can do without them . . . They're all the same . . . By having nothing – like me – seeing, hearing, everything . . . Or like others, learning not to be . . . People are now; or they've become; well, people without stories – or too many – that's TV . . . I mean people without stories like before . . . People are; people have become people without people. Yes, people without people to be . . . See . . . Persons. Others . . . Yes – the others, we say, not us, have become people without persons.

> *Pause. Kim approaches. She has blood on her hands. She sits a little away from Jim. She listens to him as if being told a story.*

. . . They've; we've, heard too many stories . . . (*Pause.*) So people are lost; and not lost because there's so little to find . . . (*Pause.*) Little Kimmy here, she has a story to tell . . . (*Pause.*) I can't hear no more – it'll surely kill me if I listen. But then again, it won't, because I've heard it all before. Let us get a little sleep, Kimmy, we know how bad it is – your face tells us the story . . . The worst can only be someone else's death . . . Death is the end of everybody's story to tell . . . Come on, Kimmy – what is it now . . . ? We're listening but we must get some sleep.

SCENE TWO

Jim and Kim.

Kim I went back there – Charlie's . . . Charlie hadn't been back . . . He went off with the money . . . The money of William Goodchild . . . Bill . . . I found him. There. Knew I would . . . Bill. Loved him. In his way.

Jim (*half asleep*) You loved who?

Kim Just like I left him . . . Starved . . . He must have starved . . . Charlie hadn't come home and Bill, he couldn't move.

Jim (*half asleep*) Bill? Who's Bill? Didn't know him, Kimmy . . . Sorry he's dead though . . . Wish I was dead – perhaps I'll sleep . . . Cold now . . . Winter's drawing in.

Kim I looked . . . Lying there . . . Felt . . . ? First – nothing . . . Then. (*Sniffs.*) Smell . . . Then so many things – but he looked so quiet . . . Not since Mother died have I wanted to cry. I didn't cry then. Looking at him so quietly . . . Peaceful – and I didn't cry.

Jim I won't be having you crying.

Kim Not for long; the wanting to cry . . . Didn't last long . . . (*Pause.*) Numb . . . (*Pause.*) Wanting to cry . . . (*Pause.*) Numb . . . Didn't last long, the wanting to cry . . . Then I felt . . . With every bit of me I felt, it wasn't crying. Him lying there peaceful with his smell of starvation death . . . (*Pause.*) Anger it was. Anger . . . Charlie . . . (*Pause.*) Anger . . . So, I waited with anger – and the anger grew. (*Pause.*) Anger. Inside – then outside as well . . . With me in the room with the old man dead and still . . . (*Pause.*) And I waited . . . (*Pause.*)

Jim (*who seems to have been asleep*) And . . . ?

Kim I killed him, Jim; Charlie, with a knife. Stabbed him. Anger killed him . . . Oh, only an hour ago . . . Look, blood.

Jim looks as if he is asleep again.

Don't trust 'em, the old woman said, and where's *she* gone? Charlie's dead . . . They'll get me. I know . . . (*Pause.*) I hope they do . . . If they don't I'll give myself to them.

She leaves. Jim sleeps.

SCENE THREE

Josh, Marie *and Jim. Jim watches the action. Josh and Marie move forward. She is pushing an old-fashioned pram. He carries two small bags. As they enter Stuart and Nancy establish their domestic area as for the beginning of the play.*

Josh Marie?

Marie What?

Josh Bigger than Littleport, eh?

They laugh.

Marie She's wet again. London . . . Away . . . Away; from all that shit and crap; and family this and that . . .

Josh Everyone says they need people; London. That's what they says.

SCENE FOUR

Stuart and Nancy. They are sitting together watching television. Pause.

Stuart Girl comes up to me today . . . (*Pause.*) Real rough she was . . . (*Pause.*) She comes up to me, right, in the street . . . Right up to me, and she says . . .

Nancy I'm trying to watch, Stuart . . . You know I like to watch the news . . . (*Pause.*) Don't ask for much do I?

   Pause.

Stuart I'm telling you she comes up to me; she says to me that she's killed a bloke . . . Knifed him . . . (*Pause.*) What d'you think of that then?

Nancy What?

Stuart She comes up and says she knifed a bloke . . . She said other things I couldn't get . . . Irish.

Nancy Who's Irish?

Stuart This girl. I said I thought she was Irish. Anyway could have been.

Nancy I'm trying to watch the news, love . . . Tell me later. I want to hear, only not now . . . Tell me later . . . (*Short pause.*) Oh, look at that. I don't know. Good job you're a policeman.

   Pause.

Stuart They'll lock her up. End of story.

Nancy We've got to find someone for that room. Fancy them two just leaving like that.

SCENE FIVE

Josh and Marie. With pram. They move past Stuart and Nancy. As they do so, Stuart and Nancy leave.

Josh We got to find somewhere. Else we're fucked.

Marie Right. (*Pause.*) Perhaps we shouldn't have come.

They approach Jim.

Josh We'll be right . . . They need people.

Jim Who's that?

Josh Everyone says they need people . . . London.

Jim Who's been telling you that?

Marie Everyone. Saw it on telly . . . Anyway, who's asking you. Josh, tell him to fuck off and leave us be.

Jim There's no need for that. I'm a gentleman. Now, you can stop here with me if you care to . . . We'll find something together in the morning.

Jim lies down as if to sleep. Josh and Marie lie down beside him. Pause.

Josh Marie?

Marie What?

Josh What's going to happen? Tell me that.

Pause.

Marie Don't know . . . How should I? Know what's going to happen? How should I? Don't know. (*Pause.*) She's sleeping though; and that's a blessing . . . Got to look to her, that I do know . . . (*Pause.*) She's warm anyway.

Josh and Marie are still on stage. They are asleep next to the pram. Holding each other beneath a blanket. Jim stands behind the pram.

Jim (*monologue*) Ah, yes indeed . . . We must look to the children, with the winter drawing in.

He moves downstage, away from Marie and Josh,

towards the audience. His speech is uninterrupted.

Indeed. The winter it's drawing in and it's to the children we must look.

TROUBLE SLEEPING

Rage gathered throughout Thomas's large frame with a silent ominous intensity, like a mob assembling.

Flannery O'Connor, 'The Comforts of Home'

CHARACTERS

Terence Daley Late thirties. He works on the railway. He speaks with a regional accent.

Rosemary Daley Aged sixty. Terence's mother. Her accent is less marked.

Ursula Walker Aged seventy-six. Rosemary's sister.

Angela Early twenties. From London.

PLACE

Near Wisbech, East Anglia

TIME

The present

Trouble Sleeping was developed at the National Theatre
Studio in London and first performed on BBC Radio 3 on
22 May 1990, with the following cast:

Rosemary Patricia Routledge
Terence Jim Broadbent
Ursula Constance Chapman
Angela Miranda Foster

Directed by Nick Ward

Act One

SCENE ONE

The setting: two rooms, connected by a door, occupy the centre. On the left the kitchen/living room and on the right a cluttered bedroom overlooking some flower beds. A staircase at the rear of the kitchen leads to a landing with two doors.

The general atmosphere is of a farmhouse which no longer commands a farm. The place has been inexpensively furnished and decorated according to Rosemary's idea of homeliness.

Framing this domestic centre there is a less naturalistic playing area.

Terence *is meticulously cracking open a boiled egg.*

Rosemary (*monologue*) Now my father was a farmer – in point of fact, farming goes back even farther than him . . . His name were Albert Chapman – but as I say the Chapmans as farmers go back farther – oh, I can't say how far. But it was always around here – the edge of Fenland – where the silt begins to start. Flat as the fen, but the soil's nowhere near as black. Very good for bulbs . . . Anyway, it's on account of the farming in my forebears that me and Terence is still here. Only it ain't been a *farm* house for ever such a long time, well, since Albert Chapman's time, because he lost the farm itself to the Chorleys. Got into some trouble and sold up to them . . . My dad was Harold Chapman and he never were a farmer. He were on the waterways first, and when they closed them down – though not without my dad and others giving up a fight – he went on the railway. That were 1927 . . . If he were alive now he'd be ninety-seven,

241

but he died when he were my age – that's sixty. He seemed ever so old to me at the time – must have been the work. It were when he were on the railway that he were my dead husband Horace's boss – that were how I met him. His people come from Scotland, so he were on his own. Anyway, so this used to be a farm, but my grandfather were careful enough to keep the house. So, that's why it's bigger than it should be given what my Terence earns, and why we're stuck out here in the middle of all these Chorley fields. No end of times they tried to shift us . . . Terence works on the railway like both our dads – Harold Chapman and Horace Daley.

Rosemary *joins Terence. She pours herself some tea.*

What was it like then?

Terence I liked it.

Rosemary What was it about?

Terence What?

Rosemary What was it *about* if you liked it so much?

Terence I didn't say I did like it *so much*.

Rosemary You'd have said nothing if I hadn't asked.

Terence True.

Pause. Terence eats.

Rosemary Aren't you going to tell me then?

Terence You should have stopped up.

Rosemary I was ever so tired.

Terence Why?

Rosemary No reason.

Terence There's a reason for everything.

Rosemary True.

Pause.

Old age.

Terence PPPFFF!

Pause.

Rosemary That's what it is.

Terence You don't look old, you . . .

Rosemary . . . Not to you I don't . . .

Terence . . . you don't look any different . . .

Pause.

Rosemary I'm sixty years old, Terry. That's the age Horace was when he passed away.

Terence Yeah, well, women live longer than men, don't they? (*Slight pause.*) No, you should have stopped up . . . I bet you didn't sleep.

Rosemary Did so . . .

Terence I bet you lay there wide awake . . .

Rosemary I didn't.

Terence . . . worrying about this and that. I know you. I wish you wouldn't an' all. It's not worth it.

Slight pause.

Rosemary I *feel* old.

Terence *You don't look old.*

Rosemary I know what I feel.

Pause.

Terence I'll be late if I don't look out.

Rosemary There's no rush.

Terence S'pose not . . .

Terence has finished his boiled egg.

Rosemary How was it?

Terence Perfect.

Pause.

Rosemary Have some toast.

Terence I'm going to. (*He does so.*)

Rosemary I want you tell me what it was like.

Terence I can't remember everything.

Rosemary Tell me what you can remember.

Terence Maybe later.

Pause.

Rosemary Things'll be more difficult when Aunt Ursula arrives.

Terence I'm not a kid.

Rosemary What?

Terence She's your sister.

Rosemary Well, I know that.

Terence Why'd you call her *Aunt* Ursula, then?

Rosemary That's what we've always called her – me and you.

Terence Exactly my point . . .

Rosemary Ursula, then.

Terence Right . . . So what? 'Things'll be different' – in what way?

Rosemary *Difficult.* They could be difficult, Terry, in lots of ways.

Terence Of course they will – it'll be three rather than two.

Rosemary It's the least we can do.

Terence Well, I'm not happy about it.

Slight pause.

Rosemary She's got to be easier than she was.

Slight pause.

Terence She's not been well.

Rosemary That's all over now. We don't speak about that, all right?

Terence *We* can.

Rosemary Yes. But, not in front of Ursula. Dr Rodger says it's best we don't. He says we should continue as normal.

Terence I don't need Dr Rodger to tell me that.

Rosemary starts clearing the table.

Rosemary All I meant was the less said the better, and that when Ursula arrives we won't be able to talk about things as much as we do at present. That's all . . . Like what the film was about – things like that – won't be so easy.

Terence Don't forget Hunstanton.

Rosemary This time of year? Are you sure?

Terence You promised . . .

Rosemary . . . only teasing.

Terence Oh . . . (*Pause.*) I'll get the stuff out now.

Rosemary There's no need.

Terence It's no trouble.

*Terence collects some clay-pigeon-shooting equipment –
trap and clays – for which he clears a space on the table.
He returns for a gun.*

Rosemary Put some newspaper down.

Terence You know what I'd like? A thirty-inch
Montecatini trap gun – this old thing's no good.

Rosemary Are you listening to me? You're scratching the
table.

Terence All right.

*Terence picks up a tabloid newspaper and starts to take
it apart.*

Rosemary Terence! That's today's.

Terence You never read it. I'll save the telly page.

Rosemary You don't know if I do or don't – you don't
know what I do when you're not here.

Terence Don't start that again. I know you don't.
Sometimes I leave it in one place on purpose, and when I
get in, you int touched it . . . You don't even read the telly
page till I get in . . . and, when you do, it don't *mean*
nothing, 'cause you'll only watch what you know's on
anyway . . . because you're just not interested.

Rosemary You know my nerves are bad, what with
Ursula coming . . . I don't want her here.

Terence Calm down.

Rosemary You're winding me up.

Terence Only teasing. (*Pause. Terence is looking at his gun.*) Trouble is, that'll be damned expensive.

Rosemary There's nothing wrong with that one . . .

Terence What do you know . . .? Course things'll be easier when Ursula get here.

Rosemary What?

Terence She's got no end of money, you said.

Rosemary You'd better be nice to her then.

Terence I'm always nice.

Slight pause.

Rosemary Terry . . . ? Summer's coming.

Terence What's that got to do with it?

Rosemary Well, I was thinking, on the way back from Hunstanton we ought to call in at that garden centre – you know the one – it's on the way . . . because we ought to brighten up the garden for Ursula.

Terence You won't get me out there.

Rosemary You'll give me a hand, won't you?

Terence No . . . The garden looks fine to me . . . anyway, you don't even know if Ursula likes flowers.

Rosemary Everybody likes flowers, Terence, even you sometimes.

Terence Yes, and who's paying?

Rosemary Don't be cruel, Terry. I don't ask for much . . . I help you with your old clay pigeons.

Terence Need you to. Can't do trap and gun on me own, int got two pairs of hands.

Rosemary I like to. I'm just saying.

Terence All right . . .

Rosemary So, we'll go there on the way . . .

Terence *All right*, I said.

Rosemary Right.

Terence I will be late now.

Rosemary Course you won't.

Terence Best be off . . . (*Terence stands up and puts his jacket on.*) See you later on then.

Rosemary Give me a kiss, then.

Terence kisses her, then leaves.

(*monologue*) My dead husband, Horace. In a way, although there's not that many folk out this way – we was at the centre of them that were . . . But, after Horace had his tumour – well, that's what we found out it were just before he died – we soon found out what kind of centre of things we was. We found that out just before he died and the tumour had changed him. Well, they do . . . Before that happened I always tried to both think and see the best in people – but, a thing like that teaches you a thing or two. That suspicion's not such bad thing – sometimes it's even necessary. Makes you want to close your door. S'pose that's what me and Terence have done in a way. No, he hasn't many friends, and I can't sleep at night . . . Horace hardly knew me at the end, he was so changed. Though none of them round here could understand – and, to think it was me and Horace established the darts down the Black Horse – hard to believe now. You see Horace was a much loved man, but none of them could stand by me when he was changed, towards the finish. It was nothing out of the ordinary though. Brain tumour – does things to

one – and it was hard for Horace. No one could see that
. . . Not even me, really. (*She is holding back tears.*)
Anyway, so that's me and Horace. It's made me think I've
got to look to Terence, 'cause he's a Daley, and I don't
think the Daleys have the constitution of the Chapmans –
that's why I wouldn't complain if he gave up that job. I'd
quietly encourage that – 'cause overwork can kill a man
. . . About me sister Ursula. First off, it gave me the shock
of my life when Dr Rodger rang me out of the blue. He's a
very nice man I've since found out – we've talked now, oh,
a dozen or more times – always on the phone. Now Dr
Rodger runs one of them special homes, and it came some
surprise to learn that that's where my Ursula wound up.
Me and her lost touch years ago. She went off with Alan
Walker – married him. He were real rich. I never knew
him, but, she becomes a Walker in 1937 and left us all
behind. Now, her and Alan Walker never did have
children, so it were through that marriage how come
Ursula came into all her money . . . which she still has, of
course . . . Dr Rodger says that Ursula's problem is that
she thinks of herself as two people – and he gave it a term.
Only she, he says, doesn't know herself that's what it is.
He says we all do it to a certain extent. I said, 'Speak for
yourself, Dr Rodger. Terence and me never done nothing
of the sort.' He laughed at that, he's such a lovely man,
and said, 'Mrs Daley, I think you might teach me a thing
or two.' He's ever so charming. I don't know what he
looks like, but he's got a lovely sense of humour. I said to
him, 'Don't you worry about old Ursula, she's been quite
enough trouble already. She'll be in very good hands with
me and Terence.' He said he thought that was right, but
any problems and I must give him a ring. I said it would
be my pleasure . . . I've since then thought a bit about
what he said. Maybe what he thinks is wrong with Ursula
– her thinking, as he puts it, that she thinks she's two
people, but doesn't know it – was what was wrong with

Horace, just before he went. It would certainly go some way to explaining why he was so very different to the Horace I knew, that's for sure – but, then again, I don't know . . . Dr Rodger's such a clever man, though, to tell the truth, I don't believe in half of what he says – it's interesting though but, if you ask me, Ursula's problem is that she's been spoilt, and that from day one. Well, she won't get no spoiling here – she'll get brought right down to earth again with me and Terry. What I've got to talk over with him is how we should work things out. It seems a folly for him to go on working as such. Course even if I get the OK from Terry, which won't be at all easy – I'll still have to bring it up with Ursula – and I don't even know if we're going to get on. So, it's early days, but I'm working out my secret plan. Got to go careful with it, though, that's for sure . . .

SCENE TWO

The same evening. Rosemary and Terence enter. Rosemary puts some bedding plants on the table. Terence sits down and starts to clean his gun, which makes a squeaking noise.

Rosemary Flowers look lovely.

Terence Should do, amount they cost.

Rosemary I'll put that nice lavender bush in first – just underneath her window – if I'm clever it'll look like it grew there on its own.

Terence Thirty quid, you didn't have to go mad.

Rosemary Then, I'll put those nice pinks with tobacco plants, pansies and them petunias – along beside.

Terence I'm not doing no digging.

Rosemary You never do.

Terence And, who's going to make my tea, if you'll be digging?

Rosemary I'll do the digging after tea.

Terence Oh, all right then. (*Pause.*) I was thinking I ought to enter a competition. Only it'd be no good with this old gun.

Rosemary She gets here next Thursday. Not long . . .

Terence . . . Look at it! (*Slight pause.*) Not even worth cleaning it.

Rosemary Leave it alone, then.

Terence That'ud be damned dangerous.

Pause. Rosemary stands.

Rosemary Terry. I've got a plan . . . No, listen, Terry . . .

Terence Why don't you sit down?

Rosemary sits.

Rosemary We'll put her in your grandfather's old room . . .

Terence Put her where you like.

Rosemary . . . that way she won't have any stairs to climb, after all, she is seventy-six.

Terence So, do you reckon Ursula 'ud buy me a new gun – one of them Montecatinis? Look 'ere.

He shows her a gun brochure.

Rosemary Doesn't look any different to me.

Terence You want to put your glasses on. (*Pause. Terence continues to clean the gun, muttering under his breath.*)

251

This thing's no good, no bloody good at all.

Rosemary I can hear you, Terence, you want to watch your language. (*She stands up again.*) No, Terry – the reason I want you to be nice to Ursula is that I've been thinking . . . Listen to me, Terry . . .

Terence What?

Rosemary I've been thinking – you wouldn't say no to more time for your clays, would you . . . ?

Terence What?

Rosemary . . . and if you had more time you'd be able to do a bit of fishing again . . .

Terence I don't like fishing. Not since I took up clays.

Rosemary You used to . . . Well, anyway, more time would be a good thing – especially if you're going to start doing competitions.

Terence Always find time for things, if you need to . . .

Rosemary You know what? Ursula's *real* rich. Dr Rodger filled me in.

Terence Did he?

Pause.

Rosemary I look at you some nights, when you get in from work (*suddenly choked with emotion*) and I think to myself you're going the same way old Horace did.

Terence You can get her to pay them people from the video rental, then, 'cause we're behind.

Rosemary We don't ever watch it.

Terence *I* do.

Slight pause.

Rosemary Do you get what I'm driving at, Terry?

Terence I'm not thick.

Rosemary I know that. (*Slight pause.*) Anyway, that's all I meant when I said you've got to be nice to Ursula.

Terence All right, then. Don't go on.

Rosemary Be nice to her, then.

Terence *Don't go on.*

Rosemary Right.

SCENE THREE

Rosemary has just planted the lavender bush, she is patting the earth down with a shovel. Terence is in the kitchen. **Ursula** *and* **Angela** *are at a pay phone. The phone rings in the kitchen. Terence ignores it. Rosemary eventually answers it.*

Rosemary Wisbech 2–8–6– . . . (*She waits for Ursula's coin to drop.*) Wisbech 2–8–6–0 . . . Hello.

Ursula Rosemary. It's Ursula . . .

Rosemary Ursula . . . (*She puts her hand over the receiver; to Terence*) It's *her* . . . (*to Ursula*) We're both looking forward to it very much . . .

Ursula Rosemary . . . ?

Rosemary (*to Terence*) She's gone a bit deaf I reckon . . . (*She speaks to Ursula slowly, as if to a child.*) We're both looking forward to seeing you on Thursday. Terence is going to drive his van to the station to meet . . .

Ursula (*interrupting*) . . . but we're already here, my dear.

253

Rosemary You're what?

Ursula We're early. I hope you don't mind. At least it should stop you going to any trouble – because we wouldn't want that, would we Angela . . . ?

Rosemary (*to Terence*) She's got here early . . . Now, she's talking to herself . . . It's what Dr Rodger talked about . . . (*to Ursula*) Where are you?

Ursula Peterborough Station.

Terence (*overlapping Ursula*) Where is she?

Rosemary Peterborough Station.

Terence She isn't . . .

Ursula Rosemary, are you there . . . ?

Rosemary . . . but, we're not ready for you, Ursula. You weren't meant to be coming till Thursday . . .

Ursula You don't have to do a thing . . .

The money is running out. Ursula struggles to find another coin.

Terence What's going on?

Rosemary I don't know.

Terence Well, find out . . . I don't like the sound of it.

Ursula (*overlapping Terence*) Rose . . . ?

Rosemary Are you alone, or what?

Ursula No, I told you, I'm with Angela.

Rosemary Who's Angela?

Ursula Angela is a very special girl, a new friend whom I met this afternoon . . . She's a little down on her luck at present . . .

254

Terence (*overlapping Ursula*) Who's that? Angela? Who the hell's Angela . . . ?

Rosemary (*to Terence*) . . . I'm just this minute finding out, Terry. I'm finding out . . .

Terence Well, you'd *better*.

Ursula . . . so I'm bringing her with me . . .

Rosemary You're doing what?

Terence What's she done . . . ?

Ursula I'm bringing her with me.

Rosemary (*to Terence*) Ssssshh . . . ! I'm finding out . . . (*to Ursula*) You're doing what?

Ursula I'm bringing her with me. Is there a fault on your line?

Rosemary You're bringing her here?

Ursula That's right, isn't it, Angela?

Terence (*overlapping Ursula*) *What?*

Rosemary (*overlapping Ursula, to Terence*) She's bringing her here.

Ursula She's just here, you see, Rosemary. She needs a little looking after herself, don't you . . .

Terence (*overlapping Ursula*) What's she on about now, then?

Rosemary (*overlapping Ursula, to Terence*) Sssshhh!

Terence Don't you 'shush' me.

Ursula . . . Angela, and when that's been done, you'll look after me. We're going to look after each other, Rose . . . and we're both waiting for Terence to drive that nice van you told me about to the station, to pick us up. Aren't we, Angela?

Angela Right.

Rosemary (*overlapping Ursula, to Terence*) You've got to pick her up.

Terence (*overlapping Ursula*) When?

Rosemary Right now.

Ursula We'll be waiting for him outside the amusements arcade.

Rosemary Amusements arcade?

Terence (*overlapping Ursula*) Amusements arcade?

Ursula (*overlapping Terence*) That's right. All right?

Rosemary Right.

Terence (*overlapping Ursula*) What?

Ursula Bye.

> *Ursula puts the receiver down. After a slight pause, Rosemary does the same.*

Rosemary Oh, dear God, better make a list.

Terence No time for lists. You should have bloody well just told her, there and then – we're not having anyone but her – and told her she's damned early an' all . . .

Rosemary Everything's falling in on top of me. I'll make a list.

Terence I'll be off, then.

Rosemary I said you would be.

Terence I don't know . . . *You* . . .

Terence leaves.

Rosemary (*to herself*) Now, Rosemary, you'd better make a list. You know what you're like. First things first . . . I don't even know *Ursula*, and she's meant to be my sister . . . I don't know, I never should have agreed. 'She belongs at home,' Dr Rodger said, 'and it's her *right*. . .' Ring Dr Rodger. Can't do that . . . I'll cheer up in a minute . . . Let alone *Angela*, whoever that is . . . I don't like things when they fall in on top . . . Put some nice music on . . . (*She does so: a Country-and-Western female vocalist on cassette. She sits down.*) That's it . . . (*She sings along for a few bars.*) Put the kettle on, why don't you . . . ? No . . . Put your feet up . . . Have to make up another bed . . . Weight of the legs. Haven't been shopping. Finished in the garden . . . Terence is on his way. She's waiting. Peterborough Station. I just don't know what's going to happen. I don't. (*She falls asleep.*)

SCENE FOUR

Rosemary is still asleep. Ursula enters, followed by Terence and Angela. Terence can't keep his eyes off Angela.

Ursula (*on entering*) Dear me! I'd hardly have recognized the place, I remember it all as being rather grand . . . Now, where is she?

Terence Mum . . . ?

Rosemary (*waking up*) Hello . . . ? Hello . . . ?

Terence Aunt Ursula's here.

Rosemary Oh, dear, I must have dosed off. (*She stands up.*)

Ursula Look at you!

*Ursula advances and holds Rosemary tight, which takes
Rosemary by surprise. She sees Angela for the first time
over Ursula's shoulder. Rosemary exhales sharply,
making a strange noise. Rosemary and Ursula separate.*

This is Angela. Angela, this is Rosemary.

Rosemary How do you do?

Angela Not bad.

*Rosemary involuntarily sniffs the air: Angela is very
dirty.*

Ursula Come on, my dear, let's get you in that bath. We
can all catch up with each other later on.

*Ursula leads Angela off. A silence. Rosemary and
Terence are stunned. Rosemary puts her hand to her lips
and makes a shushing sound. She then, very nimbly,
creeps off after them. Left alone, Terence looks at
himself in the mirror and plays with his hair. After a
short while the sound of a bath running. Rosemary
returns. On hearing her coming, Terence springs away
from the mirror.*

Rosemary Well, what do you think of that?

Terence It won't do.

Rosemary They're both sitting in there. In the *bathroom*. I
mean what do you think of that . . . ? Bit damned peculiar
if you ask me . . .

Terence Telling me.

Rosemary The way she was looking at you, Terry, the
way she was looking at you.

Terence What do you mean?

Rosemary You know.

Terence I don't . . . You want to tell your sister this int no hotel. I mean, I'll be buggered.

Rosemary I will, Terry, that's right . . . But, it could be difficult.

Terence What d'you mean?

Rosemary Keep your voice down.

Terence (*whispering*) What d'you mean?

Rosemary Ursula said she hadn't even known her before today.

Terence I know.

Rosemary She could be lying, of course. Dr Rodger said to look out for that.

Terence What's he got to do with it?

Rosemary She looks like she's come straight off the street. Ever so dirty. Got a dirty look and all . . .

Terence What d'you mean, 'difficult'?

Rosemary What do you think of Ursula, then?

Terence She seems all right.

Rosemary What I mean is, this is her house as well.

Terence So what?

Rosemary Well, I'm just saying, because it could make things difficult, Terry.

Terence I'm not with you.

Rosemary Getting rid of the girl.

Terence I don't care. Difficult or no. She's not staying.

Rosemary You're right. I'll sort it out with Ursula.

SCENE FIVE

Ursula is in her new room. Rosemary knocks on the door. Pause. Rosemary knocks again.

Rosemary (*through the door*) Ursula . . . ?

Ursula Hello, Rose.

Rosemary enters, but lingers at the door.

Rosemary You'll be comfortable in here then?

Ursula Oh, yes. Perfectly.

Slight pause.

Rosemary Look at you! Tucked up already . . .

Rosemary has moved into the room.

Ursula I always sleep better during the day, don't you find that?

Rosemary I can't say I've ever tried it.

Ursula Of course, father would have frowned on it.

Rosemary Oh, I wouldn't know.

Ursula But, you know, Rose, there's nothing *wrong* in doing it – if you want.

Rosemary I suppose there isn't, if you want, as you say. Well then.

Pause.

Ursula I'd forgotten how dreadfully flat it is around here. Still the old house hasn't really changed, beneath the surface. It's a shame the farm had to go.

Rosemary Farm? But there hasn't been a farm since Harold Chapman's time.

Ursula Still it's a shame. I always imagine it with a farm.

Rosemary Oh no, the Chorley's own the farm.

Slight pause.

Ursula Chorley doesn't ring any bells.

Rosemary It wouldn't do. (*Slight pause.*) No end of times they tried to shift us and Richard Chorley's got it in for Terry, he says the clays buggered up his harvester.

Ursula Clays?

Rosemary Clay pigeons. Terry shoots them for a hobby.

Ursula Does he, by God.

Rosemary He does, only now we have to go all the way to Hunstanton.

Ursula I like the sea.

Rosemary So do I.

Slight pause.

Ursula Lovely old room, this one . . . With a touch of redecoration.

Pause.

Rosemary Now, about Angela.

Ursula Isn't Angela a lovely girl?

Rosemary Is she?

Ursula I've told her she must make herself at home. (*Slight pause.*) Garden looks lovely, Rose.

Rosemary Oh, d'you think so?

Pause.

Ursula Terence is on the fat side.

Rosemary Oh, yes. He eats me out of house and home.

Ursula Does he just?

Slight pause.

Rosemary He's a lovely boy, though, when you get to know him . . . Bit shy.

Ursula Is he . . . ? (*Slight pause.*) I gather you're a Christian.

Rosemary I am.

Ursula Go to church, do you?

Rosemary Oh, yes. Tomorrow morning. Terry doesn't though.

Slight pause.

Ursula I gave young Angela one of Terry's shirts to put on – I found it in the cupboard in the bathroom – it will do for the time being, until we can get something more suitable.

Rosemary Oh, he's very particular.

Ursula I'm sure he won't mind. Rosemary! You should have seen the colour of Angela's bathwater. Black.

Slight pause.

Rosemary Well, then, we'll catch up with each other a bit later on.

Ursula All right, Rosemary, my dear.

Rosemary starts to leave.

Rosemary Right then. Nice to see you.

Ursula You won't even know I'm here.

Rosemary Right then.

Rosemary leaves.

SCENE SIX

Night. Ursula is lying in bed with a bedside lamp on. Terence is alone in the kitchen with the lights off. He puts a video in the recorder. He turns the television on – we see him illuminated by the flickering light of the screen. He hears someone coming. He switches it off and quickly moves away from the television. He sits down. Angela enters. She switches a light on. For a while she doesn't see Terence. She starts to search the kitchen for food. She takes some food out of the fridge.

Terence Oy!

Angela is startled.

Angela For fuck's sake, what's your game?

Terence Help yourself, why don't you?

Angela That's what Ursula said.

Terence Did she just?

Angela puts a plate of cold meat down roughly on the table.

Watch the table!

Angela Well, I wouldn't make it up, would I, would I, Terry?

Terence Terence.

Angela What?

Terence My name is Terence.

Long pause, while Angela eats. Terence keeps stealing sideways glances at her.

That's my shirt. (*Slight pause.*) Oy!

Angela It's yours, is it?

Terence Are you wearing my shirt?

Angela Look, what's your problem?

Terence That's my work shirt – for Monday.

Angela Work shirt, eh? So what d'you do?

Terence Never you mind.

Angela Ursula gave it me.

Terence Yeah, well, she had no business doing so.

Angela If it's making you so uptight – why don't you stop staring at it?

Terence What?

Angela I said, stop staring . . .

Terence Take it off. Right now . . .

Angela Piss off . . .

Terence . . . I mean, who d'you think you are, coming in here?

Angela (*leaving*) Keep your hair on, Terry.

Angela exits with the plate of food.

Terence Right. We'll see about this.

Terence goes to Rosemary's bedroom door.

Terence Mum, are you in there?

Rosemary Of course I am. (*Pause. She opens the door.*)
Keep your voice down, Terry. (*She comes out. She is
wearing a nightdress.*)

Terence She's wearing my shirt.

Rosemary I know. Never mind.

Terence 'Never mind'!

Rosemary I can always wash it, Terry.

Terence That's not the point . . . but, you'll need to.
That's right . . . Well, did you tell her?

Rosemary What?

Terence Did you tell Ursula that we won't have it?

Rosemary Not quite.

Terence What's that s'posed to mean?

Rosemary I was building up to it.

Terence You were doing what?

Rosemary I'll tell her in the morning, when she's settled in
. . . No. Will you do it? Will you tell her in the morning,
Terry? I'm useless.

Terence You *are*. I will. 'Building up to it'! I don't know.

Rosemary She is my sister . . . and she's our guest. Well,
more than that . . .

Terence What?

Rosemary I said, she's more than that . . . She does *own*
the house – along with me, that is . . .

Terence . . . and what about me?

Rosemary No, that's what I'm saying, you don't *own* the
house, Terry. At least not until I'm dead.

Terence Don't I?

Rosemary No, you just live here.

Terence Yeah, along with a few others.

Pause.

Rosemary When I'm dead, you'll get my half – unless Ursula gives you her half as well, after she's gone.

Terence I see.

Rosemary But she can leave her half to anyone she cares to.

Terence Can she just?

Rosemary She can. (*Slight pause.*) Anyone at all.

Terence Oh!

Slight pause.

Rosemary So, you'll have a word with her in the morning?

Terence I will . . .

Rosemary . . . and don't forget the other thing.

Terence What other thing?

Rosemary What we talked about – what you need to ask Ursula for, but don't rush her, mind, one thing at a time, eh? She's not been well. She mustn't be demanded upon, Dr Rodger said.

Terence Yeah, well, he doesn't have to live with her.

Rosemary Terry, so first things first.

Terence Right.

Rosemary And getting rid of that dreadful girl comes top of the list.

Terence That's right.

Rosemary She's got a real look in her eye.

Terence That's right.

Rosemary Is it?

Terence What?

Rosemary You noticed it as well.

Terence So, you think I should ask Ursula about the other thing an' all?

Rosemary Maybe. See what you think.

Slight pause.

Terence You mustn't worry about a thing. I'll sort it out.

Rosemary Good for you.

Terence Goodnight, then.

Rosemary Goodnight.

He kisses her.

Terence You know she's eaten all the food.

Rosemary She hasn't.

Terence She has. All tomorrow's food.

Rosemary I wish you hadn't told me that – I won't sleep now.

Terence Course you will, 'cause I'm going to sort it out tomorrow while you're at church. So you sleep easy.

Rosemary I'll try.

Terence Goodnight, then.

Rosemary Goodnight.

SCENE SEVEN

*Terence is boiling an egg. After a long pause, Angela
enters, having just woken up. She is still wearing Terence's
shirt. She sits down. Terence looks at his watch – timing
the egg. A very long pause.*

Angela Make me a cup of tea, Terry.

Terence Terence. Terence. Not Terry.

Angela I like Terry.

Terence I don't care.

   Pause.

Angela Make me a cup of tea.

Terence I'm not making you tea.

   *Angela switches the kettle on and waits for it to boil.
   She puts a tea bag in a cup. She is now standing very
   close to Terence. Long pause. Terence looks at his
   watch again. He takes the egg out of the pan and puts it
   on a carefully prepared tray, with toast and a pot of tea.
   He starts to leave for Ursula's room.*

Angela Nice try, Terry, but she won't thank you for it.

Terence I won't tell you again, it's Terence.

Angela (*quickly*) What you going to do if I call you Terry
again, Terry?

Terence Shut up.

   *Angela remains in the kitchen. Terence, having knocked
   cautiously, enters Ursula's room with the tray. He
   tiptoes across the room. Ursula is asleep.*

(*whispering*) Aunt Ursula? Aunt Ursula?

Ursula opens her eyes and sees Terence. She shrieks with surprise. Terence almost drops the tray with the shock, but manages to hold on to it after a strange little dance.

Angela What *are* you doing, Terry?

Terence I brought you an egg.

Angela I hate eggs.

Terence Oh, dear.

An awkward silence. Ursula is still half asleep. Terence stands very still. The two of them are simply looking at each other. Ursula sits up slowly.

Ursula (*kindly*) You eat it, though.

Terence I've already had two today, thank you.

Ursula Where's Angela?

Terence Through there.

Ursula Give it to her then. It's a shame to waste it.

Terence I'll try and find room.

Ursula Sit down.

Terence Thank you.

He sits down on the chair by the bed and nervously starts to eat the egg.

Ursula I'll have a cup of tea though.

Terence Oh, good.

He stops eating the egg and pours her a cup of tea.

Ursula Thank you. Sorry for barking. You gave me a turn.

Terence That's all right.

Slight pause.

Ursula Do you ever think you're asleep?

Terence Come again.

Ursula Do you ever think you're asleep when you're awake?

Terence I often doze off in front of the telly.

Ursula It happens to me all the time. Just now I thought you were a bad dream, but when I woke up you were still here.

Terence Oh dear . . . (*Eating the egg.*) Mmmm! Just right! (*Slight pause.*) There's something we need to discuss, Aunt Ursula.

Ursula Oh, my dear, must you keep calling me that? It sounds terribly funny – especially with you pulling that long face. Don't you think it sounds funny?

Terence S'pose it does really.

Ursula *Aunt* Ursula! And it makes me feel terribly old – a grown man like you.

Terence Well, Ursula, then. Me and Mum's been thinking . . .

Ursula I haven't seen much of her since yesterday afternoon – I hope she isn't upset about anything.

Terence Oh, no.

Ursula I heard her banging about earlier.

Terence She can be clumsy.

Ursula You don't think she'll mind that I've asked Angela to give this room a lick of paint.

Terence Oh, no.

Ursula That's good, because you know something, Terry?

Terence What's that?

Ursula I wasn't sure at first, but now I know that coming here is a good thing.

Terence That's good.

Ursula Yes, I feel better already.

Terence You do?

Ursula No, I'll go further – I feel calm and *stable* for the first time in ages.

Terence That's very good. (*Pause.*) See, the thing is . . .

Ursula (*interrupting*) I really do. I want to be *happy* here.

Terence Good.

Ursula . . . and I'm ready to help others now. Look outside more . . . Help you and Rose, in whatever way I can . . .

Terence About Angela.

Ursula Oh, yes, of course – I want to help Angela as well, poor girl.

Terence Um . . .

Ursula (*interrupting*) You know, Terry, just between you and me, she's been in prison – she told me.

Terence Doesn't surprise me . . .

Ursula . . . and when she came out, she went home to her mother, the one place, you would have thought, that she could be sure of finding love in the world, but no, her mother just turned her away . . . Can you imagine, Terry, how you'd feel if Rosemary turned you away?

Terence Um . . .

Ursula She stole a cheque book, she said. But she was *forced* into it by some man . . . and she loved him, Terry. Don't you think that's sad?

Terence I s'pose it is.

Ursula No, it's worse than sad. It's *tragic* what some men do to the women who love them. I had forty years of it, Terry, so I know what I'm talking about.

Terence I'm sure you do, Aun . . . Ursula, sorry.

Ursula I hope you're not like that.

Terence Sorry?

Ursula Poor Angela.

Pause.

Terence Ursula?

Ursula She hasn't told me about *him* yet – but I'm sure she will – when the time is right . . . I know what you're thinking, Terry. You're thinking that she's only after my money.

Terence Well . . .

Ursula . . . and you may be right. But you've got to give people a chance . . . and there's something in her I recognize. Do you understand that, Terry?

Terence She'll be staying for a bit, then?

Ursula I hope so.

Terence Right.

Ursula Oh, yes, we have a real understanding. It was instant. (*Pause.*) Have you got a girlfriend?

Terence What . . . ? I mean, not yet . . . I mean, not at present.

Ursula Well then, Terry, now's your chance. It's not as if you're married, is it? But, if you don't mind me saying, you could do with losing a bit of weight. She's very attractive, don't you think?

Terence (*panic*) Mmmmm?

Ursula So, you never know, eh, Terry?

A silence. Terence crushes the empty eggshell.

Oh, yes, I want to help you all, in any way I can. So, if you want anything, you mustn't hesitate to ask.

Terence Right. Thank you very much. I'll be off then.

Ursula All right, my dear.

Terence starts to go. Angela, in the room next door, hears him coming and leaves quickly.

Ursula Oh, Terry?

Terence Yes?

Ursula Tell Angela, I've decided on white.

Terence Right.

He leaves Ursula's room. Once in the kitchen, he unplugs the television set and video recorder and carries them up to his room.

SCENE EIGHT

Rosemary returns from church. She is wearing her Sunday best. She goes to Terence's door.

Rosemary (*a loud whisper*) Terry, I'm back? Are you in there?

A pause. The sound of Terence rigging up the video.

Terry . . . ? What *are* you doing?

Terence Wait a minute. (*He opens the door.*)

Rosemary What were you doing, Terry?

Terence Just rigging the video up.

Rosemary What's it doing in there?

Terence I moved it in there, didn't I?

Rosemary I can see that. What for?

Terence Because that's where I want it.

Rosemary What for?

Terence I just do – I don't see why I should share it. If they want a video they can get their own.

Rosemary What if *I* want to watch something on telly – like the news, say?

Terence You can watch it in there, if you ask – it's *my* telly.

Rosemary I don't know what's got into you – what if Ursula wants to watch it?

Terence She won't. I asked her.

Rosemary Did you?

Terence She said she didn't like watching telly . . . anyway you hardly ever watch it, on purpose.

Rosemary Have it your own way. You're not very nice, Terry. (*Pause.*) Well, what did she say?

Terence She's off her head.

Rosemary Do you think so, Terry?

Terence She spoke all kinds of nonsense – said she was still asleep – things like that – and other things I won't repeat.

Rosemary What other things?

Terence Things about *you* – I won't repeat.

Rosemary Did she, Terry?

Terence She did.

Rosemary What? Unkind things about me?

Terence That's right.

Rosemary Well, there's gratitude for you.

Terence Well, she did.

Rosemary I never should have agreed – I should have made excuses – it was Dr Rodger talked me into it.

Terence You wouldn't listen to me.

Pause.

Rosemary Well, what about the girl?

Terence We didn't get that far.

Rosemary Why not, Terry? You got as far as the telly.

Terence We started with the telly.

Rosemary Yes, and what's more important? The telly isn't important at all.

Terence Is to me.

Rosemary You said you would, Terry.

Terence The time weren't right.

Rosemary What did you talk about, then – apart from the telly?

Terence Not a lot.

Rosemary You're useless, Terry. I was expecting more. I was expecting to get back from church and find her gone. That's what I was expecting. (*Pause.*) Did you talk to *her*?

Terence What?

Rosemary The girl?

Terence No.

Rosemary Are you sure?

Terence Well, I told her she weren't welcome – and left it at that.

Rosemary What else did you say?

Terence Nothing.

Rosemary What else did she say?

Terence Nothing.

Slight pause.

Rosemary She must have said something.

Terence She said nothing. I reckon *she's* soft in the head an' all.

Rosemary Do you think so, Terry?

Terence I do.

Slight pause.

Rosemary Is she still wearing that shirt of yours?

Terence She is.

Rosemary She gives me the creeps. (*Slight pause.*) So, you'll sort it out with Ursula, then?

Terence I will.

Rosemary You said you would before. You've let me down.

Terence All right. I've said I'll do it.

Rosemary You want to come straight out with it.

Terence I *will* . . . *and*, ask her the other thing I have to ask her an' all.

Rosemary All right, then.

Terence All right.

Rosemary All right.

Terence All right.

Act Two

SCENE ONE

Ursula is in bed. Angela is laying down newspaper in preparation for painting. The room has been stripped bare.

Ursula Put plenty of newspaper down, won't you?

Angela Right.

Angela continues to put down newspaper.

Ursula I don't know what Terry sees in that paper.

Angela 'Spect he likes looking at the pictures.

Ursula How dreadful.

Pause. Angela starts painting.

I think we'll need two coats.

Angela Right.

Ursula Where did you put all that wallpaper?

Angela Binned it.

Ursula I hope Rosemary didn't mind.

Angela Rosemary did mind – I heard her tell Terry.

Ursula Oh, well, you can't please everyone.

Angela That's right.

Pause.

Ursula Well, it's only been two weeks – but, already I'm beginning to feel at home.

Angela That's good.

Slight pause.

Ursula Thanks to you. (*Pause.*) The white looks lovely. So clean and fresh. Like the crest of a wave . . . We'll have to get rid of the furniture next – it's so cluttered in here – oppressive. Reminds me of my father.

Angela Know what you mean.

Slight pause.

Ursula Terry said that . . .

Angela You don't want to listen to him.

Slight pause.

Ursula If it's only money you want, you can have it.

Angela stops painting.

Angela What's he been saying?

Ursula If you're only staying here because you want money – then, I'll give you what you want, and you'll be free to go. I don't want you staying if you don't want to.

Angela is suddenly very upset, although she tries to hide it.

Angela, my dear, what's the matter . . . ? Angela . . . ? What is it . . . ? (*Slight pause.*) Angela? Oh dear, I'm not very good at this.

Angela (*through tears*) You want me out.

Ursula I didn't say that.

Angela You do.

Ursula No, no . . . I want you to stay.

Angela Why?

Ursula Because I like you.

Angela Why?

Ursula For lots of reasons . . . But, I don't want to keep you here – if you want to go. (*Pause.*) You find life difficult. Like me. That's why I like you.

   Pause.

Angela I'll finish this off later, if you don't mind.

Ursula So, you'll stay, then?

Angela Right.

Ursula For as long as you want?

   Angela nods.

Good.

   Angela leaves with the dirty paint brushes.

SCENE TWO

Angela is washing out the brushes. Terence enters.

Angela Terry . . . !

Terence (*taking off his jacket*) What?

Angela What's got into you?

Terence What?

Angela You're back early.

Terence I'm not, and it's *Terence*.

   Slight pause.

Angela Ursula says she doesn't want you in there in the mornings.

Terence And don't talk to me about her.

Angela I'm telling you what she said . . .

Terence . . . I don't want to know.

Angela She also told me to tell you to stop trying to get on the right side of her, 'cause it'll do you no good, 'cause she knows very well that you're after something.

Terence What d'you say to her?

Angela Nothing. She just told me to tell you that it's my job to do things like that.

Terence What, things like getting on her right side, eh?

Angela Now, now.

Terence 'Cause don't think I don't know what you're after.

Angela No, Terry, things like waking her up in the mornings. Things like that. She likes me, you see, Terry.

Terence Phew!

Angela She likes me because she trusts me, Terry.

Terence Yeah, well, she won't for much longer.

Angela I'm not with you, Terry.

Terence sits down. Pause.

Terence Yeah, you want to watch out, 'cause I know about you. And, I'll tell her. What you're after and what you done.

Angela Tell her what you like.

Slight pause.

Terence So, what do you do in London? I know what you do in London, don't think I don't. I know your type. I know exactly what you do in London.

Angela My type, eh, Terry?

Terence That's right.

Angela So, what do I do, then?

Terence I *know* and don't think I don't.

Angela You know *nothing*. About me nor London . . .

Terence . . . and it weren't what you told Ursula it was. I know that an' all.

Angela Tell her what you like – 'cause you know nothing. (*Slight pause.*) Though there's a thing or two you'd *like* to know, eh, Terry?

Terence You what?

Angela There's a few things you'd like me to have done an' all.

Terence What d'you mean?

Angela But, there's a few things *I* know about you – and it ain't guesswork, neither.

Terence Ppphhh!

Terence reads the paper. Pause.

Angela Do you like me, Terry?

Terence What?

Angela Do you like me? Do you like being with me?

Terence Course I don't.

Angela What you sitting in here for then, if you don't like being with me?

Terence I don't want you here.

Angela I think you must like me, Terry, otherwise, why don't you go into your own room?

Terence None of your business.

Pause.

Angela You've got a very nice room.

Pause.

Terence I'm sorry? Did you say you've been in my room? (*Pause.*) Have you been in my room?

Slight pause.

Angela Maybe. (*She leaves.*)

SCENE THREE

Very noisily, Terence is putting a new lock on the door. He uses a hammer and chisel. Rosemary enters. She's been shopping.

Rosemary (*excited*) Terry? Terry? I've got good news. (*Pause.*) Terry? What are you doing?

Terence Putting a lock on my door.

Rosemary What for?

Terence Security.

Pause.

Rosemary But the telly's in there.

Terence So what?

Rosemary I might want to watch it.

Terence You can if you want.

Rosemary I won't be able, if you're not here.

Terence True. (*Slight pause.*) You'll have to listen to the radio then, won't you? Or, wait till I get in and we can arrange it.

Pause.

Rosemary Terry?

Terence I'm busy. What?

Rosemary I hope you're not up to anything.

Terence What?

Rosemary Behind my back.

Terence *What?*

Rosemary Have you spoken to that girl again?

Terence No.

Slight pause.

Rosemary What, not at all?

Terence No.

Slight pause.

Rosemary What's the lock *for*, Terry?

Terence I just told you.

Pause.

Rosemary You're trying to lock me out.

Terence Don't be daft.

Rosemary Well, you're making me suspicious.

Terence That's your problem.

Pause.

Rosemary Oh, that banging's putting me on edge.

Terence Nearly finished.

Slight pause.

Rosemary I've had a word with Urse. Good news.

Terence Oh, it's *Urse* now, is it?

Rosemary Of course it is.

Terence Yeah, well, I have to call her Urs–*ula*.

Rosemary Well, that's all right. She *is* my sister, Terry. Urse is what we used to call her. (*Slight pause.*) Anyway, I mentioned that matter we discussed – remember – the reason why you have to be nice to her.

Terence Course I do.

Rosemary Well. She said she'd love to help.

Terence stops banging.

Terence Did she?

Rosemary She did, but she said that you must bring it up with her yourself – but that, in principle, she'd love to help.

Terence Right then. I'll finish this off after, then. (*He downs tools.*)

SCENE FOUR

Terence and Ursula are sitting together in her room.

Ursula So, what exactly *is* the difference?

Terence What?

Ursula What's the difference between what you've got now, and the one you want?

Terence Do you really want to know?

Ursula Of course I do, I wouldn't be asking if I didn't.

Slight pause.

Terence Mum never wants to know.

Ursula Well, *I* do.

Terence All right then. (*Pause.*) You really want to know?

Ursula I do.

Terence Well, then . . . What I've got is an old Browning, must be third even fourth hand, I'd say. Now, that's not even intended, strictly, as a trap gun . . . and what I want is a Winchester Grand European Montecatini Trap thirty inch.

He points to a picture of the gun in a brochure. Ursula's eyesight is not too good. She strains forward to look.

Ursula Why do you particularly want one of those?

Terence It's in the features it's got.

Ursula So, what are its special features?

Terence Do you really want to know?

Ursula I really do.

Slight pause.

Terence Right then, well, first off, you've got to look at the length.

Ursula The length.

Terence That's right – the length of the barrel. What I've got at present's only got twenty-seven and a half inches, whereas, as I say, the Montecatini's got thirty, which in the competition situation would make me swing steadier and give me that much more control.

Ursula I see.

Terence That's got *two* sights, one on the end – that's usual – but, another *midway* down the barrel . . . and, in addition it's got a screw-in, variable, multiple choke.

Ursula What on earth is that?

Terence That's what controls the spread of your shot. It doesn't want to be too tight – despite you getting a better kill at close range – or, too spread, when you'll fail to kill anything – despite hitting, if you see what I mean.

Ursula Oh, yes.

Terence Anyway, I'll be able to get it just right – with a bit of trial and error, that is . . . The Montecatini's got a lovely-looking stock – made of walnut – that's the bit where your gun meets your face, and that'll fit me cheekbone like a glove . . . and the stand – that's the end what meets your shoulder – int too pointed at the toe . . . the toe's the bottom end.

Ursula Doesn't look like a toe to me.

Terence S'pose it doesn't . . . but, anyway, that's what it's called. (*Slight pause.*) The comb . . .

Ursula As in *comb*.

Terence That's it. The comb is the height – a Montecatini'll shoot one-third above, and two-thirds below your target – which is just right.

Ursula Why?

Terence 'Cause then you can see what you're shooting at, without blotting it out.

Ursula I see.

Terence And, although it's only got a single trigger, it's got a barrel selector on the safety catch – which is what you want for clays . . . and it's got a real light trigger pull – about seven pound – which'll take a bit of getting used to, to be honest, 'cause my old Browning needs winch and tackle gear . . . (*Laughs. Pause.*) . . . and if you look at the fore end, the Montecatini's got a beautiful tapered one, whereas my old thing's got one of them clump beavertails – which int at all pretty . . . (*Pause.*) Well, in a nutshell, that's about it. Without going into specifics.

Ursula I think I get the picture. (*Pause.*) Terry?

Terence Yup?

Ursula Do you mind if I ask you something?

Terence Fire away.

Ursula Why do you think you like guns so much?

> *Pause.*

Terence Don't know – just do. (*Pause.*) Exciting.

Ursula I see.

Terence Yup, that's it – exciting.

Ursula How fascinating.

Terence That's it. (*Slight pause.*) Mum's not interested though.

Ursula I'm sure she is.

Terence No, she's not – not at all.

Ursula I think she just pretends not to be. She doesn't want to show too much interest, that's all.

Terence Oh, I don't know about that. (*Slight pause.*) So, what do you say?

Ursula Mmmm?

Terence What I mean is – do you think you'll be able to get me a Montecatini, then?

Ursula If it's something you really want.

Terence It is . . . that'll be expensive though, Ursula, you do know that?

Ursula (*with a smile*) That's the least of our problems.

Terence That's good. (*Slight pause.*) So, you'll get me one then?

Ursula Of course I will.

Terence Thank you.

   Pause.

Ursula How are you getting along with Angela?

Terence Not too bad, thank you!

Ursula She tells me that you're putting a new lock on your bedroom door.

Terence That's right.

Ursula I used to feel like that.

Terence Oh . . . (*Pause.*) Well, thank you again. We'll be able to sort out the money side, then.

Ursula Yes.

Terence When? I'm in no hurry, mind.

Ursula Later on.

Terence All right, then. (*Pause.*) Well, I'll be off, then.

Ursula What about the other thing?

Terence What other thing?

Ursula Rose said that . . .

Terence . . . Yeah, well, you mustn't listen to her.

Ursula I'm sorry.

Terence She's taken against Angela, see. Real bad. Don't take no notice.

Ursula Has she? (*Slight pause.*) No, I meant about your job on the railway.

Terence What about it?

Ursula She told me that you wanted to talk to me about giving it up.

Terence What?

Ursula She said you wanted to give up your job.

Terence She done *what*?

SCENE FIVE

Terence continues to put the lock on his door. Angela enters.

Angela What *are* you doing?

Terence What's it look like?

   Pause.

Angela Terry, you're looking pleased with yourself.

Terence Maybe I am.

Angela Getting a new gun, I hear.

Terence None of your business.

   Pause.

Angela Well, that lock'll do you no good.

Terence It'll keep you out.

Slight pause.

Angela Yeah, well you want to keep the noise down.
Ursula don't like it.

Terence You can tell her I'll be finished with it in a
minute.

Angela Not *that* noise . . . I'm talking about the noise you
make – in the night.

Terence What?

Angela In your bedroom – in the middle of the night. You
want to keep it down. (*Slight pause.*) You want to turn the
volume down on your video.

Terence What?

Angela Do you want me to *spell* it out, Terry?

Terence No.

Angela Oh, right, so we're talking about the same thing,
then?

Terence No. What? I mean, what?

Angela 'Cause you want to remember you got me on one
side and Ursula underneath . . . and she don't sleep at
night. (*Slight pause.*) But your secret's safe with me –
'cause I'm sure Ursula won't say nothing to Rosemary . . .
She's not like that . . . (*Pause.*) . . . and I don't think your
mum should know, do you?

Terence What?

Angela Surprises me you ain't been hit by a train, in that
job of yours . . .

Terence What?

Angela 'Cause your hearing ain't at all good . . . You get me, though, don't you, Terry?

Terence What?

Angela (*slowly*) I don't reckon your mum should know – with me? – what you get up to – want me to go on? – in your room, in the middle of the night . . . all on your own. (*Quickly.*) I don't think she should know, right?

Terence (*very quietly*) Right.

Angela Right. (*Slight pause.*) See you then, Terry (*She leaves.*)

SCENE SIX

Rosemary and Terence.

Terence What did you tell her I wanted to give up me job for?

Rosemary Don't you adopt that tone with me, my boy.

Terence I asked you why you done it?

Rosemary I don't know what you're talking about, Terry. All I can hear is the tone.

Terence (*speaking slowly*) I said, why'd you go and tell Ursula that I didn't want to do me job no more?

Rosemary We agreed. That's why and don't you try telling me we didn't.

Terence Yeah, well, we did nothing of the sort. And you know it.

   Pause.

Rosemary Well, you got what you wanted . . . You are selfish.

Terence What?

Rosemary Selfish. You heard. And, what's more, you know you are.

   Slight pause.

Terence (*under his breath*) I'll be damned.

Rosemary You never think of me, no more. You *will* be. That's right.

Terence I don't know what you're on about.

Rosemary Right under my nose.

Terence What?

Rosemary Don't 'what?' me.

   Pause.

Terence Oh, well, never mind . . . You going to come with me, then?

Rosemary What?

Terence Try out the Montecatini what Ursula bought.

Rosemary I don't see why I should. We agreed, Terry, you're going the same way Horace went.

Terence What you on about? Fresh air'll do you good. You could do with some, I reckon. Listen to you.

Rosemary Don't see why I should.

Terence Don't be daft, you'd like to.

Rosemary I don't know why you don't go with *her*, seeing as you get along so well.

Terence Don't be *daft*. She can hardly get out of the bed – let alone operate a trap. (*Laughs.*)

Rosemary Not her. I meant Angela.

Terence What?

Rosemary (*quickly*) I don't know why you don't get *her* to operate your damned trap – seeing as you're so keen.

Terence What d'you mean?

Rosemary Don't think you can fool me, Terry. I know you very well.

Terence This time, I think you're fallen right off your trolley. That's what I think.

Rosemary Well, I don't know why you don't . . . What d'you talk to her about, anyway?

Terence Who?

Rosemary You know.

Terence Don't know what's got into you – that's all I know.

Rosemary Who'd you think?

Terence Who?

Rosemary Angela.

Terence I don't have to tell you nothing . . . but, if you must know . . . I don't talk to her about nothing. 'Cept to say I don't even like her. Don't like her at all . . . In fact, I hate her and I wish she weren't here. So.

Rosemary Well, she likes you.

Terence I tell her exactly what I told you I'd tell her, that she'd best be getting off out of it . . . and quick too . . . But, Ursula wants her. So there.

Rosemary Little hussy. (*Slight pause.*) No, don't think you can fool me. I know you *too* well.

Terence Shut up, will you?

Rosemary In my own house . . . and you've no time for me any more.

Terence Shut up. Why'd you tell her that I wanted to give up me job?

Rosemary Because we agreed. We didn't want you going the same way your dad went – anyway, it's me that's upset about that.

Terence We never did. (*Slight pause.*) We never said nothing at all. You had no right.

Rosemary Don't you talk to me about *right*.

   Pause.

Terence I'm nothing like me dad.

Rosemary You can't see it.

Terence I'm nothing like him . . . For one thing . . . (*Slight pause.*) For one thing, *I'm* not going to go soft in the head.

Rosemary What d'you mean?

Terence Like him. 'Cause, he went soft in the head.

Rosemary How dare you speak like that about your own father.

Terence Well, he weren't no one else's.

Rosemary He had a brain tumour, Terence.

Terence That were neither here nor there. He went soft. And you most probably drove him there . . .

   Slight pause.

Rosemary Terence, I am going to try very hard to ignore what you just said.

Terence Do what you like. (*Pause.*) What'd you mean,
'she likes me'?

Slight pause.

Rosemary You don't mean what you just said, did you,
Terry?

Terence What?

Rosemary About me driving him there . . . ? Did you?
Terry?

Terence Course I didn't. What d'you mean, 'she likes me'?

Rosemary Promise?

Terence Promise. Heat of the moment. (*Slight pause.*)
What d'you mean, 'she likes me'?

Rosemary She likes you.

Terence Well, that's always possible. I hadn't thought of
that. (*Slight pause.*) Now, are you going to give me a hand,
or not?

Rosemary So, you admit it then – there's something going
on?

Terence Are you going to help me?

Rosemary I've told you what.

Terence Yes or no?

Rosemary Things are getting very difficult for me – very
difficult . . . and you're no help . . . and there's nothing I
can do . . . I'm helpless.

Terence You're *hopeless*, more like (*Laughs.*) Come on.

Rosemary Don't laugh at me, Terry . . . I can't cope. I *am*
hopeless. It's all come in on top.

Terence No, it hasn't.

Pause.

Rosemary Ursula told me.

Terence What?

Rosemary She's told me.

Terence What's she told you? You don't want to listen to her.

Rosemary She told me you like Angela.

Terence Yeah, well, she really *is* soft in the head.

Rosemary Well, that's what you'd have me think – I don't know who to believe.

Terence Are you calling me a liar?

Rosemary No, of course not.

Terence I hope *not* . . . Phew! I don't know what to do about you. (*Slight pause.*) Come on. Cheer up, then.

Rosemary is crying.

Are you going to help me try it out then?

Rosemary I will not.

Terence What?

Rosemary I will not. You can do it on your own. I'm going out. (*She starts to leave.*)

Terence (*raising his voice*) You better not.

Rosemary Do it without me.

Terence Come back here.

Rosemary Don't you shout at me. That should teach you a lesson.

Terence Come here.

He grabs her. Rosemary struggles to get out.

(*shouting*) You're going nowhere.

Angela comes in.

Angela What *is* going on, Terry?

Terence Get out, you.

Angela Beating up your mum now, Terry?

Terence lets Rosemary go.

Pick on someone your own size, Terry.

Terence Shut up.

Rosemary (*very agitated*) You'll help Terry with his traps, won't you, Angela?

Angela What you on about?

Terence Shut up, both of you. (*He leaves.*)

Angela What's got into him, then?

Rosemary *You.* Don't talk to me.

Angela Suit yourself.

Rosemary (*leaving*) It's all your fault. (*She leaves.*)

SCENE SEVEN

Rosemary is outside the house, alone.

Rosemary (*shouting*) Terry . . . ! Terry . . . ! (*Pause. She walks in silence for a while. She stops walking. To herself*) Phew . . . ! It's so hot. Even the old house has got a frown. (*She keeps walking. Shouting – as if to a dog*) Terry . . . !

Terry . . . ! (*Slight pause. She stops walking again.*
Shouting) I know you're out there somewhere. The van's
not gone. (*Pause. She keeps walking.*) Terry . . . ! *Please,*
Terry . . . ! (*Pause. She stops walking.*) Terry . . . ! Where
are you? (*Pause.*) Terry, I want to talk to you. (*Quieter.*) I
can't cope. (*Shouting*) Terry . . . ! (*She leaves.*)

SCENE EIGHT

*A different place, outside the house. Terence is sitting
alone with his new gun. Rosemary enters.*

Rosemary There you are, Terry. You could have shouted
back. What *are* you doing?

Terence What's it look like?

Rosemary You know what Richard Chorley's like.

Terence What's he got to do with it?

Rosemary It's his land, Terry. That's what he's got to do
with it . . . Oooh! It's too hot. (*Slight pause.*) Don't you go
shooting anything out here. He'd have you up for that.

Terence Not going to.

Rosemary Well, then, stop pointing it like that.

Terence (*angry*) Well, you won't help me.

Rosemary Of course I will. That's what I've come out here
to tell you.

Terence You will?

Rosemary Of course I will . . . but not until you get rid of
that girl. I want her out . . . (*With rising hysteria*) I want
her out . . . Until she is, I won't help . . . Terry, you've got
to help me as well . . . So, get rid of her for me. She's no

good. She's causing no end of grief for me . . . and *you* . . . and you can't even see it.

Terence You never should have said what you said to Ursula about me job.

Rosemary I don't see what that's got to do with it.

Terence Oh! Don't you just . . . anyway, I don't know what you're getting so damned agitated about . . .

Rosemary (*desperate*) If you don't get rid of her, Terry . . . I . . . I . . . don't know what I'll do.

Terence Keep it down.

Rosemary I *won't*.

Slight pause.

Terence So, what you going to do then?

Rosemary *Something.* (*Slight pause.*) So, if I was you I'd take that stupid gun of yours, and point it straight at *her*. *Right* at her. Until she goes, and when she has gone, everything will be all right again. You can't see that. I mean Ursula's no trouble . . . and I'm sorry I said what I did . . . as long, that is, as you're not lying to me about not knowing that's what we both wanted, because of Horace dying the same age I am now. Things like that – like we talked about.

Terence I don't know why you're bringing *him* into it.

Rosemary No, you *don't*.

Slight pause.

Terence You're in a right old state. 'What we both wanted'!

Rosemary I am in a state.

Terence But, you're the selfish one, because you think you're the only one.

Rosemary What?

Terence What about *me*?

Rosemary What?

Terence I'm in a state.

Rosemary I know you are, Terry. That's why I'm saying you've got to get rid of her, then you won't be.

Terence You may be right.

Rosemary I *know* I am. (*Slight pause.*) Are you going to get rid of her, then? (*Slight pause.*) Well? (*Slight pause.*) Terry?

Terence All right.

Rosemary Then I'll give you a hand with your new gun and things like that . . .

Terence All right.

Rosemary Go on, then. It's ever so hot out here. I don't know how you can stand it. I'm boiling. It's like that hot year all over again . . . So, you'll do it then, you'll get rid of her?

Terence I'm going to.

  Slight pause.

Rosemary You're going, then?

Terence (*impatiently*) *All right.*

Rosemary You don't look like you are. You look like you're just sitting there in Richard Chorley's wheat.

Terence Do I?

Rosemary Terry? (*Slight pause.*) Terry? (*Slight pause.*) Terry, if you don't go this minute, I'm going to scream – because I'm desperate – at the top of my lungs . . . so, *get up* and go in there and get rid of her.

Terence I'm going. (*He gets up.*) I was just working it out.

Pause. Rosemary sits down.

What *are* you doing?

Rosemary Sitting down *here*.

Terence What on earth for? That wheat'll bring on your hay fever.

Rosemary It already has. But, I don't care. I'm not shifting till I see *her* walk out of that door. (*Slight pause.*) Terry . . . ?

Slight pause.

Terence No. Now, you listen to me – and I'll take charge – you don't want to sit out here – 'cause I'm going to need you in *there* . . .

Rosemary What for?

Terence You've got to go in with Ursula – just in case she tries to stop me getting rid of Angela. With me?

Rosemary Are you sure about that?

Terence I *know* it. You've got to go in with Ursula, and lock the door.

Rosemary Clever boy. So, I've got to sit in with Ursula – with a bit of luck she'll be fast asleep – and when she wakes up, Angela will have gone.

Terence That's it.

Rosemary It'll be just like she's had a bad tooth pulled.

Terence That's it.

SCENE NINE

Ursula is asleep. Rosemary enters quietly. She closes the door behind her. Terence is sitting next door, with his gun, waiting for Angela.

Rosemary Urse . . . ? Urse . . . ?

Pause. She goes to her bedside. She lowers her voice.

You asleep, Urse?

Ursula (*in her sleep*) Hello . . . ?

Rosemary Never mind. You sleep.

Slight pause.

Ursula (*in her sleep*) Never mind . . .

Pause. Rosemary speaks very quietly – as if to herself. As Rosemary speaks, Ursula breathes heavily in her sleep.

Rosemary If I listen out carefully, I might be able to hear what he says to her . . . He said he'd just sit in there with that new gun you gave him and wait for her to come in. What a relief, eh . . . ? When she gets in, he said, he'd sort her out . . . Not before time if you ask me . . . Ever so calm, he said he'd be – wouldn't make a song and dance about it – he'd just tell her in plain language what's what . . . So, if you don't mind, Urse, I'll just sit in here with you until he's done it. (*Pause.*) Can't hear a thing . . . Oh, well – won't be long . . . (*Slight pause.*) . . . then we'll be able to work out what's best to do next . . . Look at you – you still look real pretty, in a way – when you're asleep, at least – real *peaceful*. (*Pause.*) I was always the plain one of

303

the two – I know that. You were father's favourite, that's
for sure. I never measured up in his eyes. You broke his
heart when you went away, he always spoke of it. The
gap's always made me suspect that I weren't meant. Still.
(*Slight pause.*) Though I reckon you've been through it as
well, in a way . . . I must remind myself to ask you to tell
me all about that Dr Rodger – I still think of him ever such
a lot, and all those things he said . . . but I haven't got the
full picture . . . though I can hear his voice. Friendly. He
seemed like such a gentleman. Though I've seen no
evidence of what he said to look out for in you. I told him
I'd soon have you sorted out, in only the way a sister
can . . . (*Pause.*) It's not too cosy in here, since you had it
painted – it's a bit on the bleak side, if you don't mind me
saying. I was rather fond of that wallpaper. Each to his
own. (*Pause.*) Still, you can smell the flowers coming
through the window – which must be nice for you.
(*Pause.*) *Still* nothing happening out there. (*Pause.*) I
wouldn't care if I never saw that horrible girl again in my
whole life. That's the truth. (*Slight pause.*) . . . and I
haven't given up on Terry giving up his job, I just didn't
bring it up the best way. (*Slight pause.*) As for you, Urse,
we'll be able to get to know each other a bit better now. I
mean, you've been with us nearly a month and we've
hardly spoken. It'll be easier when she's not in the way,
wrecking everything. Terry said, you'd said, she's been in
prison, didn't surprise me, the way she was giving Terry
the eye from the start . . . To be quite honest, I don't know
why you brought her. I don't. (*Pause.*) Oh, I think I can
hear something.

Angela enters.

Terence Where you been?

Angela What's it to you, miss me did you, Terry?

Terence You've got to go.

Angela Who says?

Terence I do.

Angela Oh, well, that's all right then.

Slight pause.

Terence Did you hear what I just said?

Angela Did you sort it out with your mum, then, Terry?

Terence What?

Angela Looked to me like you had a little problem to sort out.

Terence She wants you out, an' all.

Angela Does she *really*? I never would have guessed. Thanks for telling me, Terry. (*Slight pause.*) What a lovely big gun, Terry. I bet you're feeling pleased with yourself.

Terence I want you out.

Angela Wrong. Your mum wants me out. You don't want me *out* – you just *want* me.

Pause. Terence stands up.

Don't you, Terry? (*Slight pause.*) What's it like, then, Terry – to want *me*?

Terence I want you *out*.

Angela Just like you want all them little girls on your videos, eh, Terry? But, the thing is, you know no girl's ever going to want you and even if they did – you wouldn't know what to *do* . . . Pig!

Pause.

Terence Get out!

He moves towards her.

I want you out.

Angela So you said.

Terence Get out!

Angela You don't frighten me, Terry.

Terence stops.

Terence Get out!

Angela If anyone's going, Terry – it'll be you. (*She raises her voice.*) Tell that to your mum.

Terence Shut up.

Angela Because when I tell her what her little boy does when she's not looking . . .

Terence Shut up, I said.

He moves towards her again.

Angela Put the gun down now, Terry.

Terence Ha! Not frightened, eh?

Silence. He stops moving and points the gun at her.

Not frightened? I said.

Angela Terry, listen to me, Terry.

Terence I'll teach you.

They are in the corner of the room. Terence holds on to the gun with one hand and reaches out for her with the other.

Teach you a lesson.

Angela (*shouting*) Get off . . . ! Get off me . . . !

Terence has pushed her down.

(*screaming*) Get off! Wanker! Fuck off!

Rosemary enters. She sees them.

Rosemary Terry . . . ! Terry . . . ! What are you doing?

She rushes across the room, grabbing Terence from behind. There's a struggle. They all get hopelessly tangled up. The gun goes off. The three of them lie there immobile. The lights fade to black.

SCENE TEN

Angela alone.

Angela (*monologue*) The gun goes off. We all go down. Tangled up. Terry with his gun. Happened quick. Must have been an accident – 'cause it were damned stupid otherwise. So, this bang goes off and I know someone's dead. That's a smell of death. I knew it weren't me. Like a kid, I'm saying, well, I'm alive. It int me. Hear meself breathing. Least think it's me. Live another day – just like inside, 'cept, then you don't care whether it's night nor day. So, I'm thinking there's a difference between me then, and me now, which is something . . . I'm saying to meself, it int me. Next I'm thinking it's Terry's topped himself – 'cause he's right on top of me. Fat slob. Wanker. Mummy's boy . . . So, what about her? She's the one. She's lying there, across his legs. Her eyes are staring at him and her tongue's poking out. Right at him. He's gone and done his own flesh and blood. Then I saw me dad standing there, in the room with us, looking at me, looking at them, down there on the floor. Her with all that blood coming out her side . . . and he was smiling . . . and, I wished I'd done to him what Terence done, accident or not, to his mum. I didn't fear Terry. Not now. Even though it was me he meant to get. You'd think I would, get out quick, but I didn't, 'cause I knew no harm 'ud come to me from him . . . So, I got up, pushed him off me first. He lay there like he was dead and weighed as much. And, I stood up and looked at them lying there on the floor, and just like my dad, I felt like laughing.

Reveal Ursula and Terence who are in the garden. Rosemary has been laid out.

Ursula Terence . . . ? (*Slight pause.*) Terry . . . ?

Terence Mmmm?

Ursula Angela told me everything.

Terence Angela?

Pause.

Ursula The earth is very dry. We need rain . . . What a summer . . . ! Rosemary's flowers are dying . . . Look! Those ones are dead already . . . I can never remember their names. She must have neglected them of late. Sad . . . I think that's why I've always preferred wild flowers. It's never sad to see them die. Their deaths are natural – whereas Rosemary's flowers were so *dependent* . . .

Slight pause.

Terence What are we going to do?

Slight pause.

Ursula Look at the sky, Terry. Not a cloud in sight.

Terence There's one or two over there.

Ursula So there are. But, they're very white. No chance of any rain there.

Terence S'pose not.

Ursula And we need more than rain – we need a deluge.

Pause.

Terence What are we going to do?

Ursula It needs to rain and rain and rain.

Terence When they find out?

Ursula Do you ever just look into the sky?

Terence What then, Ursula?

Ursula I love the sky best of all. I like to look at the sky even on rainy days – when it's grey and samey – because it's never the same. Always changing.

Terence Ursula?

Ursula At times like this, I always look at the sky and watch it change. It's beautiful.

Pause.

Terence What's going to happen?

Ursula Oh, they'll find out. They always do. We could say she's gone away – but they'll find out – sooner or later. No doubt the people from the church will be first.

Terence What then?

Ursula We'll tell them the truth. That it was an accident – which it was – but it'll do us no good. (*Slight pause.*) They'll lock you up. (*Slight pause.*) And, they'll send me back. (*Pause.*) Terence?

Terence Mmmm?

Ursula Maybe we should bury her . . . We could tell them before we do – but what difference does it really make? She'll get buried that way as well – but they always make such a fuss . . . I'm against them. (*Slight pause.*) Terry . . . ? Very deep it has to be . . . You can dig it in her favourite spot . . . Which was Rosemary's favourite spot?

Terence Lavender bush.

Ursula That's a nice idea.

Terence Where's Angela?

Ursula She's gone. I gave her some money.

Terence She's gone?

Ursula I thought it would be best all round, after she told me what happened. She won't say anything.

  Pause.

Terence I liked her.

Ursula I know you did, you just had a funny way of showing it . . . I liked her too . . . Terry?

Terence What's that?

Ursula I think you've woken up. Never mind. It's better that way – in the long run . . . You'll look after me, won't you? Until they come, that is?

Terence Course I will, Ursula.

Ursula So, until they do, I'm afraid we'll have to let that job of yours go.

Terence Right.

SCENE ELEVEN

Angela alone. The sound of a train.

Angela (*monologue*) You're in a room, and there's no way out. No way out of a room – your only world. Then your brain begins to eat in itself, then when your brain eats itself, it starts on your heart and everything else. But

what's left is saying all the time – don't want no pity,
'cause it's the other world of out, that's done it, that's set it
on itself – brain eats itself and eats you all. But, that don't
make you special – makes you just like all the others. Feel
like you lost someone you love real strong. Feel . . . numb.

My Summer of

LISA GREENWALD

Pink & Green

AMULET BOOKS

NEW YORK

PUBLISHER'S NOTE: This is a work of fiction. Names, characters, places, and incidents are either the product of the author's imagination or are used fictitiously, and any resemblance to actual persons, living or dead, business establishments, events, or locales is entirely coincidental.

The Library of Congress has catalogued the hardcover edition of this book as follows:

Greenwald, Lisa
My summer of pink and green / by Lisa Greenwald.
p. cm.
Sequel to: My life in pink & green.
Summary: Rather than a summer of fun transforming her family's pharmacy into an eco-spa, Lucy Desberg must face her sister Claudia's new boyfriend Bean, investor Gary's irritating daughter Bevin, and a spa coordinator who is put in charge of the plans.
ISBN 978-1-4197-0413-0 (hardback)
[1. Buildings—Repair and reconstruction—Fiction. 2. Health resorts—Fiction. 3. Family life—Connecticut—Fiction. 4. Cosmetics—Fiction. 5. Green movement—Fiction.] I. Title.
PZ7.G85199Mys 2013
[Fic]—dc23
2012040936

ISBN for this edition: 978-1-4197-0931-9

Text copyright © 2013 Lisa Greenwald
Photography copyright © 2013 Jonathan Beckerman
Book design by Chad W. Beckerman

Originally published in hardcover in 2013 by Amulet Books, an imprint of ABRAMS. This edition published in 2014. All rights reserved. No portion of this book may be reproduced, stored in a retrieval system, or transmitted in any form or by any means, mechanical, electronic, photocopying, recording, or otherwise, without written permission from the publisher.

Amulet Books and Amulet Paperbacks are registered trademarks of Harry N. Abrams, Inc.

Printed and bound in U.S.A. 10 9 8 7 6 5 4 3 2 1

Amulet Books are available at special discounts when purchased in quantity for premiums and promotions as well as fundraising or educational use. Special editions can also be created to specification. For details, contact specialsales@abramsbooks.com or the address below.

THE ART OF BOOKS SINCE 1949
115 West 18th Street
New York, NY 10011
www.abramsbooks.com

For my brothers David and Max Greenwald, who make everything better just by being there

Lucy's tip for a great summer:
Appreciate every moment.
Summer is fleeting and goes by fast!

School got out a week ago, but it doesn't feel like summer yet. It will soon, though. As soon as Claudia drives up and gets out of the car and runs to hug me, then it will feel like summer. The best feeling in the whole, entire world.

"It's gonna be a Jetta," Yamir says. "College kids always drive Jettas." We're sitting on my front porch drinking my mom's famous homemade mint iced tea: me; my best friend, Sunny Ramal; her brother, Yamir; and our friend Evan. He's pretty much Sunny's boyfriend, but we're all friends with him too. The others always turn their noses up at the mint iced tea, but once it's in the special tall glasses with little pieces of mint floating on the top, they can't resist. It's just too refreshing.

"I don't think so; Jettas are fancy, aren't they?" I ask. We're guessing cars because Claudia's driving home with a friend from school. If Claudia were flying home from Chicago, we'd pick her up at the airport and I'd even make one of those name signs that professional drivers use. But she got a ride home instead. Mom and Grandma were all worried about the long drive, and they insisted that she stop and stay overnight somewhere. Her friend Lauren is the one driving her; she lives in Fairfield, which is like an hour from here.

"It's gonna be some old car," Sunny says, standing up. She wants to be the first one to see Claudia coming, but I don't see how that's going to happen if we don't even know what car she's coming in.

"No way," I add. "Girls named Lauren don't have beat-up old cars. Maybe a Honda, but a new one."

"Maybe it's a motorcycle!" Evan shouts. "Wouldn't that be hilarious?"

I give him a stare-down. "No, Evan Mass, it would not be hilarious, because my mom and grandma would probably pass out from shock. Then we'd have to take them to the hospital." I keep up my stare-down. If he's going to be my best friend's boyfriend, then he can't say dumb things like that. "Motorcycles are really dangerous, you know."

He cracks up, and Sunny and Yamir do too.

I don't see what's so funny. "They are. I'm serious."

Sunny pats my knee. "He was just kidding, Lucy."

Thankfully my mom comes out with a tray holding a full pitcher of more mint iced tea and a bowl of strawberries and breaks the tension. "Hungry?" she asks. When none of us answer, she says, "You know, you guys can go swimming. I'm sure Claudia will come on back when she gets here."

The pool! OK, I changed my mind. It will really feel like summer when we're all in the pool. Claudia will probably run inside and throw on her favorite red-and-white gingham bikini and then she'll race out to join us. We'll have diving contests and make Sunny be the judge. She always gives me a ten. And we'll go down the spiral slide a billion times. Sometimes I even sit on Claudia's lap when we go down the spiral slide. It makes Grandma nervous, but we do it anyway.

Claudia's friends will come over and BBQ like crazy— Grandma always lets them use the grill even though she says I'm not old enough. They'll make hamburgers and hot dogs, and portobello burgers for their vegetarian friends. They'll hang out for hours, and they'll let me hang out with them too, some of the time.

It will feel like summer will last forever, and I'll keep telling myself that it won't last forever but that I need to appreciate it and savor every second: every sip of Mom's iced tea, every trip down the spiral slide, every diving contest.

"She's here!" I scream. I know it's her because the windows are rolled down and her head is out the front passenger side like she's a golden retriever.

They pull into the driveway.

"A Subaru!" Yamir says. "We should have known. College kids always drive Subarus."

I don't even care to discuss with him about how he knows that. I'm too excited to see Claudia, to give her hugs, to talk to her about everything—especially the opening of the spa—that I just don't have time to deal with Yamir.

He's been so weird lately. He doesn't get why it's such a big deal that Claudia's coming home. He takes it for granted that his sister is home all the time, but I haven't seen Claudia since September, since she didn't come home for Thanksgiving. Then she was in El Salvador over winter break, and she went to Ghana for spring break. For an eighteen-year-old, she travels a lot.

I run over to the car and Claudia hops out and we hug for a million years like I thought we would. "I missed you so much," I whisper in her ear.

"I missed you too, Luce!"

Her friend Lauren starts unloading the trunk and I'm thankful that Yamir goes over to help. He can be a gentleman sometimes, but then other times he can act like a complete doofus. Grandma says that's just how boys his age act. But I don't really believe her—can't he just act nicer? For me?

"These are yours, right, Claud?" Lauren asks her, holding up a duffel. Claudia looks over, and that's when I notice that there's another person here. A tall, skinny guy, standing right near the car talking to Evan about the Subaru's muffler or something.

"Yeah, those are mine. Bean's are the ones in the backseat."

"Bean is here?" I ask without thinking.

Claudia does a head-jerk motion in his direction, trying to get his attention, and he comes over to where we're standing. I look around for Mom and Grandma. The moment we've all been waiting for—Claudia coming home—is finally here!

"You must be Lucy," this Bean guy says, with a hand up to high-five me.

"I am." I smile and high-five him back. "And you must be Bean? Well, duh, I mean I know you're Bean, Claudia just said that. But I remember your name. Claudia said you helped look over the grant application a few months ago."

"I did. I did." He nods like he's so proud of himself. "I'm pre-law."

"Huh?"

"It means he's going to be a lawyer, Lucy," Claudia explains.

I feel stupid. I could have figured that out.

5

"But it's a dual major with the business school," Bean adds.

I nod. Bean sounds like he's on a job interview. I'm not really concerned with his major right now. It's summer! He shouldn't be thinking about school anyway.

"Welcome home!" Mom yells, running outside, a dish towel over her right shoulder. "Ma, Claudia's home!" she yells back into the house.

A few seconds later, Grandma comes out, and then we're all together. I don't even realize that Sunny, Yamir, and Evan went back onto the porch until I hear the click of Yamir's iPhone camera taking a picture of all of us standing around in the driveway.

"Such a photo op," he says with a grin. "Right, Luce-Juice? You're all about the photo ops, especially one like this."

Sometimes I feel like Yamir knows the right thing to do and he does it, but then he says something obnoxious while doing it, and that takes all the goodness out of it.

"Thanks." I put my hand on my hip and go into a model pose and he snaps another shot.

"So, Mom, Grandma," Claudia starts. "This is my friend Lauren, and this is Bean."

I wonder why Claudia doesn't refer to Bean as her friend.

"Lovely to meet you, thank you for driving her home, Lauren," Grandma says. "You probably want to get going. I

6

bet your parents are worried sick about you doing so much driving and all the crazies on the road."

"Grams, it's OK." Claudia pats her shoulder. "She's meeting them nearby, and then they're going to their beach house in Newport for the summer."

"That's lovely," Mom says. Everything's lovely, apparently.

I'm still standing there, wondering if it's too soon to go change into bathing suits and jump in the pool. I wish Lauren and Bean would just leave already so I could have Claudia to myself.

"What a lovely tote," Mom says about this long bag that Lauren has over her shoulder. It's just a canvas tote with the word *Tranquility* embroidered in pink letters. It's nothing that special, really.

"Thanks. It's from Etsy." Lauren smiles. "It's basically the only place I shop these days."

"Oh, I know," Mom says. "It's just so fabulous that artists can sell directly to—"

"So, Mom, Grandma, Lucy," Claudia interrupts, thankfully, because this conversation about Lauren's tote bag was getting really boring for everyone except Lauren and Mom. "I know this may come as a shock to you, but it was a really last-minute decision."

I look at Claudia and then at Bean and I start to get a bad feeling.

Did they elope?

"I invited Bean to come stay with us for the summer."

I gasp. I feel like someone sucked all the water out of our perfect pool with a straw and there will never be water in it again. Everything I had been looking forward to just evaporated.

"What?" I ask.

Claudia ignores me and looks at Mom and Grandma, who haven't said anything. After a second she continues. "Bean has a great mind for business and he's going to be a huge help with the opening of the spa. His parents travel a lot for work, so there was really no point in him going back to Pittsburgh."

Grandma seems skeptical, but Mom nods like it's a totally genius idea.

"And we're in love," Claudia says, grabbing Bean's hand. "We're really in love."

"What?" I ask again. She cannot be serious. She's in love with Bean? First of all, what kind of a name is Bean? He's probably called that because he looks like a string bean. A long, skinny, dried-out string bean.

"Oh, that is wonderful, Claudia," Mom says. "I remember when your father and I felt like that. Like we could conquer the world together."

When Mom brings up Dad in this fairy-tale, romantic

comedy kind of way, I wonder why their relationship isn't like that now. I get all these hopeful thoughts and start to think that maybe it will be like that again someday. But I hate to think like that, because it means I'll just get my hopes up and then be disappointed again. Dad lives in England and has this big, important professor job there. I don't know if he'll ever be able to come back permanently, or even if he'd really want to.

Grandma shoots Mom a look and shakes her head. I can almost read her thoughts. They're saying: *And I remember when you had no money and lived here and had your head in the clouds.*

"Jane, may I have a word with you, please?" Grandma asks, and takes Mom's hand and leads her to the side of the house. I need to walk away too, so I go and join Sunny, Evan, and Yamir on the porch.

"What's going on?" Sunny asks. "And can we go swim? It's really hot out here."

I plop down on the porch, not even caring if I get any splinters in my legs. "Bean is staying with us for the summer. They're in love. Can you believe it?"

"Really?" Sunny asks.

Evan and Yamir don't have anything to say. Clearly they don't understand why this is a big deal.

"Yup. Unless my mom and grandma say no or something. But I doubt they'll do that."

"Maybe he'll be cool to have around," Sunny says. "Maybe he can be your chauffeur. You can even make him wear a hat and open doors for you."

I roll my eyes at her. "We don't have an extra car, but good thought."

No one else says anything. We're just sitting here staring at Claudia, Lauren, and Bean in the driveway. Bean looks nervous.

"Bye, Lucy," Lauren yells. "Nice to meet you!"

I wave good-bye and Lauren gets back in the car and drives away. Bean's and Claudia's bags are just sitting in the driveway now. If Grandma and Mom do say no to Bean staying, I have no idea how he'll get home. Lauren's off to her fabulous beach house and we're stuck with Bean.

We have so much work to do. The ground-breaking ceremony for the spa is tomorrow, and we waited until Claudia got home before having it. It's two weeks later than it should have been because she claimed she was busy setting up this summer camp for poor kids in Chicago. She was probably just busy spending more alone time with Bean.

"Eww," Sunny says, and we all look over to the driveway again. Claudia's giving Bean a massage, and it's grossing all of us out. "We're going to swim, OK, Lucy?"

"Fine," I groan.

"Do you want me to stay with you?" Yamir asks, and he has his nervous face on, the one that makes the left side of his mouth twitch a little.

I smile. I'm so proud of him for saying the right thing that it doesn't really matter if he stays or not. "No, it's OK. You can go swim."

"Is the code for the gate still 1818?" Sunny asks. My grandma is so paranoid about people drowning that we still have a gate for the pool, and she really doesn't like people to be back there without an adult.

"Yeah," I say. "Be really careful."

Mom and Grandma come back around and walk over to the driveway to talk to Claudia and Bean. Thankfully, Claudia has stopped the massage. It's too hot out for massages anyway. I don't know why you would want someone's sweaty hands on you.

I wonder if I should go over and join them. But I'm so annoyed that I'd rather stay here, in the shade of the porch, on one of the wicker rocking chairs. I can hear everything they're saying anyway.

"We really wish you had told us in advance," Grandma says. "There's so much going on with the spa opening that it's going to be hectic having someone else around the house. I wish I'd had time to prepare."

"I know, Grams," Claudia says. "But Bean won't be a hassle. He's a good cook too!"

"Oh, I'll be a huge help, Mrs. Desberg," Bean says. "I can cook, do laundry, go grocery shopping, drive people around, you name it."

"You're hired!" Mom says, and laughs, even though no one else does.

Grandma shakes her head at Mom and looks back at Claudia. "You have to know there are some ground rules," Grandma says. "Separate rooms. Bean can sleep in the attic guest room. I'll turn on the air-conditioning up there and take my winter clothes out of the closet."

"The attic? He can just sleep in the guest room on the second floor," Claudia says.

"No. I said the attic," Grandma says.

Grandma's a smart lady. The stairs up to the attic creak so loud, the whole neighborhood can hear them. She'll know if Bean's not where he's supposed to be.

Grandma continues, "And we need Bean pitching in."

"He said he would," Claudia says, looking at him.

Grandma leans in to whisper something in Claudia's ear. And then they walk off to the side a little bit. I bet it's about me. I bet she's telling her that they have to include me, and spend time with me, like I'm some kind of charity case.

Well, I'll show them. I'll be busy too, with Yamir and Sunny and Evan. We have plans to go to the beach and we'll be busy with the Earth Club stuff. Mrs. Deleccio wants us to come in a little over the summer to work on the Going Green school board proposal.

I try to eavesdrop, but I can't really hear much.

"Next time, we'll need a little more notice," Grandma says to Claudia, no longer whispering. "This isn't a hotel, and bringing a boyfriend home is a serious thing."

The thing is, Claudia's not the only one with a boyfriend. I sorta have one too. I mean, yeah, Yamir and I haven't come out and said it, really. We don't go around telling the whole world how in love we are or anything.

But I'm pretty sure he's my boyfriend. He looks out for me, pays attention to me. We see each other almost every day. It's in a group, but it's still seeing a lot of each other. So that's gotta mean something. I always get excited to see him, and it seems like he gets excited to see me too. That's really the most important sign of a good relationship, I think.

Their conversation ends and Claudia and Bean walk over to me. "Wanna go swim, Luce?" Claudia asks. "I've been practicing my dives. You're not even gonna believe my flip."

"Liar. You swim in Chicago?"

"Oh, does she swim!" Bean exclaims. "She's practically a fish."

I don't want to be happy; I want to stay mad at Bean for being here over the summer. But at this moment, all I can think about is the pool in the backyard and Claudia being home and dumping buckets of ice water on her stomach while she's sleeping on the lounge chair next to me.

It's summer. Claudia's home. The ground breaking for the spa is happening tomorrow. Even with Bean here, I have to be a little bit happy.

When Claudia's around, it's not just that everything feels better. Everything *is* better.

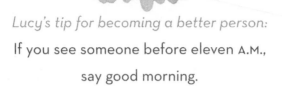

Lucy's tip for becoming a better person:
If you see someone before eleven A.M.,
say good morning.

I wake up ridiculously early the next day. This always happens to me when I'm really excited about something or really nervous about something. And in this case, it's both.

It's almost seven and no one else is up yet. I can't believe it. We have to be at the pharmacy by nine. Mayor Danes said to be prompt, and we can't just run in when all the news crews are there—it would look so unprofessional. Besides, they're going to want interviews and stuff. I can't look sweaty and frazzled.

I walk around upstairs and try to make as much noise as possible—loudly closing the medicine cabinet door, slamming down the toilet seat, flushing a few extra times. Nothing's working.

And then I hear creaking on the stairs from the attic to the d floor. And then I remember: Bean. Figures that Bean the first one up. Now I'm going to have to see him all awkward in the morning in his pajamas with messy hair before he's brushed his teeth. It's grossing me out.

"Good morning, Lucy!" he says, so cheery. And then he does this weird salute thing that I don't really understand.

"Good morning," I mumble, not looking at him.

"Ready for your big day?"

I like the fact that he's calling it *my* big day, which it kind of is even though it's everyone's big day too, but I can't focus on that because all I'm thinking about is that he hasn't brushed his teeth yet. I am a brush-your-teeth-as-soon-as-you-get-up kind of person.

Soon everyone's getting up, and since I was awake and ready before everyone else, I take it upon myself to make breakfast. I scramble some eggs and fry some French toast and I even put a carton of orange juice in Mom's fancy pitcher. I want this to feel like a special day since it really, really is.

"Thanks for breakfast, Luce," Claudia says after a sip of juice. "So what exactly happens today? I was thinking I'd throw my beach stuff in the car, and Bean and I will probably go there for the afternoon."

"You're going to the beach?" I ask, with my mouth half-full of French toast.

Claudia makes a disgusted face. "Eww. Don't talk with your mouth full." She shakes her head at me like I've completely lost all sense. "Yeah, we're going to the beach. The ground breaking won't take all day."

I finish chewing and then speak. "Claudia, don't you realize how much work we have to do? This is just the official ground breaking, so construction has already started, but we still need to order everything, hire staff, all of that stuff." I look over at Bean to see if he'll agree with me. He's sipping coffee and reading the newspaper, and I bet he's not even listening.

"Relax, Lucy." Claudia smiles her you're-insane smile and pulls her chair back from the table.

A little while later, Mom, Claudia, and Bean are still doing who knows what in the house, so Grandma and I are waiting in the car for them.

"Lucy, doll," Grandma says, looking back at me from the front seat. "You know I am so unbelievably grateful for all that you did to help save the pharmacy, right?"

I nod. She's told me like a billion times. She's said over and over again how smart it was for me to apply for that Going Green grant and how entrepreneurial it was of me to start doing the makeovers and to create the Relaxation Room. I don't know why she's saying it again now.

"But here's the thing, love," she goes on, and I know that

whenever she starts a sentence like that, whatever follows will definitely not be good. "I don't expect you to totally take care of opening the spa on your own. What do we know about opening a spa? If we're going to do it right, we need a professional to help us, don't we?"

I'm not really sure what she's getting at. Is she telling me I'm fired? If you're not an official employee, can you really be fired anyway?

"You're still going to be a huge help, though," Grandma continues. "You'll be—"

"Hola, amigos!" Bean yells as he's getting in the car. "Doris, if you ever want me to drive, just say so. I have a clean driving record. I could be the Desberg chauffeur!"

I roll my eyes. "You mentioned that yesterday."

Grandma cracks up. "Thanks, Bean."

"OK, you can be the family driver, but only if you wear a uniform and a hat and call me m'lady," I add.

Grandma shoots me a look. "Lucy," she warns.

I wish Claudia would hurry up instead of leaving me in the backseat with her dumb boyfriend. He totally interrupted Grandma's train of thought when she was telling me what I'd actually be doing at the spa, since apparently I'm not "professional" enough to be in charge.

Finally Mom and Claudia come out. Bean slides over so

that he and Claudia can sit next to each other, which works to my advantage because Bean gets stuck in the awful middle seat. Plus, he's really tall, so the top of his head hits the roof.

I'm about to laugh when I notice that Claudia and Bean are holding hands, which makes the whole situation no longer funny, just ridiculous. They don't really need to hold hands right now, when we're all in the car together.

"I just got a text from Gary," Grandma says. Gary's our investor; he's known Mom and Grandma forever. "They'll be able to make it today after all."

It's still really funny to me that my grandma knows how to text. I wonder if all grandmas do, or if she's just incredibly hip.

"What? Really?" Mom asks. "Ugh, I needed to prepare for that. Gary's not a person you just spring on others."

"Yeah, not like Bean," I say sarcastically under my breath and then regret it.

"Lucy!" Claudia hisses.

Mom and Grandma are arguing in the front seat about Gary and I don't need to hear this same conversation for the millionth time. "Why is your name Bean, anyway?" I ask him.

"Well, my real name is Noah Beanerman, but everyone has always called me Bean."

"Even your parents?"

He laughs. "No, I mean, like my friends and stuff."

"Got it." Am I the only one who notices that he really does look like a string bean, though? He's so tall and thin. I think about bringing it up, but I'm not sure if Claudia would find it funny.

We get to the pharmacy and there are already a million people there, just like I thought there would be. OK, not exactly a million, but at least fifty or sixty. They're taking up the whole sidewalk, all the way down to the car wash.

My stomach starts getting that rumbly feeling and soon everyone's out of the car and off in a million directions and I don't even know where to go. It's my family's store, and for the first time I feel like I'm lost in it, like I don't know my way around.

I know Sunny and Yamir and their parents are coming, so I decide to make finding them my project. I hope that when I find them, Yamir is nice and supportive to me. Sometimes he's nice, but sometimes he's weird and aloof and only half-paying attention to me. That makes me wonder if we're boyfriend and girlfriend or not. It's not clear-cut like it is with Evan and Sunny or Claudia and Bean.

With Evan and Sunny, he basically just said he wanted to be her boyfriend one day when they were waiting on line to buy slushies at the movies. And she said OK, and it's been that way for two months now.

But with Yamir . . . nothing. We hang out and we have fun together, and sometimes I think we are boyfriend and girl-friend, but we might not be anything more than friends. It used to be that just being friends was good, and I liked the way things were, but is there something wrong that he doesn't want to be my boyfriend? Am I missing something?

Everyone's standing on the sidewalk in front of the phar-macy. As I'm about to walk in, someone hands me a hard hat, like I'm a real construction worker. This is what happens at ground-breaking ceremonies, so I put it on happily.

"Oh, Lucy, I'm so glad you're here!" I hear someone say, and turn around. It's a tall woman in a white sundress. "I'm Amelia, Mayor Danes's chief of staff. It's a pleasure to meet you." She shakes my hand while staring down at her iPad. "Your whole family is here now?"

I nod, still in awe of the fact that this woman does all of her work on an iPad. Does that make the clipboard obsolete? I always thought clipboards were so cool. But I have no idea why I am thinking about something as insignificant as clip-boards at such an important time.

Amelia takes her cell phone (an iPhone, obviously) out of her dress pocket. "Phil," she says into the phone in half a second. I don't even know how it had time to ring on the other end. "The Desbergs are all here. Let's get started."

I'm still thinking about the fact that this super-important chief of staff woman knew who I was and recognized me, when I see Gary coming into the pharmacy.

Oh joy. Where's my mother? I need to warn her. I could say it in code, like "The eagle has landed" or something. She should know what that means.

"Lucy!" a little pip-squeaky, whiny voice yells, and then I see a short, chubby girl running up to me. One of her socks is higher than the other and she has a huge wet spot in the middle of her T-shirt. "Remember me? Bevin! We spent that whole afternoon having raft races in your pool that time we were eight. Remember?"

"Yeah. Hi, Bevin." I smile. "How are you?"

"I'm *grrrreat!*" she yells so loud that people turn around to look at us.

"OK, Lucy, we need you." Amelia grabs my arm and pulls me away. I wave good-bye to Bevin, but I'm relieved not to have to talk to her anymore.

Amelia leads me outside and that's where we find Mom, Grandma, Claudia, and Bean.

"Hello, Desbergs!" Mayor Dane, says, going down the line shaking each of our hands. "The day is here! Can you believe it?"

"Well, we began construction a month ago," Grandma says.

"But yes, we appreciate the town's commitment to our store and this wonderful celebration you guys are having for us."

"Of course, Doris." He smiles in his politiciany way.

It's funny because Grandma has known Mayor Danes since he was a little kid. He grew up in Old Mill and went to a school that was around the corner from the pharmacy. It was turned into a supermarket about ten years ago.

I wonder if it's hard for Grandma to take Mayor Danes seriously since she remembers when he would get milk mustaches at the pharmacy counter and count out his spare change to see if he had enough money to buy a pack of bubble gum.

Soon we all have our hard hats on and we're standing in front of the entrance of the pharmacy with Mayor Danes. There are a few news crews here and writers from the *Old Mill Observer* and the *Connecticut Chronicle*.

There are people standing all around us and when I look into the crowd, I spot Sunny, Yamir, and their parents. Sunny's waving at me and Yamir is looking down at his phone or his handheld game or something.

"Thank you all for coming out today for the official ground breaking of the Pink and Green Spa at Old Mill Pharmacy," Mayor Danes says into his megaphone, and everyone starts clapping. It's so loud that I wonder if people sitting in the movie theater are able to hear it. But then I remember that it's only nine thirty in the morning. I don't think movies ever start that early! "As I'm sure you all know, Old Mill Pharmacy is a local business that embodies community. It is where we go for prescriptions, where we go for advice when every lotion on the market will not help our dry skin." He pauses and everyone laughs. Who ever thought dry skin could be so funny? "But it is also where we go when we need some advice on anything from meddling mothers-in-law to the best method for making chicken soup. It is where we go for a smile after a hard day or a friendly face after a long winter. It is Old Mill's home away from home, and we are all so lucky to have it."

I look around the crowd again and I recognize so many of the faces—Meredith Ganzi and her mom from the movie theater down the street; Eli from the video store that the spa is expanding into; Mr. Becker and his baby son, Wyatt. Even my makeup client Courtney Adner and her parents came out. And everyone seems so happy to be here. It's early in the morning on a hot summer day and they're standing on the sidewalk, and yet they really seem happy.

"And now this pharmacy will be even more than a pharmacy," Mayor Danes continues. "It will be a spa. A place for beauty and rest and relaxation. And a green spa! Not only are the Desbergs of Old Mill Pharmacy saving us from life's pharmaceutical and everyday woes, but they are now saving the environment, too!"

After that there's more applause and I look around to see if I can find Mrs. Deleccio. She said she was going to come. After all, it's her Earth Club that got me into caring about the environment and the research during that club that helped me to find the Going Green grant for local businesses of Old Mill.

"And who would believe that the person behind all of this expansion and vision was a thirteen-year-old girl with a big heart and even bigger dreams?" Mayor Danes looks at me, and Claudia whispers in my ear, "He is *soooo* cheesy."

She's right, but she doesn't have to say it. He's saying amazing things about me, and I don't care if they're cheesy—I like hearing them.

"Thank you, Lucy, for all you have done, and all you will no doubt continue to do!" Mayor Danes says, and I bet if we weren't all already standing, people would give me a standing ovation. It just feels like that kind of moment. "So, let's all go inside, make sure your hard hats are on, and we will continue with the official ground breaking!"

I hope people don't mind that the wall between the pharmacy and the video store was already torn down and other walls for the treatment rooms have already been put up. I hope this ground breaking doesn't feel anticlimactic. We learned that word in English this year, and I think there are a lot of anticlimactic things in life. Come to think of it, Claudia coming home ended up being a little anticlimactic. I was all excited about it, and then . . . well, it hasn't been quite what I hoped for. But I guess that's just the way it is sometimes.

We all shuffle in and stand near the wall. Mom, Grandma, Claudia, and I are up front, and I'm glad that Bean is toward the back a little bit, because it means he realizes he's not part of the family. Not yet anyway.

The wall is mostly torn down and the archway is in the process of being remodeled, but we left a little bit up just for this purpose.

Mayor Danes hands me a sledgehammer. "Would you like to do the honors, Lucy?"

I look at Mom, Grandma, and Claudia and they're all nodding at me.

In my head I can hear Erica Crane saying something about how this is such a liability and her uncle who's a lawyer could totally report us or something else about the law and codes that really doesn't make any sense.

I quickly scan the crowd for her, but I don't see her. I'm relieved, even though I didn't really expect her to come.

"OK," I say, and I take the sledgehammer and slam it as hard as I can into that plaster wall. As I'm doing it, I'm imagining everything I've been angry about—Yamir acting dumb, Erica Crane being mean in Earth Club, my dad postponing his yearly trip to the United States, Claudia bringing Bean home for the summer. I guess I'm not very strong, because even using all of my strength, my hits don't do very much damage—barely any plaster falls off, and the hole isn't even very big—but as I'm hitting, all the anger I've been feeling seems to dribble away a little bit. I take one more slam and then put down the sledgehammer. I take a bow and everyone claps.

"Doris and Jane," Mayor Danes says, turning to face them. "Would you like to give everyone a little tour of the new space?"

"Phil," Grandma says, nudging him in her direction so she can say something to him quietly. "Is this safe? I mean, there's some loose flooring, a bunch of open wiring, and who knows what else?"

"It's OK, Dor," he says. "We do this all the time."

She shrugs.

"Follow the Desberg ladies!" Mayor Danes yells out to the crowd, and soon everyone's following us through the half-torn-down wall and the archway into the old Fellini & Friends video store.

It's hard to believe that within weeks, Pink & Green will really be open. Customers—brides-to-be, prom goers, bat mitzvah girls—will be coming in for makeup and massages and facials.

As we're walking in, I feel someone put their arms on my shoulders and when I turn around, I see that it's Sunny. She reaches over to give me a hug. "I am so proud of you, Luce! You really did it. Oh, and when did your mom and grandma agree to the name? You never told me it was officially going to be called Pink and Green."

I'm distracted as I'm talking to her because I'm looking around at everyone who is coming in with us, especially keeping an eye on Yamir. But I try to focus. "Well, the official name is 'Pink and Green: The Spa at Old Mill Pharmacy,' but everyone liked just 'Pink and Green' by itself. My grandma was worried people wouldn't know what it was, so she added that little bit at the end."

"Makes sense," Sunny says, peering around a corner. We've separated from the rest of the tour, but it's not like we really need to be with the group. I know my way around here. "That's the makeup chair?" she asks, pointing to a huge chair covered in plastic in the corner.

"Yup!" I walk over to it, and Sunny follows. "Isn't it so amazing? We ordered it special from this beauty supplies catalog. It has all these different settings, so I can make it higher or lower depending on how tall the people are."

"Let's unwrap it!" Sunny says.

"No, we can't. It'll get all dusty from the construction," I say. "But I promise you will be one of the first people to sit in it."

"Cool," Sunny says, seeming bored all of a sudden. I look away from the chair and back at her and I notice she's not even paying attention or seeming excited about the chair anymore. She's looking down at her phone, reading a text message or something. Finally she looks up. "Oh, sorry. Evan was just texting me, asking if I wanted to go to the carnival at Old Mill Elementary later."

"I thought they had one a few months ago."

"They did, but they're having another, and it's a fund-raiser. They need money for that new music wing." She shrugs. "Should be fun, though."

Is Sunny really going to something and not inviting me? I don't know what to say. I just stay quiet. It'll come. She'll say *Do you want to come with us?* any second now.

But she doesn't. It feels like an hour goes by without either of us saying anything.

"Lucy, we need you," Grandma calls. "This lovely woman wants to ask you some questions."

"OK, so I gotta go, Sunny," I say, and give her one last chance to invite me.

"See you later! Go be your important spa-owning self." She smiles and blows me a kiss. But no invite.

If you can, go swimming every single day.

𝒪he next few days seem to go in slow motion. I expected everything to happen superfast as soon as Claudia was home and we had the ground breaking, but instead it feels like I'm just sitting around all the time.

Every day I go to the pharmacy and help out with my usual stuff—the magazines, the hair products, keeping the Relaxation Room nice and neat—but I want to be doing stuff for the spa! I hang around the construction area and watch the workers handle the installations and the lighting and I page through spa catalogs, folding down corners.

Right now Mom and Grandma are in the back office looking at the calendar trying to figure the best day for the grand opening of the spa. I don't understand why they don't know the perfect day right away. It's so obvious.

I'm glad my eavesdropping skills have improved so

much and that I can hear them talking. I put the stack of magazines on the Relaxation Room table in a neat pile and run over to them.

"Hey, Lucy," Grandma says.

"Hi." I plop myself down on the office couch. "Whatcha talking about?" See, I can't make it too obvious that I'm a master eavesdropper, because if I do, they won't talk so loudly anymore and I'll never be able to hear what's going on.

"Just trying to figure out scheduling," my mom says, sounding worn out. "Ma, don't forget I have that wedding in August."

"What wedding?" I ask.

"Oh, a friend of Dad's and mine from Yale—her name is Esme. She and her fiancé live on a commune in New Hampshire. They're finally getting married," Mom says. "She's really crazy, but we—"

"OK." Grandma puts a hand on my mom's shoulder. "We don't need every single detail, Jane. Just remind me of the weekend."

"It's the weekend before Labor Day weekend. So we can do the grand opening before or after."

"Are you guys serious?" I ask. They look at me, confused. "It's ridiculously obvious that the grand opening of

Pink and Green needs to be Labor Day weekend. Hello, Boat Fest!"

Grandma raises her finger in the air like she's so excited about what I said, and then she pats me on the back. "Genius! My granddaughter, she's a genius."

I smile. "Well, how did you guys not think of that? I mean, all the fancy summer-home people are in town, lots of weddings go on over Labor Day weekend, and practically every single person in Connecticut is out and about that weekend!"

"OK, so it's settled!" Grandma declares. "Follow me."

We follow her over to the spa area. "Hey, Johnny," Grandma yells out over the noise of the drill and the sander and the other tools they're using. "Can we have everything ready to go by Labor Day?"

He turns off the drill. "Our part should be done, yeah. But y'all need equipment, lighting consults, all that other jazz."

I look at Grandma. I wonder if she realizes this is what I've been saying all along, but she doesn't look at me. She nods and Johnny turns the drill back on. We all cover our ears at the same time and leave the spa area.

"OK, time to return Gary's call," Grandma says. "He came into town for the ground breaking, but we didn't get a chance to chat. We need to make plans."

I look at my watch. Claudia was supposed to be here ten minutes ago to drive me to Earth Club. She's late. Since Bean's been here, she's always late.

"Ma, Gary's just the investor," Mom says to Grandma. "I don't think you need to consult him about every little thing." Mom's still stuck on the fact that she was set up with Gary years and years ago. I'm sure Gary's moved on and doesn't even think about it anymore, but for some reason my mom gets all weird whenever Gary's name comes up. Too bad for her, though, because Gary's a huge investor in Pink & Green, and I have a feeling he's going to be around a lot this summer.

Grandma ignores her and gets Gary on the phone. "Gary, hi, it's Doris." She pauses and waits for him to talk. "Oh, that's great," she goes on. "OK, well, fabulous, that's exactly what I was thinking. I'm glad you beat me to it." She nods. "And you're on top of compensation?" She's writing something down in her little red notebook. "Got it. See you tomorrow."

Grandma hangs up and Mom and I just sit there staring at her, waiting for her to tell us what that was all about.

"So, Gary's hired a spa consultant to help us get up and running," Grandma says, still writing stuff down in her notebook. "She's coming tomorrow, so we'll really start to get the ball rolling."

"But Grandma," I say, kind of in shock. "I know what we need to order. We don't need a consultant."

"Lucy," Grandma says in her letting-me-down-easy tone that I really, really hate. "We talked about this."

I should tell her that we started to talk about it but never really finished because Bean interrupted us.

Mom stands up and folds her arms across her chest. "Ma, who knows who this consultant is? She needs to know we're doing this all green. We can't just have any old person coming in here and telling us how to run the place."

"Relax, please. Both of you." Grandma sighs. "It's all going to be fine. Now, please excuse me so I can get back to the prescription counter. We are still a pharmacy, you know!"

Grandma leaves the office and my mom and I just stare at each other.

"Don't worry, Luce," my mom says. "You'll still play a huge part in the opening of the spa."

"Uh-huh," I grumble, then hear the car horn. "I gotta go to Earth Club. See you later."

I leave the pharmacy without saying good-bye to Grandma. She's busy filling prescriptions for the new local news anchor anyway.

Well, there's nothing I can do about the fact that both Grandma and Gary feel that the spa needs some kind of consultant. But I'll show them how much I can do. Let the consultant come. We can work together. She'll be so impressed with me. Grandma and Mom will be even prouder of me than they were when we got the grant. I'm not threatened by this spa consultant. Not at all.

"Hey," I say to Claudia and Bean when I get in the car.

"Hey, darlin'," Bean says. "We got you a surprise."

Claudia hands me one of those giant gobstoppers wrapped in waxed paper. "You used to love these," she says. "We saw them in a big bin at the mall, so we had to get one for you."

"That's sweet," I say, and crack up. "No pun intended."

I sit in the backseat and eat my gobstopper. I still can't believe that we actually agreed to work on school projects during the summer, but I guess it's OK because it's something we feel is important.

Today Earth Club is doing a beach cleanup. It's not exactly lounging at the beach, but it is better than sitting inside somewhere.

"Hey, you," I hear someone say as I'm walking through the entrance to the beach. Usually this is the place where you pay, but since it's a weekday before the height of the season, none of the guards are here.

It's Yamir. I could tell his voice anywhere, even with the sound of the ocean all around us.

"Hi," I say. "Waiting for Anthony?"

"No, I was waiting for you. Dummy." He hits his elbow against my arm.

"Oh." I smile. "That was nice."

"But now I have to wait for Anthony," he says.

I can't tell if he's serious or not, so I just wait to see what he does next. He sits back down on the bench. I'm actually a few minutes early to meet everyone by the lifeguard chair, so I sit with him.

"So what's new?" Yamir asks me.

"Ugh, everyone's annoying," I start. "Claudia's boyfriend is living with us for the summer and now Gary's hired this spa consultant, and I don't really have anything to do for the spa now, and no one cares about my ideas."

"Oh, boo-hoo, poor Lucy." He rolls his eyes. "You complain a lot. Did you know that?"

I stand up. "I'm going to find everyone now," I say, and start walking away from him. "You know we're here to clean, not just sit around, right?"

He doesn't respond.

I know I like to complain, but I never realized other people noticed how often I do it. It's not fun to have your bad habits pointed out. And I used to be such an optimistic person. It's just that now it seems like no one even cares if I'm around. Claudia is busy with Bean, and Sunny and Evan are lovebirds who are just happy hanging out with each other. And Mom and Grandma don't even really need my help around the pharmacy anymore. The grant led to all this awesome publicity, which led to business picking up, so they were able to hire our beloved pharmacy workers Tory and Charise back.

I'm practically useless to everyone.

"Lucy, what are you doing?" Mrs. Deleccio runs up to me. I decided to walk along the boardwalk for a few minutes before meeting up with everyone. I guess Mrs. Deleccio saw me and got worried. "We need you. There's more beach littering than you'd think; we have a lot to do."

I nod. "OK, I'm coming."

"I was really impressed with that organic food supplier you found," she says as we're walking over to the rest of the group. "And it seems like you're able to negotiate with them to get us a good rate, right?"

"Uh-huh."

"Lucy, you know you're an instrumental member of this club, right?" Mrs. Deleccio says when we're a few feet from everyone else. "I hope you'll still be able to give it your all even though you'll be really busy with the spa opening." She smiles at me. It's like she read my mind or sensed how I was feeling, but she said exactly what I needed to hear. Sometimes teachers just know these things; it's like they have psychic powers or something.

But the thing is, I want to be instrumental in other areas of my life too. Earth Club is barely even meeting over the summer; it can't be the only thing I work on. And maybe the pharmacy doesn't need me anymore, and the spa work is above my head. But I can do something else. I know I can. I just have to figure out another project, somewhere else I'm needed.

I walk over to the group, and Sunny and Evan are off to the side laughing about something.

"Hey, guys," I say.

"Oh hey, Luce," Sunny says. "Where's Yamir? He said he was waiting for you."

"He was." I pick up a shell and tell myself not to take any shells home, as much as I want to. I have so many shells at home already. "But then he said he had to wait for Anthony."

"Dummy." Evan crinkles his brow. "Anthony's not coming today. I just told him that. I bet he's just too lazy to actually do the beach cleanup."

I shrug.

"OK, Earth Club!" Mrs. Deleccio yells. It's very windy, so she needs to be loud to get our attention. "We're going to cover the strip of beach from this red flag to the one all the way down there." She points to the red flag on the far end, near the snack bar. "Meet back here in about a half hour. I have garbage bags for each of you." Mrs. Deleccio hands us each a garbage bag and I start walking toward the water to pick up trash that may have washed up during high tide. I look behind me to see if Evan and Sunny are close by, but they're traipsing behind.

"Are you guys coming?" I ask Evan and Sunny. They just keep cracking up. I have no idea what's so funny. I stop for a second and wait for them to catch up.

"Hello, I am Mr. Shell," Evan says, holding a shell and talking to Sunny. He bursts out laughing. Sunny does too, like he just said the funniest thing she's ever heard.

Sunny's holding up a shell too. "Hello, I am Mrs. Shell."

I don't know why they find the silliest things funny. They're acting like two little kids, and I really don't get it. And they obviously don't even care that I'm here.

I walk away. I can collect litter on my own. Maybe a quiet walk along the beach by myself will be good to clear my head.

Yamir comes down to the beach and catches up with me, with only about twenty minutes left before it's time to go.

"Sorry," he says. "I was confused. Anthony's actually not coming." He walks along with me, but doesn't get a garbage bag of his own. Instead, he puts whatever trash he finds in my bag.

"Uh-huh." I'm not really paying attention to him.

"Anyway, do you want to go see that new Spielberg movie next week?"

"What's it about?" I try not to act too excited about the fact that Yamir's asking me to hang out. It's been forever since we hung out alone, and I didn't even think he noticed.

"Kids solving this mystery about this campground or something," he says. "It looks freaky but not too scary."

I finally look at him. He looks so cute with his dark shaggy hair and his long eyelashes. "Sure, I'll go."

"Cool. Movie times aren't out yet, but I'll let you know."

"Yamir, I notice you don't have a garbage bag," Mrs. Deleccio says, coming out of nowhere. "If you're going to be here, I'd like you to participate."

"On it, Mrs. Deleccio." He stands up and marches over to the box of garbage bags, and takes one.

Mrs. Deleccio sighs.

"Mr. Shell, do you like living at the beach?" Sunny asks in this fake British accent.

I try to tune them out and focus on other things.

Mrs. Deleccio said I'm an instrumental part of this club, and I try to believe her. I really care about this, and even if I'm not needed at the pharmacy, I am needed here.

And Yamir asked me to go to the movies. Things aren't so bad. Maybe a little bit of an optimistic attitude would go a long way.

Lucy's tip for becoming a better person:
As hard as it is, try to put yourself in someone else's
shoes, and see how they might be feeling.

I don't ever knock on wood because I'm Jewish and my grandma told me once that Jews don't knock on wood. But sometimes I feel like I need something to ward off bad luck. Like right now. I want to knock on wood because things seem like they're working out, getting better even, and I feel like if I don't knock on wood, I'm taking it for granted and they could fall apart again.

Before we got the grant, I made this pact with God that if we got the grant and things worked out and we were able to open the eco-spa, then I wouldn't complain again. Even when I was making the pact, I knew it was kind of ridiculous and that I wouldn't be able to keep it because I sort of like to complain. Not to be annoying but to let off steam. But I made the pact anyway, hoping that just the fact that I made it would help keep me from complaining.

Anyway, every time I get down about stuff, I try to remember the pact and I try to think about knocking on wood (but not actually knock on it) because, basically, I just don't want to take any good things for granted.

I'm having this deep conversation with myself as I'm getting dressed and ready to leave for the pharmacy to meet Gary and the new spa consultant.

I remind myself about how nice it was for Claudia and Bean to think of me and get me the gobstopper and drive me around everywhere, and I'm also thinking about something else.

Yamir asked me to the movies. It's a big deal.

He didn't ask Sunny and Evan to come too. At least I don't think he did, because Sunny didn't mention it and she usually mentions these things immediately.

He asked me. One on one. And it's actually a movie I'm pretty interested in seeing, not something weird like aliens that creep into your brain or elevators that come alive and swallow you whole. That was the last movie he was obsessed with.

"Lucy, five minutes and we're going," Grandma yells to me from downstairs.

"OK!" I call back.

I usually don't take this long to get ready, but this fancy spa consultant person is coming from New York City and I bet she's going to look all chic, and I can't just stand there in my cutoff shorts and a pocket tee. I need her to take me seriously.

I walk downstairs and decide to take a granola bar on my way out for breakfast. It's not the kind of breakfast Mom usually approves of, but I took so long to get dressed and I don't want to be the one responsible for making us late.

"Lucy!" Claudia says as soon as she sees me, and then Bean does that obnoxious whistle thing that guys do to girls sometimes, even though he's totally doing it in a joking way. "You're so decked out."

"I'm not! It's just a sundress." I shake my head and turn away from them, but I can still hear them whispering.

"You look like you're going to a wedding," Claudia says. "Go change."

"Oh, Claudia, leave her alone," Mom mumbles, still half-asleep. Her hair is all frizzed and tied back into a ponytail. She's wearing one of those T-shirts that are meant to look faded, but hers looks a little too faded. "Be nice to your sister."

"I am being nice!" Claudia grabs one of my spaghetti straps and pulls me back closer to her. "I'm being nice because I'm being honest, and you look too overdressed to be going to spend a day on a construction site. You're wearing heels!"

I inch away from her and go out to the car. So what if I look overdressed? I want to wear this. And Claudia doesn't know I have flip-flops in my backpack and my hoodie to wear over my dress. The pharmacy gets freezing in the summer anyway. This outfit is just to make a good first impression.

When we get to the pharmacy, there's a town car pulled up in front and people are getting out of it. If Gary and the spa consultant really took a car service all the way from New York City, she's even fancier than I thought.

We drive into Grandma's regular spot in the parking lot and hop out of the car. Bean has his headphones on and I wonder if I should tell him to take them off. Claudia should probably be the person to do that, but she's not. And why is Bean even here? Claudia says he comes to the store so he can learn about business and stuff for his major, but I don't see him taking any notes. He spends most of the day staring at the mini fountain in the Relaxation Room.

"Hello, Gary!" Grandma says, and reaches out to hug him.

"Doris, you look more and more beautiful each time I see you," Gary says, and I hear Claudia mumble the word *barf* under her breath. Bean starts laughing, of course, because he laughs at everything my sister says, and then everyone looks over at us.

And that's when I notice it's not just Gary and the spa consultant getting out of the car. There's someone else here. Bevin. Gary's obnoxious daughter, who was born three days after me. She should be back home by now. She came for the ground breaking, but I figured that would be it.

"Lucy!" Bevin screams so loud that my mom covers her ears. "I am so so so so so so so excited to see you. We didn't really get to talk the other day."

She runs over and hugs me and I just stand there being hugged, not hugging her back. But if I act like she's acting, the spa consultant won't take me seriously.

"We have so much to catch up on," Bevin says. "We haven't really talked since we were in sixth grade."

"That was only, like, a year ago," I say to Bevin.

She doesn't seem like she hears me. "And I told everyone in my school about how you saved the pharmacy, and they were all, like, really impressed. They think you're *sooooo* cool."

"Why don't we all go into the Relaxation Room so we can sit down and discuss the plans?" Grandma says, like it's an instruction and not a suggestion. "It's right over there. Lucy can show you the way."

I nod. Phew. For a second I thought Grandma was going to make me take Bevin to another part of the store and work on cleaning or something just to entertain her. But no! I'm part of the discussion because I'm part of this business. If anyone should be entertaining Bevin, it should be Bean, the interloper.

We all sit down on the Relaxation Room couches and Mom brings over a tray with pretty little mugs and her floral teapot, which is probably her most prized possession.

"Green tea," my mom says. "Who would like some?" She's talking in her quiet voice. She woke up two hours ago, but I know she's not really awake yet.

Everyone says they'd like some, and Bean runs back to the office to get some more mugs. It's good to see him making himself useful.

"Our goal is to open the spa Labor Day weekend," Grandma says. "That's a really big weekend around here." She's talking directly to Gary and the spa consultant. And that's when I realize I don't even know this person's name.

"I'm sorry to interrupt," I say to her. "But I didn't introduce myself. I'm Lucy, Doris's granddaughter."

"Lovely to meet you, Lucy." She smiles. Her teeth are insanely white and perfectly straight. "I'm Anais."

She's probably one of the prettiest people I've ever seen in my life. She's got clear, dark skin, and she's wearing a long white skirt and a beaded black tank top. She looks like the kind of person who never sweats. I want her to like me. I want to work with her. I want her to think I know what I'm talking about, or *know* that I know what I'm talking about.

Anais crosses and uncrosses her legs and looks down at

her notebook. "Well, there's a lot of work to do. I'm glad the construction has begun. From what I can tell, the rooms are already done. We need to work on the waiting area, get all of the furniture, supplies, etc. And then of course we need to work on marketing, signage, all of that."

Mom nods. "I'm in charge of all the publicity. I've already reached out to the local papers. I've gotten in touch with my contacts. I'd love to work with you on the best design for the sign, stationery, all of our branding stuff." Mom pauses and sips her tea. She immediately winces, which must mean she has burned her tongue.

"Excellent."

Anais is writing in her notebook when Grandma looks at Gary and says, "So, Gar, what's your plan, your role in all of this?"

He puts his mug down on the table and when a little tea spills, he wipes it up with the sleeve of his flannel shirt. Yes, he's wearing flannel in late June. I can see why Mom's really not into him.

"Well, Dor, to be honest, it's a little much to travel back and forth from the city so often. I was looking into renting a place here for the summer, but they're pretty pricey. I guess things have changed since I was a kid." He picks at his chin hair and it's grossing me out so much that I have to look away.

"And I really want to be involved with everything. I know you're in good hands with Anais; she's done this many times. She helped open the Great Jones Spa in Manhattan, one of the best in the world. But I'd still love to be here if I can."

Mom's flipping through one of Anais's spa supplier catalogs, and Claudia and Bean are trying to discreetly play the can-knock-down game on Bean's iPad.

"It's settled, then," Grandma says to Gary, and I notice I'm the only one paying attention. Bevin has fallen asleep in the Turbo Massage Chair 7000. I don't think she realizes it's still on and massaging her back. "You'll move into the upstairs apartment. It's cleaned out and everything; we scanned all the paperwork so it's digital now and so it's no longer needed for storage."

"What?" I ask, but no one hears me.

"I've got Bevie with me for the summer. Her mom's on some photography assignment in Senegal." He rolls his eyes and I look over at Bevin to make sure she's still asleep. I know how it is when one parent is annoyed at the other parent. Just two weeks ago we found out that my dad's trip to the United States was postponed because of extra teaching commitments. He comes every year at the end of June when school's out, and he usually spends two weeks or more. He stays at this amazing bed-and-breakfast on the water, and he gets a suite so Claudia and I can have our own room. It's usually the best time ever. My dad is honestly a kid disguised as a grown-up—he always gets waffles with ice cream for breakfast and encourages us to do the same. He stays up late, and if it's raining, he takes us to see three or four movies in a day!

He apologized a million times and I said it was OK, and that I understood, but deep down I'm so disappointed, and kind of mad too.

The thing is, I was really little when he first moved away to England, and so I didn't really get it. But now I do get it, and I miss him, and I wish he were here more. So his visits are extra-important.

And if he's going to just postpone his trip like it's no big deal, how can I ever really trust him? I think all of these things but I can never say them out loud—not even to Claudia or Sunny.

"There are two bedrooms up there!" Grandma says, like Gary's an idiot and he should have known that. "Bring Bevin, she can hang out with Lucy and Claudia. It'll be great. We'll put her to work, though, I'm warning you now."

"What?" I ask again, louder this time, but still, no one's paying attention.

What is wrong with these people?

Grandma ignores me, and Anais is still writing down notes.

I can't imagine what she's writing, but she's gotten up three times to go look at the spa area and no one's even noticed.

"Oh, Dor, wouldn't that be a huge nuisance?" Gary asks.

Yes, yes it would be! I'm screaming in my head, but I'd never be so rude to scream that out loud. Why did Grandma just offer that? Has she totally lost her mind? Did Mom put some crazy ginseng or something in the green tea?

Grandma waves her hand in that *pshaw* way people do when the other person is saying something outlandish. "Not a bit. But you'll kick in a little rent, maybe that'll ease your mind?" Grandma smiles. "I know we got the grant, thanks to Lucy, and this spa is very exciting, but money's still tight, you know."

"Ma! Enough with that!" Mom finally tears herself away from the spa supplier catalog. "How many times in my life am I going to hear you say that?"

"That's fair," Gary says.

"So it's settled then," Grandma says, completely ignoring Mom's comment. "Go back to Manhattan, get your stuff, move in whenever. OK, back to business." She turns to look at Anais.

Mom and I are staring at each other, wondering if what happened is what we think happened.

What on earth am I going to do with Bevin all summer?

"I've made a list," Anais says, pouring herself another cup of tea. "I can see, and also Gary has told me, that this is truly a family business. You all want to be involved, and that is wonderful. I've divvied up responsibilities, and then you can tell me if the fits seem right."

I nudge Claudia with my elbow and they finally turn off the iPad and pay attention. Bean is such a bad influence on her. She could do so much better, but now isn't the time for me to tell her that.

Anais stands up and does some yoga-like stretching and then begins reading off the list. Bevin is still asleep. Clearly she's not going to be much help around here, but that's OK with me. I can do it fine on my own.

"Jane will be in charge of the publicity and the branding. She has connections to local news sources and she has an eye for design, I can tell from the wonderful relaxing atmosphere in here." She looks over at Mom and Mom starts to say, "Well, that was really Lucy's doing," but then Grandma shuts her up, and Anais goes on.

"Claudia and Lucy and Bevin, if she's here, will be in charge of the hiring process. I've spoken to Claudia about this and she seems up for the task. Gary and I will be making the final decisions, but you can do the initial groundwork." Anais looks at Claudia.

"Bean can help us with that too." Claudia smiles. "His dad is the vice president of HR for JetBlue."

"Got it." Anais pulls her hair into a low ponytail. "Doris, Gary, and I will oversee the operations, handle the supplies, setting everything up, and preparing for the grand opening. And you'll keep running the actual pharmacy." She looks down at her notebook one more time. "Any questions?"

"I'll also oversee the eco-spa aspect of it, focusing on the eco," Mom says. "That was Lucy's vision, that's why we got the grant in the first place, and we must make sure that everything is up to the correct environmental standards." Mom looks at me. "Right, Lucy?"

"Right."

"OK, I will make a note of that," Anais says. "So if we're in agreement, I'd like us to all walk over to the spa area together, and we can discuss how we envision the entrance area."

Gary goes over to the Turbo Massage Chair 7000 and taps Bevin on the arm. "Bevie," he whispers. "Come on. Get up."

Bevie? If he keeps calling her that, it's going to get very annoying.

As we're walking over to the spa area, Grandma whispers to Mom, "Anais is great, isn't she?" For the first time in a while, Grandma actually seems relaxed. Even though every single thing about this spa opening is annoying me, I'm happy to see Grandma relaxed. I need to appreciate that.

"She seems very amenable to us all working together," Mom admits. "And she's very calming."

"I agree," Grandma says, and she puts her arm around Mom.

Deep breaths, Lucy. Deep breaths. I say that to myself over and over again. I can't always be complaining, like Yamir said I was.

Anyway, things aren't so bad. Anais understands that we all have a role here. It's going to be OK.

And based on today, Bevin will probably be sleeping the whole summer anyway.

Lucy's tip for a great summer:
Spend some time just watching the ocean.
It's better than any TV show or video game.

Anais is the kind of Consultant who's always traveling. She'll help open a spa in Boston one month and then be sent to Arizona to open a spa there the next month. Her housing is paid for by her company, and I have to admit . . . it's my dream job. I know I talked forever about becoming Laura Mercier and having my own makeup line and everything, but guess what? I'm thirteen and I can change my mind. Or maybe I can have two dream jobs for now, and then decide when I actually have to work.

Right this minute, I want to be a spa consultant and travel all over the country—and the world. Anais said she was helping a spa in Paris a few months ago. Paris! Unbelievable.

The best part about Anais being here is that we don't have to pay her anything. I didn't realize this until I overheard Grandma, Mom, and Gary talking the other day. Gary was saying how her salary is included in his part of the investment. He wants to make sure the spa gets off to the best start possible. And I agree 100 percent. For once, Gary and I are on the same page.

Gary and Bevin are moving into the upstairs apartment today, and Anais is moving into her apartment. The Fourth of July is this weekend, and then we will have less than two months to get the spa open. That's not that long. It feels like after today things are going to go really, really fast.

Claudia put an ad online that the soon-to-be-opened Pink & Green: The Spa at Old Mill Pharmacy is looking for employees: facialists, makeup artists, waxers, and all kinds of aestheticians and beauticians.

She's really good at writing stuff like this, and Bean said he knew how to word it since he's helped his dad with human resources stuff before. I wanted Anais to look it over, but she said it was OK to start out and she'd help us if we needed it.

We're waiting for the first interviewee to arrive when my phone starts buzzing in my pocket.

"Whatcha doing?" Sunny asks me when I answer. "I'm so bored."

"Where's Evan?" I ask, and I know I've got an attitude, but the truth is, she pretty much spends all her time with him anyway.

"At his grandparents' in the Berkshires for a few days," she grumbles. "See why I'm bored?"

She doesn't even try to pretend that Evan hasn't pretty much replaced me. Sunny doesn't understand that's something she should try to do.

"Sorry. I'm busy, Sunny. We have an interview coming in."

"Fine." She stops talking like she's waiting for me to change my mind. "Call me later. OK?"

"Sure." I won't say this out loud or anything, but I'm not going to call Sunny a million times over these next few days while Evan is away. I want her to miss me.

Mom and Grandma are helping Gary and Bevin move in upstairs, and every other minute I hear something drop and Mom or Grandma curse and then yell at each other for a few seconds. I'm glad I'm not up there right now. But I kind of wish I was helping Anais move into her apartment. She's renting this place right on the water. You walk outside the main door to her apartment building and there's the ocean. And they also have a pool for the people who live there. It sounds like paradise, but it's right in Old Mill, Connecticut. But when I asked if she needed help, she told me she's all set. Her company even pays for movers and unpackers and people who set up her electronics and everything.

See what I mean? Dream job.

"Hello, I'm looking for . . . uh . . . ," a girl says as she's walking into the pharmacy and then she looks down at a crumpled slip of paper. "Claudia Deszszsberg." She doesn't know how to pronounce our name. Few people do. It's Desberg, with a soft *s,* but some people pronounce it with a *z* sound.

"Hello, I'm Claudia." My sister reaches over to shake her hand. Claudia's wearing a gray pencil skirt and a crisp white button-down. Does she realize she's not the one being interviewed? No one told me to dress up. I'm in khaki capri pants and a striped T-shirt. But even Bean looks dressed up, or as dressed up as Bean can really look. His camel cargo pants are a little wrinkly and so is his button-down, but at least he's wearing a tie. It has pink flamingos on it, but it's still a tie. It's obvious he tried.

"A pleasure to meet you, Claudia," the girl says, a little more relaxed. "I'm Diana. I have a ten-thirty appointment."

Claudia nods. "Of course. Right this way."

Claudia and Bean lead Diana through the pharmacy to the spa area, where there's a tiny little meeting room. It's barely set up, but Anais made sure there was a small couch, two rolling desk chairs, and ample lighting. I follow behind them.

"It's still very much in progress, as you can tell," Claudia says.

Diana sits down on the little love seat and Bean and

59

Claudia get to the rolling desk chairs before me. Then I'm left standing, not knowing what to do. I look over at Claudia, but she's already staring down at the list of questions we came up with last night.

"So tell us about your experience at the Coral Reef Spa in Florida," Claudia starts. "You were there a while?"

Diana opens her mouth to answer, but they can't expect me to just stand for the whole interview so I say, "Um, I'm just going to go find another chair." All three of them look up at me and then go back to what they're doing.

I go scavenging around the spa area for another chair, but I know I won't find one there. I'll just go take Mom's chair from the pharmacy office and return it when I'm done. Mom won't mind since she's busy helping Bevin and Gary move in.

I can't believe this. Claudia acts like I'm so important and such a vital part of the spa. But that's only when the grown-ups are there. When it's actually time to do something, she pretty much ignores me. She and Bean planned to dress up and look all professional for the interview, but they never told me! They wanted me to look young in my ratty clothes, and they planned for me to not have a seat. This is a conspiracy! A conspiracy for me to quit working at the spa and go find some kid activity to do. Well, it's not gonna happen.

I'll bring my own chair if I have to!

That reminds me of one of Claudia's friends who didn't get into Yale. It was her dream her whole life, and she's kind of an "outside-the-box thinker." She was so determined to get there somehow that she purchased a folding chair and a lap desk and wrote a letter to the dean. She included the receipts for the purchases with the letter and basically said something like: "I will attend Yale, and sit in the back of the room, on my own chair, not disturbing anyone. Thank you."

They ended up letting her in after she reapplied the next year, and she's doing really well so far. That's what Claudia told me anyway.

That's just one of those stories that proves someone can really do what she sets her mind to. So if people don't want to include me in the opening of this spa, then I will literally bring my own chair! I will make it happen!

I'm walking over to grab the chair when I get a text from Sunny.

SO BORED. PLEASE HELP.

It seems to me Sunny should have more of my "bring your own chair" philosophy and find something to do.

I'm about to barge into the office to grab Mom's desk chair when I notice the door is closed, and then I hear voices.

"Lucy's asked me seven times when you're coming," I hear my mom say, and when I don't hear anyone say anything back, I figure out what's going on. She's on the phone with my dad. "Please do not disappoint her. Claudia doesn't care; she's busy with her boyfriend. But Lucy was really looking forward to your visit."

That's not true—Claudia cares too. She's just not as open about it as I am. I wish I knew what they're talking about. It could be scheduling or—worst-case scenario—maybe Dad's moved on and has a new family. It seems out of the blue, but I guess it could happen.

"Oh, that's an idea!" Mom says, and I can tell even through the closed door that she's excited. She gets that high-pitched squeak in her voice only when she's excited about something. I love that squeak.

"She would freak, Sam," Mom continues. "You know she would." She pauses for a second and I wish so much that I could see her facial expression right now. "But then how much time would you really have with the girls?"

Silence again. If I wait any longer, I'll miss Diana's whole interview. I need to get that chair. I need to be in that interview so Bean and Claudia know that I care.

I knock on the door and then I hear Mom say, "OK, Sam, I gotta run. E-mail me your tentative plans and I'll go from there. I think we still have a few weeks until the RSVP date." She hangs up and then sings, "Come in!"

"I need a chair," I say right away so she doesn't think I've been listening. "Claudia and Bean didn't even get me one for the interview. And they didn't tell me they were dressing up."

Mom's sitting there, staring at me, and then it occurs to me that complaining like a little kid won't help them take me more seriously. It will just remind them that I'm a kid.

"Anyway, can I borrow your chair?"

"Take Grandma's," Mom says, but she's already turned back to the computer, looking at that site that lists every airline's flight prices. "Oh, Luce, I probably won't see you later. I have that Green Entrepreneurs lecture this afternoon. Give me a kiss."

I kiss my mom on the cheek and peek over at the computer. There's a minimized tab on the bottom of her screen that appears to be an e-mail, with the subject heading "RE: summer plans."

My dad's up to something. It could be a big surprise, like maybe he's coming to Connecticut to pick us up and then take us on a cruise around Europe. Or maybe even a cruise *to* Europe. But there isn't really time for all that, not with the opening of the spa in less than two months.

Well, he's got to be planning something, that's for sure.

And as long as he's planning something, I know he's thinking about us. And if he's thinking about us, I know he cares.

By the time I get back with Grandma's desk chair, Claudia, Bean, and Diana are shaking hands again. "We'll be in touch," Claudia says.

"Thanks again. This is going to be an amazing spa," Diana says as she's walking out.

Claudia and Bean leave the spa and plop down in the Relaxation Room. "She seemed smart," Claudia says. "But I think she may be too expensive."

Bean nods. "Yeah, she has tons of experience. Of course she's expensive."

They look at each other for a few seconds.

"So when's our next interview?" I ask.

"Luce, we can handle this. And you really don't know anything about interviewing people," Claudia says in her fake-sweet voice, like she's trying so hard not to hurt my feelings. "I'm sure there are other things you can help with. Just ask Anais."

"She said I should help with interviewing."

"Fine." Claudia turns away from me. "Be stubborn. But please be quiet. Our next interview is in twenty minutes, and we want to take a power nap."

Please. They're so tired after one interview? They didn't

even wake up today until nine A.M. I was up at eight, making coffee for them and Mom and Grandma. I'm the only one who seems too excited to sleep, and yet I'm being left out of everything.

I leave Claudia and Bean to their nap, and if they don't wake up in time for the next interview, I'll just do it myself. That'll show them.

I walk back over to the pharmacy and I quickly tidy up the facial products aisle and the makeup aisle. We can't have it looking like a total mess if we're interviewing people for the spa. Those aisles will be the first place they look!

I hear the door chimes and I look up thinking it's the next interviewee, but it's actually Anais.

"Anais!" I jump up and walk over to her. "How's moving in?"

"Fine, Lucy." She smiles, but it seems forced, not relaxed like I'd seen her up until now. "Where's your mom?"

"Some Green Entrepreneurs conference," I say. "Can I help you with something?"

She smiles that forced smile again. "Where's your grandma?"

I shrug. "I can help you, I'm sure. I know everything about this place."

"Thanks, Lucy, but we actually have a small issue with

scheduling the inspection for the spa." She pauses. "I really need to speak to an adult. Have you seen Gary?"

"Nope. Sorry."

I leave her in the middle of the makeup aisle. I get why she needs to speak to an adult, because obviously I don't know anything about inspections, but it still stings. I decide to play a computer game while I wait for the next interview.

I'm beating the computer at Scrabble better than I've ever beaten it before when I get interrupted by a text. Why is Sunny bothering me again?

But when I look at my phone, I see that it's not from Sunny. It's from Yamir.

My stomach starts doing flips, like the kind Claudia can do off the diving board. I'm excited, then nervous, then excited again.

Gotta bail on the Spielberg movie. Clint's dad got free passes to a screening in NYC.

I should have expected this. Clint's dad does lighting for movie shoots and he always gets free passes. Why did I even get excited in the first place?

"Hey, Lucille," Bevin says, and she plops herself down on the office floor. She knows my name isn't Lucille, but for some reason she always feels the need to call me that. I really don't understand it.

I don't answer her.

"Whatcha doin', Lucille?"

"Playing Scrabble," I grumble.

My whole summer flashes before my eyes—it won't be like I planned, hanging out with Claudia, swimming, working at the pharmacy, and getting the spa ready. No. It'll be me hiding in the office while the grown-ups do cool stuff, and then Bevin coming to bug me. And Yamir won't even want to hang out with me. And Sunny will be busy with Evan.

"Can I play?" Bevin asks.

"It's a solo game and I play against the computer." I talk to Bevin while staring at the computer screen. I don't feel like being nice right now.

"What's wrong, Lucille?" Bevin takes a pen off Grandma's desk and starts drawing on her hand.

Aren't we a little old for pen tattoos?

"Nothing."

"Liar."

"I'm fine, Bevin, but thanks."

"Liar again."

Bevin might be the most annoying person on the entire planet. And of course she finds me to hang out with because she probably knows no one else can stand her. Either that or she figures they're all busy and I'm just a kid, so what do I have to do, just like everyone else thinks.

"Just tell me."

Finally I turn around. She's not going to stop until I say something. "Fine. If you must know, I'm annoyed that people still don't take me seriously around here, even though I'm the one who found the grant and got this whole spa thing going in the first place! And I'm annoyed that Claudia's busy with Bean and Sunny's busy with Evan and I'm totally left out of everything. And I'm annoyed that Yamir, who I think is my boyfriend but I don't really know for sure, asked me to go to the movies and then totally bailed so he could go with Clint!"

Bevin gets up and closes the office door. I guess she's worried everyone's going to hear me yelling, but I don't really care, and I'm done now anyway.

She sits back down on the floor. "OK." She takes a deep breath. "First of all, you have a boyfriend and I didn't even know that. So. Tell. Tell everything."

I squint at her. With everything that's going on, what's most important to her is Yamir. Strange.

"You're so lucky." She's braiding the threads on her cut-offs. "He must be really cool."

"Thanks," I say. "But maybe he doesn't even think he's

my boyfriend. I don't know. Sunny and Evan hang out all the time, but Yamir and I rarely do."

She shrugs. "So invite him to hang out! Invite him over to the pharmacy. Tell him to bring friends." She smiles. "Imagine if I met a boyfriend in Connecticut this summer and then I could go back and tell everyone at school. That would be amazing."

This conversation makes me realize that Bevin is even more pathetic than I am, which in a really, really mean way kind of makes me feel better.

Lucy's tip for becoming a better person:
Ask people questions. It shows you're interested.

$\mathcal{E}$*very time* $\mathcal{I}$ *asked* Mom and Grandma about the inspection scheduling problem that Anais was freaking out about, they told me that everything was fine.

I have this weird feeling that I shouldn't believe them, but I'm not going to worry about it now. It's the Fourth of July, one of my favorite holidays, and I can't waste it worrying!

I check my e-mail one last time before we head out for our big Fourth of July celebration. I get really excited when I see I have an e-mail from my dad.

Hey Lulu!

Just wanted to wish my girl a happy 4th o' July. I know it's your favorite, and it's sad to be somewhere that doesn't celebrate it.

Stay tuned for details about our reunion!

Oodles of Noodles,
Dad

Well, that didn't say much at all. But at least he's thinking about me today. It's pretty much more important to me than my own birthday, even! I wonder what he means by details and why he's being so vague. But I can't spend my day worrying about this—as frustrating as it is. It's the Fourth of July and we have a huge evening planned.

Anais's apartment is right on the beach where the Fourth of July fireworks are taking place, so she invited us all over for a champagne toast before. I try to put all of my frustration about being left out of things at the spa out of my mind.

"Are you always this chummy with the spa families you're working with?" I ask her, after a sip of my sparkling apple juice.

"Lucy," Claudia says in her I'm-horrified tone, but I really don't understand why that was such an inappropriate question.

Anais laughs. "No, no, that's a good question." She smiles at me and I look over and glare at Claudia. Since Bean's been living with us, Claudia thinks she's like the queen of etiquette or something. Anais goes on, "The truth is, most of the spas I work with are owned by some sort of larger corporation, so I'll meet the manager and maybe the CEO a few times, but it's not like this, where there's a great family who owns the place and really cares about every single detail."

"We're just the best," Mom says, staring at Anais's floor-to-ceiling window with the most unbelievable view of the beach. "Aren't we, guys?"

Everyone else in my family rolls their eyes at my mom, but at this moment I just want to run up and hug her. Maybe that's what we need—a little unity, a little family pride.

After our champagne toast and tour of Anais's apartment, where we debate which room has the best view of the ocean, we all head down to the beach. Anais suggested that we could watch from her balcony, but we have our traditions. The Desbergs do the Fourth of July the same way every year, and we can't change that.

Mom carries backpack beach chairs—she can carry three at once, and it's so impressive. Grandma brings a huge picnic blanket that folds up into a tiny square. And we have the best picnic food ever: sandwiches from the deli—turkey, mozzarella and tomato, grilled vegetables and Brie—and bags of potato chips and fresh-baked chocolate chip cookies. We always get to the fireworks a few hours early so we can get a good spot and enjoy our picnic without everyone stomping all over us looking for a spot.

The Ramals usually find us and put their blankets and

chairs near ours. When we were little, Sunny and I would pretend each of our blankets was a little island and if we stepped on the sand, we'd drown. So we'd hop from blanket to blanket.

It was such a silly game, but we had so much fun doing it. And sometimes we'd try to push Yamir off the blanket and pretend he was drowning.

I'd never do that now. Now I wish he'd sit with me on our blanket. I'd be so happy to have him there, but I'd never tell him that. I guess I could ask him, but he'd probably make a joke and embarrass me.

We set up our space. Bean arranges the chairs around the blanket, and Gary and Bevin bring a sushi boat as an appetizer. It's one of the really pretty ones too, with all the rolls arranged in a cool way and flowers made from the ginger. I don't know how they got it here still looking so perfect after a walk across the sand.

"Do you like sushi?" Bevin asks me. She pops a spicy tuna roll into her mouth. "It's my favorite."

I can't help but laugh because food is falling out of her mouth and she doesn't even seem to be embarrassed. I take a piece of yellowtail and scallion. "I love it too. And I'm so glad you got it from Sushi by Gari—it's the best in the area. They have locations in New York and Japan too."

"Really? Authentic!"

"Yeah, Gari bought a summer home here, so he opened another location." I smile, dipping a roll in soy sauce. "Lucky us."

Soon the Ramals find us, and set up their blanket and chairs. Sunny's mom always brings Indian food for their picnic and it always stresses me out. It's just so messy. The containers usually leak and Sunny usually ends up upset because there's dripping sauce on her leg.

Picnics are more fun when the food is easy to eat—sandwiches, sushi, stuff like that.

Actually, that's a rule I just thought of: Picnic food should start with *s*: sandwiches, sushi, soda, salsa, salami. And then I run out of other *s* words.

I turn away to grab a piece of tuna sushi and when I turn back around and look at the Ramals' blanket, I notice someone else is there with them.

"You're back?" I say, when Evan makes eye contact. "I thought you were in the Berkshires until the tenth."

He takes a piece of naan and dips it in the curry sauce. "I couldn't miss Old Mill Fourth of July! Are you crazy?"

He says that really loud and my whole family and the rest of the group turns around.

"No. I'm not crazy." I laugh. "Sunny said you were staying longer. That's all."

"I came back early," he says. "My uncle was driving back to Manhattan for work, so he gave me a lift."

"Oh." I force a smile.

"Want some of our chicken, Luce?" Sunny asks me.

"No, thanks. Too hot for me." I fan my mouth. "Temperature *and* spice!"

Bevin's the only one who laughs at my joke, but that's because she laughs at everything—and it's not just a laugh but a laugh and snort combination. It sounds so bad, it makes me not want to tell any more jokes.

Claudia is pretty much sitting in Bean's lap. Grandma and Anais are in some deep conversation about the history of Japan, Gary went to wash his hands somewhere, and Mom's reading an article on green living.

I turn back to the Ramals. Yamir hasn't even said hi to me yet, and now he's gone. Evan and Sunny are doing the slaps game where you have to move your hands away fast so the other person can't slap them.

I taught Sunny that game.

"I'll be right back, Bevin," I tell her because she's the only one who will notice that I'm even gone.

I still have a few hours until the fireworks start. It's only six, and they usually start around nine. It used to be that the hours before the fireworks were almost as much fun as the fireworks, but now it doesn't seem to be that way.

I walk across the beach and over to the carousel, and then I just keep walking. I don't know where I'm going, but I'm glad to have a break from everyone.

I keep walking, across the beach parking lot and through the neighborhood, and soon I'm in town, on Ocean Street, right near the pharmacy.

I have my own key, so I let myself in.

This is my family's store. My store. I'm allowed to be here. I have my own key and I know the alarm code. But even though I tell myself that, I still feel like I'm doing something I'm not supposed to be doing.

I go in and walk around the aisles, seeing if there's anything that needs straightening. But everything looks neat and tidy and perfect.

Now that Tory and Charise are back, Grandma doesn't even do her daily inspection of the aisles, giving me lists of what to work on. She knows the store will look perfect. Even the office is neat.

I wonder what Gary and Bevin have done to the upstairs apartment, but I know I can't go up and look. I'm sure they lock it anyway, and they have their own entrance at the back of the building, so they don't always have to walk through the store.

When I'm done inspecting the pharmacy, I go over to the spa.

The construction is nearly done. One of the treatment rooms has pink walls and one has green, and the entryway has pink and green stripes on the walls. The space where the reception area will be is all cleaned out and we're just waiting for the furniture to be delivered.

Toward the back there will be a rejuvenation area, where people can wait for their treatments. We'll have pitchers of water with fruit pieces floating in them and serene music playing. And we'll have robes that say PINK & GREEN on them. We'll have organic fruits if people get hungry, and the towels we're getting are made from some recycled materials.

At least I hope we will. That's how I envisioned all of this. But then I remember that envisioning something and something actually happening is really different. I feel like somehow I got off the path of planning the spa, and now I can't get back on.

It's strange how things can get off track so quickly. Like somehow I got replaced as Sunny's best friend, and somehow forgot how to act around Yamir, and somehow got replaced as Claudia's sidekick.

Somehow all of these things changed all at once, and now I don't know how to fix them.

I take one of the rolling desk chairs out of the interview room and roll myself through the spa area. Think, Lucy, think. I can do this. Because it's not enough to just have your own chair, you need to actually do something with that chair.

I look at my watch. It's already seven thirty. I'll stay here a half hour longer and then I'll go back to the beach. I don't want to wait too long or I'll never be able to make my way through the crowds to find our blanket.

As I'm rolling around the spa area, I notice that the high chair for hair and makeup is unpacked from its plastic wrapping. It's probably weird to say this, but this chair is beautiful. It's white porcelain with brass finishes, and the seat cushion is a navy blue corduroy. Mom, Grandma, and I picked it out as soon as we found out we got the grant and that Gary was investing.

It was one of the first things we did. And it was so much fun. We spent a whole Saturday night poring over the spa supplier catalogs Mom had ordered and we each picked out three chairs and then we narrowed down our choices and we voted.

It was unanimous. This was our chair.

It felt so real and exciting, like things were actually happening.

I quickly glance around just to make sure no one is looking in the window, and once I see that the coast is clear, I climb up in the chair, adjust the headrest, and sit back. From this high chair, I can see everything—the whole street, all the stores, people walking by. It's like a lighthouse in Old Mill, but my very own.

I look at my watch again. OK, it's almost eight. I really need to go back.

I'm climbing down from the chair backward (I've never been able to go down ladders facing front; I'm too much of a scaredy cat) when I hear sobs.

Uh-oh. I've been discovered.

I sneak around the chair and hide behind it. But the sobs keep getting louder, and then I realize I'm such a dummy because I've left all the lights on in the spa area. It's not even that dark out yet, I didn't need lights, but I left them on.

"Are, um, are—are—are you open?" I hear someone say through sobs. It sounds like a girl, but it could be a young boy. Bevin? I'm not really sure. I stay quiet. Maybe this person will just go away if no one answers.

"Hello? Anyone?"

I peek around the chair, but I still can't see the person. I have no idea what I should do. I'm not really supposed to work the cash register. Maybe I could convince the person to come back tomorrow to buy what they need. Only what if they have some sort of emergency?

I don't know what to do. But I need to be fast because I'm going to miss the fireworks.

"Hello?" the person says again, still sobbing.

"Hello!" I pop out from the chair like some kind of weird clown in one of those jack-in-the-box toys.

"Oh!" the lady screams. "I didn't see you there. Um, OK. Well, are you, um, open?" She's just standing there, sobbing, rubbing her eyes with the sleeve of her pale blue oxford shirt. She's thin with long blond hair and very short khaki shorts. She looks like a model, in a way. But a very sad model.

"Not really." I clench my teeth. "But I'm sure we'll have what you need tomorrow, if you come back then. OK?"

"You're not a spa?" She talks and cries at the same time. "I thought I read about you in the local paper, some interview with someone. Am I wrong? Oh, I'm so tired, I can't remember anything."

I pull over the other rolling chair and motion for her to take a seat. I don't know what else to do.

"No, you're right. We are a spa, but we're expanding, so we're not like officially open, but maybe I can help you anyway?" This lady looks so pathetic that I don't even know what to do. How can someone so pretty look so pathetic?

Finally she sits down in the chair and rests her face in her palms, and starts massaging her eyebrows, like she's trying to relieve the tension.

"OK." She pauses and takes a deep breath. "When will you be open?"

I can't help her if she doesn't tell me what's wrong. I wish she'd just tell me, but I don't want to pressure her. Also, I don't know how to explain to her that it's already after eight and I really need to get back to the beach for the fireworks.

Anyone and everyone in Old Mill and the surrounding towns knows about the Fourth of July fireworks. She must not be from here. She must be new.

There must be more to her story.

"We're opening officially Labor Day weekend—it's this huge weekend around here, called Boat Fest. Everyone has their boats out. There are street fairs, a carnival on the beach, amazing food. It's the best weekend ever." I smile and try to get her to smile too, but she still looks really, really sad.

"Labor Day weekend?" She perks up, finally.

I nod. "It's really not that far away. After the Fourth of July, it always seems like the summer is over, doesn't it?" I realize that was an idiotic thing to say. That it will only depress her more, and now I feel depressed too.

"OK." She's nodding slowly like she's figuring something out. She smiles at me, stands up, and walks over to the window. She takes her phone out of her pocket and hits a few buttons. She says into the phone, "I found a place. OK? But please don't treat me like that again." She pauses. "Mom, why do you have to do that? Don't you see it's my day?" She pauses again and keeps opening her mouth but not saying anything, like the person on the other end won't let her get a word in.

Finally, after a few more minutes of that, she hangs up.

"OK, I need to book you guys for the Saturday of Labor Day weekend. Eight bridesmaids, one bride, one mother of the bride, and one mother of the groom." She looks down at her phone again. "Makeup. Hair. Nails. Whatever else people do."

It occurs to me that this girl never goes to spas, never has her hair done, never does any of this.

"We can do that." I get her name, her number, and all of her info.

"Thank you so much," she says. "And your sign is amazing."

"Our sign?" I ask.

She walks outside and I follow her. "Yeah." She points up. "Your sign."

I hadn't even seen it yet. I came in the side door to the pharmacy, from the neighborhood, not through town.

But it's there. Our beautiful sign.

The PINK part is in pink and the GREEN part is in green, obviously, and it looks so beautiful and perfect and wonderful.

"You don't understand how glad I am that I found you," the girl says once we're back inside. "I don't even read the local paper ever, but I am so glad I did. My parents just bought a place here, and they're throwing the wedding for us in their yard, which is like ten acres, and they're being so impossible. Not letting Owen and me have a say in anything. And my mom is just . . ." She curls her lips inside and starts crying again. "She just can't understand it's not about her, and I know she's excited, but it's just so stressful."

I nod. "It'll be OK." I put a hand on her shoulder. I don't know what else to say. I mean, I could figure it out, but right now I really just want to see the fireworks.

I love helping people. And so I feel selfish for thinking this, but I need to see the fireworks.

"Hey, I have an idea!" I start turning off the lights in the spa. "Come with me to the fireworks! Do you know there are fireworks tonight?"

"I don't know anything." She shakes her head. "I just got in today. And the first thing my mom said was how disappointed in me she was that I hadn't booked a spa for the wedding."

I nod. This woman clearly feels the need to share all of her family's dirty laundry with me. And I love helping people with their problems, but not now. "OK, this will cheer you up! Come with me." I make sure all the lights are turned off, and the alarm is back on, and we leave the spa.

We're walking back to the beach with exactly fifteen minutes to spare. We may not make it back to my family's blanket, but we'll make it back to the benches on the boardwalk. And I'll text Claudia and say I ran into some people, so my family doesn't worry.

As we're walking, I realize that I just wrote down this girl's name for the appointments and I already forgot it. That's embarrassing.

"I'm so sorry, but your name just slipped my mind," I say. "I'm Lucy. Did I tell you that already?"

She laughs. "You did. But don't worry. I'm Sarabeth."

"Pretty name," I say.

We get back to the beach and I see immediately it's going to be hectic to get back to our blankets.

I text Claudia.

Ran into ppl from Hebrew school. see u after fireworks. Xo

I had to say Hebrew school because if I said regular school, Claudia would tell Sunny, Evan, and Yamir and they'd never believe me or they'd need to know who it was.

She texts back.

Have fun.

Sarabeth and I find a seat on the benches and we sit together and watch the fireworks.

It isn't at all how I expected to spend the Fourth of July, but it's good.

It seems like I'm on the right track to feeling like myself again.

Lucy's tip for a great summer:
Have as many picnics as you possibly can.

Lucy! Where have you been?" Mom yelps as soon as she sees me waiting by the car. The beach is walking distance from the pharmacy, but not from our house, and even if it were, there was no way we could've walked with all the chairs and food and stuff we brought.

"I texted Claudia." I shoot my sister a look, but she's too busy playing with Bean's hair to notice. "I ran into some people from Hebrew school. So we hung out by the benches and got some Dairy Queen."

I am totally planning on telling them about Sarabeth and all the business I just brought in for opening weekend, but now doesn't seem to be the time. Grandma and Gary are struggling to get all the chairs back in the trunk and Bevin is begging her dad for an ice cream. And Claudia is still playing with Bean's hair. Can't he just get a haircut already?

"Oh, but Sunny, Evan, and Yamir were with us," she says like she knows something's up. "Yamir even asked me where you were." There's a clump of sand on the pavement and she swishes it around with her shoe when she asks me that. She doesn't want to embarrass me; I can tell.

"Oh." I shrug. "Yeah, I ran into some other kids. They don't know them." My mom probably knows I'm lying since I'm not saying the other kids' names, but she doesn't push it.

Gary and Bevin take their car (an amazing convertible) back to the pharmacy apartment and the rest of us pile into our car. Mom and Grandma get the front, and then Bean, Claudia, and I sit in the back.

"Yamir looked really upset that you just disappeared, Luce," Claudia says, nudging me with her elbow. At least she's the one in the middle seat this time and I don't need to sit next to bony Bean.

I don't know what to say. If I act excited, Claudia will continue talking about it and embarrass me further. If I don't say anything, she'll ask me a million questions about what's going on.

"He was just trying to make conversation," I say finally. "I texted him and told him I was hanging out with some other people."

Claudia glares at me. "I don't think so. They didn't seem

to have any idea where you were. Even Sunny. Seems super-weird."

"Whatever, Claudia. You're super-weird for just bringing your boyfriend home and not telling anyone."

"Lucy!" Mom yells from the front seat. "Enough. Let's have quiet for the rest of the ride."

If I had a penny for every time I've heard my mom say that, I'd be rich. For real.

We get home and Grandma asks if any of us want a cup of tea. I say yes only because I know Mom will say yes and I want a chance to sit and talk with them about Sarabeth.

We all change into pajamas and settle in the den. Bean has Claudia's Old Mill High School sweatshirt on and it looks so bizarre on him. I wish he could just wear his own sweatshirt, but apparently he borrowed it once and decided it was the most comfortable sweatshirt he'd ever worn. I wish every single thing he did didn't annoy me so much. He could end up being my brother-in-law one day, and I don't think it's good to hate your brother-in-law.

"Ah, another wonderful Fourth of July," Grandma says, putting her feet up on the leather ottoman. "There's something about the Fourth of July that feels empowering, isn't there?"

She looks at all of us.

"Well, if you're into that patriotic stuff," Mom says. "Truthfully, I'd like to see the Fourth of July become a day of service where we help those less fortunate in our communities."

I agree with what Mom's saying, but why can't we just leave a good thing alone for a minute? Fireworks, hot dogs, the beach. I mean, it's perfect as it is. Let's just enjoy it.

"Anyway," I say, trying to change the topic. "So, actually, I'm sorry to say this, but I lied."

Everyone gasps; Grandma gasps the loudest and covers her mouth. Sheesh. I can't even imagine what she thinks I'm about to say. Lying is a big no-no in our family, but still.

"No, not about anything crazy. I haven't, like, dropped out of school." I laugh, but no one else does, so I go on. "But I mean, I lied about tonight. I wasn't with some kids from Hebrew school."

"Shocking!" Claudia says, and rolls her eyes. I wonder where she thinks I was. I should've been putting up posters searching for a new sister!

I ignore her and turn to face Mom and Grandma, sitting together on the smaller couch. "I walked over to the pharmacy, just to clear my thoughts, and then a customer came in."

"Lucy, how many times have I asked you not to mess with the cash register?" Grandma says, all frustrated. No one in my family ever even gives me a chance to finish a sentence!

"I didn't use the cash register." I pause and wait for her to say something, and I can see her mouth opening to interrupt me again. "Will you please let me finish my story?"

They nod.

"Promise?"

"Just go on, Lucy," Claudia says.

Bean keeps burning his tongue on the tea and then making this ridiculous over-the-top expression. It's kind of funny but also distracting.

"So I was in the spa area, and this really frazzled woman came in. Her parents just bought this mansion summer home here, and that's where they're having the wedding, and this woman needed to find a place to do hair and makeup for her, the bridesmaids and the moms and everyone the day of the wedding."

"When's the wedding?" Bean asks. "Because my manicuring skills really aren't up to snuff yet."

Claudia hits him on the arm.

"Ow," he says, and then starts rubbing the spot.

"It's Labor Day weekend, Bean." I shoot eye-daggers at him. "So we have plenty of time. And that's our grand opening! And we have this huge wedding party! For hair and makeup."

I stand up and take a bow. "No applause. Thank you. No applause."

They laugh, but it sounds a little forced.

"That's really wonderful, Lucy," Grandma says. "I'm sorry I thought you were monkeying with the cash register. I'm glad you found these clients."

"Me too," I say. "So I didn't start telling her about how I do the makeup and everything. She seemed so frazzled and upset that I just booked the appointments and then we walked down to the beach and watched the fireworks together."

"Oh, very sweet," Mom says.

"Um, guys, I think we need to tell her," Claudia says to Mom and Grandma and then looks at me.

"Tell me what?" I ask.

"You know you're not going to be, like, the makeup artist at the spa?" Claudia says. "Right?"

"Well, I know you're hiring other people too," I say.

"OK." Claudia leans over and gives me a hug. "You're the cutest, Lucy-Luce."

People always have to say something like *you're so cute* right after they break some bad news. They must think that makes them sound nicer, but it doesn't.

I have to be allowed to do makeup, especially for my repeat customers like Kristin and Erin and Laura Gregory. That's how we got the idea to start a spa in the first place! But there's no point in arguing with them now. I have appointments booked for the next few weeks, so I'm just going to go ahead with them like nothing has changed. They'll see I'm needed on their own.

"Sarabeth is really great, though," I add.

Grandma says, "Let's make sure to tell Anais tomorrow. We want her to know about all appointments, especially the first ones, and we want her input in everything."

I nod.

"And we need to tell Gary too," Grandma adds. "Lucy, remember all of this, OK?"

"OK, will do," I say. "I'm gonna go to bed. I'm really tired."

"Night, sweetie," Mom says.

Claudia adds, "Night, Luce."

When I get upstairs, I check my cell phone.

I missed three text messages since coming home from the fireworks.

Two from Sunny:

U r so weird. Why did u disappear? On your fave night of the year?

Where r u? I am worried.

And then one from Yamir:

Didn't see u at fireworks. Skee-ball tomorrow?

I feel too tired and overwhelmed right now to respond to them. Sometimes it's just nice to know you were missed and to relish that feeling for a few minutes before you respond and acknowledge the people who were missing you.

I should be happy that Mom and Claudia and even Grandma were excited about Sarabeth being one of the first spa customers. But even with their excitement, it still didn't seem right. They just wanted me to make sure I told Anais and Gary. And then that whole thing about doing makeup was weird.

I feel like my emotions are a seesaw, and one minute I'm up and the next I'm down.

It's like those videos Mrs. Eldridge made us watch in health class about our changing moods. We all laughed about it at the time, but now I'm thinking they had some truth to them.

Lucy's tip for becoming a better person:
Listen to advice and consider it,
even if you don't end up taking it.

𝒪*he next few days are super-busy.*
Claudia told Anais all about the interviews, and they have decided which beauticians they want to call back for a second round and for sample procedures.

Claudia volunteered to be the tester-person, which basically means that these cosmetologists will come in and do sample procedures on her.

She'll be getting facials, waxing, her hair done, makeup, everything.

"OK, I've printed up these checklists so, as the people come in, you guys can be checking off the things that they do well and the things they don't do as well," Anais says to Bean and me. "But I need you to be honest, OK?"

"Sure," I respond. "But you know, I know a lot about

makeup. I think I could be a good tester-person. Can I please volunteer for at least one?"

Anais pulls me closer and whispers, "Lucy, if I let you do it, then I have to let Bevin do it, and Bevin's just not as mature as you are." She pats me on the back. "Please understand."

"Fine," I groan. But I don't really care about Bevin. Bevin should have a nanny who's taking her to the beach and the pool every day. She's bored at the spa. Right now she's playing some bowling game on Bean's iPad. She doesn't care at all about what's happening.

But I bet it will end up being so busy and hectic and Anais won't even notice when I hop up in the makeup chair. I'll find a way.

I walk over to the office to grab a Band-Aid out of the first-aid kit. These new flip-flops are cutting the skin on my toes where the rubber rubs against them.

"Well, when do you want to tell them?" I hear Mom say in the office, and then wait for Grandma's response. Tell us what? For a family who hates lying, there seem to a million secrets spiraling around here lately.

I wait a few seconds and I still don't hear Grandma's voice.

"Claudia might be heading back to school by then," Mom says. She's on the phone. Duh. Why don't I ever pick up on this? Probably because Mom hates talking on the phone. But she hates video-chatting even more because she says she's never "camera-ready."

"Because I don't know what Claudia's doing," Mom goes on. "She has her own life to lead. She's here now, but she could be gone tomorrow, for all I know. You know how it is when you're that age. She's free and she's enjoying her freedom."

Barf. I hate how it's always Claudia this and Claudia that. She basically has no rules to follow and they're all about "giving her space."

"OK, well, once you finalize everything . . ." Mom pauses. "And I mean *really* finalize, then we'll tell everyone." Silence again. "OK, right. Very good. Yes, OK. Take care."

Mom hangs up, and I knock on the office door, then walk in for a Band-Aid. "These flip-flops are killing me," I say. "How long will it take for me to wear them in?"

"I don't know, Luce," Mom says quietly, staring at the computer. "I'm late for a meeting at the *Old Mill Observer*. They want to talk about the grand opening and how everything's going. They have a special magazine section for the summer months, and I think we're going to be the cover story!"

"That's amazing!" I put on my Band-Aid and then wrap my arms around Mom's neck. "That is such awesome news. Can I come?"

She swivels around in her chair. "Luce, Anais needs you here."

I nod. Yeah, right. Everyone says everyone else needs me, but then when I think about it, I'm not sure anyone really needs me.

"Lucille!" Bevin's running through the pharmacy screaming. "Lucille! Lucille! Where *aarrreeee* you?"

Fine, maybe I was wrong. One person needs me. That person is Bevin. And I really wish she didn't.

"In here, in the office," I call back.

"I've been looking all over for you. Do you want to go see that new Princess Confidential movie? My dad said I could go. It's playing at one P.M."

My mom's still typing at her computer. Why can't she say that "Anais needs me" right now?

"I need to be here, Bevin. Sorry." I throw away the Band-Aid wrapper and leave the office. "Anais wants me to help evaluate the spa interviewees."

She follows me. "Oh. OK."

"Sorry. We can go see it later, maybe."

"Really? Oh, that's great! It's playing tonight too!" She claps. "I'm *soooo* excited. I've seen the first three. Have you?"

I don't have the heart to tell her that I only saw the first one and that's because it came out when I was in fifth grade and even then it seemed really babyish.

"So do you want to go to the six o'clock showing?" she asks.

"Um." I'm about to say yes and then I remember Yamir's text about Skee-ball. I really, really want to go down to the beach and play Skee-ball with Yamir and maybe get Frostees after. It sounds almost like a real date.

Then I keep imagining it, and instead of getting excited about the plan, I get nervous. I get that seeping-pit-of-lava feeling in my stomach.

I can't do that with Yamir. I like him. I really do. But being alone with him on the beach, at night, the moon shining over our heads, the sound of the waves hitting the shore . . .

It's all the things I love to do, but then rolled together and combined, it's scary. So scary that I want to run away. So scary that I'd rather go see that stupid princess movie with Bevin.

"Sure. That sounds perfect." I smile. "The interviews should be over by five, anyway."

"Yay!" Bevin yells, and then wraps her arms around me. "Movie buddies!"

"Yup," I say quietly, and pull out of her hug. "I need to find Anais and Claudia now. I think I hear the first candidate coming in."

"I'll come too," she says, and follows me to the spa area.

Lucy's tip for a great summer:

Wear sunscreen. You will still tan, but you won't burn.

So think of this as a sort of interactive interview," Anais tells Miranda, our first interviewee.

Miranda keeps shifting her weight from foot to foot and twirling the end of her hair. "OK, but I'm not completely familiar with these products, so would you mind just going over them with me?"

Anais scratches her forehead. "They're pretty standard. But sure."

Anais starts giving Miranda a tour of the spa area while explaining the products. Bean's unpacking boxes of supplies, and it's good to see him making himself useful. Bevin and I are just standing around because we need to observe this spa treatment that Miranda's going to do on Claudia. The longer I stand, the more nervous I get. This Miranda girl could have absolutely no idea what she's doing, and she's going to start treatments on my sister. If she doesn't know to shake out the towel, Claudia could have third-degree burns on her face! If she leaves the cold cream on too long, Claudia's face will completely break out. So many things could go wrong if you don't know what you're doing.

My mind immediately jumps to Courtney Adner and the hair trauma she had on homecoming, and how I felt so awesome the day I helped her fix her hair. I haven't seen Courtney around lately. I think she works as a counselor at summer camp. She was here toiletry shopping a few weeks ago. She spent forever in the pharmacy picking out what she needed. She said toiletries are her favorite thing to shop for, and I totally understood that.

"OK, we're ready," Anais says, a little out of breath, brushing her wispy curls away from her face. "Miranda, you'll be working on Claudia here." Anais puts a hand on Claudia's shoulder and Claudia smiles from ear to ear like she's some kind of model.

"What should I do?" I whisper in Anais's ear.

She looks down at her papers. "You'll be evaluating, Lucy, like I said before." For the first time, Anais sounds annoyed with me. "Here, Bevin, you take an evaluation sheet too." Anais rolls over the two office chairs and guides us to sit down.

I've never felt so useless in my whole entire life. Bevin doesn't know anything about these treatments, and so if she and I are filling out the same forms, those forms can't be important. Anais doesn't really need us evaluating. I bet my grandma said I need to be included, and so she found something harmless for me to do.

I shouldn't have insisted on this. Grandma and Mom said I could go to art camp at Connecticut College. They said I'd be busy with that and swimming and everything, but I told them I wanted to be around the spa as much as possible and spend as much time with Claudia as possible.

Yeah, right. It was all a mistake.

I uncap my roller-ball pen; at least Anais isn't forcing us to use golf pencils or something. That would make the situation way worse. I write Miranda's name at the top and start checking off the procedures she'll be doing.

I look up at Claudia on the fancy white table, lying perfectly flat, some kind of cold cream being spread on her face. I should be the one up there. I'm the one who knows all about spas and everything from all the research I did.

"Why do you look so upset, Lucille?" Bevin asks me, and grabs my arm like she's trying to be supportive.

"I'm fine." I force a closed-mouth smile.

"You don't look fine."

"Bevin. I'm fine."

"Fine." She cracks up even though nothing about this conversation has been funny. "I haven't seen Yamir around here lately. Did you guys break up?"

"Shhh. Miranda's trying to work." I point over in their direction and see Miranda struggling to get the cream off Claudia's face with some kind of washcloth. Doesn't she realize the washcloth needs to be wet? And it should be warm too. Even I know that.

"Did you guys break up?" Bevin asks again, whispering this time.

"No, we did not break up," I say through my teeth. "Now, shhh."

We sit here evaluating, but in almost every category, Miranda gets a "needs improvement" rating. She struggles with everything and when she finally finishes, she's dripping with sweat. You do not want your aesthetician to be sweaty.

"OK, well, thank you, Miranda," Anais says, shaking her hand. "We'll be in touch."

"When can I expect to hear from you?" Miranda asks.

"Um . . . within the next few weeks." Anais consults her clipboard, not making eye contact. "Thanks again."

Once Miranda's gone, Anais lets out her breath and plops down on the spa reception-area couch. It's such a nice couch that it's hard for me to believe it's ours. It's this beautiful brown velvet, kind of antique-looking.

Anais found it while she was antiquing in the Berkshires a few weekends ago, and she e-mailed us a picture and we all immediately approved. She had it shipped right away.

"So how did we all feel about Miranda?" Anais asks.

I look down at my sheet even though I don't need to. "She wasn't very good," I say.

"She didn't seem to know what she was doing," Bevin adds.

"Yeah, and um . . . ," Claudia starts, getting our attention. We all look up.

"Oh my gosh!" I scream. "Claudia! We need to get you to a hospital."

There are bright red splotches all over Claudia's face, kind of like she fell face-first into a forest of poison ivy. Some parts are even a dark burgundy-looking color, and one eye is starting to swell up. Miranda left the exfoliant on too long, and she probably didn't know to use one for sensitive skin!

"Claudia, come here please." Anais grabs her by the hand and leads her into the spa bathroom. She sits her down and starts blotting her face with witch hazel and dipping cloths into a cup of chamomile tea. "This will help."

It's not just that Anais is a spa consultant; she really knows what she's doing. That makes me feel a little bit better.

After Claudia's skin emergency, Mom, Grandma, Gary, and Anais go into a closed-door meeting in the pharmacy office.

Claudia's resting in the Relaxation Room with cold cloths all over her face and Bean is waiting on her like she's the Queen of England. He brings her drinks and candy and even goes down to the deli to get her favorite sandwich—Brie and apple slices.

"Bean is *soooo* cool," Bevin whispers to me as we're working in the pharmacy, fixing up the aisle with the pain relievers and cough medicine and stuff like that.

"Really?" I ask.

"Oh, totally," she says. "He's so good to your sister. And he's the kind of guy who can wear a necklace and not look dorky."

I peek around the corner and notice Bean's necklace. It's made of rope with beads on it. It looks dirty.

"Whatever," I mumble. I don't want to get into this with Bevin. What does she know about boys anyway?

We finish our work on the shelves and Mom, Grandma, Gary, and Anais come out of their closed-door meeting. It's already after five and Bevin and I should probably be heading to the movies soon.

I walk over and tap Claudia on the shoulder. "How's your face?"

"Fine. I was just falling asleep," she mumbles, and I know that's my cue to walk away. Claudia's very serious about her sleep.

"Let's go tell the adults that we're leaving for the movies," I say. "Otherwise they'll worry."

Bevin nods and skips over to the spa reception area. Everyone's sitting on the couch talking and sipping tea. It doesn't seem like they're working that hard, but since Grandma seems so happy, I decide not to worry about it.

I gauge my mood based on Grandma's a lot of the time. If she seems happy, then I feel happy.

"Bevin and I are going to the movies," I tell them. "Can we have twenty dollars for snacks?"

"Luce, just take candy from here, OK?" Mom says. "The movie theater is so overpriced."

"But we want popcorn," I whine.

"Fine, here's twenty dollars." Gary opens his wallet and hands Bevin the money.

I'm not proud of my whining, but if I'm not going to get treated like a grown-up, I may as well get treated like a spoiled kid.

"Luce-Juice!" I hear someone yelling as we're leaving the spa area. Only one person in the whole world calls me that, so I obviously know who it is.

What is he doing here?

"Luce-Juice!" he yells again, and I see Anais stand up and look around, not seeming happy about someone running through the store yelling.

Grandma goes back to the prescription counter to help some new customers. "Yamir, please, keep it down, OK?" She smiles, but I can tell she's a little annoyed.

"Lucy in the spa with Be-eh-vin," he sings when he sees us, creating a new twist on the song "Lucy in the Sky with Diamonds."

"Very funny, Yamir."

"I thought so." He raises his arms for a double high five, so I oblige him and then Bevin high-fives him too and cracks up.

"You ready?" he asks me.

"Huh?"

"Didn't you get my texts? Skee-ball competition at the beach tonight? I entered us. You're the best Skee-baller I know."

Suddenly it feels like there are clumps of cauliflower in my throat. I look over at Bevin, who has her eyebrows twisty, and she's still clutching the twenty dollars from her dad.

"We need to be there in twenty minutes, come on," he says. "I mean, I'm a speedy walker, but you can get slow sometimes." He laughs. "Kidding, kidding."

"Um, I didn't know that was officially confirmed," I say,

and then realize I sound like some kind of businesswoman. "So I, uh, made plans to see a movie with Bevin."

"Yup!" Bevin grabs my hand. "And we're gonna be late. Come on! We need to get popcorn and slushies and get good seats."

Instead of just the cauliflower lumpy feeling in my throat, now it feels like it's burning, like I swallowed a hot coal or something. I look over at Yamir and his eyes are scrunched and he's kind of frowning. It seems like hours of silence before anyone says anything.

"Oh, OK, no biggie," Yamir says finally. "Clint's free tonight. And he's really good at Skee-ball too. We'll win, for sure." He turns around and heads out of the spa area, toward the front of the pharmacy.

"Don't look so sad, Yamir!" Bevin yells.

I whack her in the arm. What is she thinking? She's yelling at Yamir right now, in front of everyone.

"Lucy likes you!" she yells, and I whack her again.

"Bevin!" I grab her arm to lead her out the back door. But she stands there, her feet firmly planted, like they were glued to the floor with rubber cement.

"Yamir! Are you listening? Lucy likes you! She really likes you!"

Now my family's out of the spa area and the Relaxation

Room and they're all standing in the doorway looking at me. Even customers are paying attention, popping up from the aisles. Every single person in Old Mill Pharmacy is staring at me right now.

It seems like Yamir is just going to walk right out without saying anything. I can't decide if I want him to say anything or if I don't. I guess I just want this moment to end. And I want to lock Bevin in her upstairs apartment for the rest of the summer.

"No time for that! I got a Skee-ball competition to win!" Yamir yells, with his back to us. "Later!"

I think I would have preferred if he had kept walking.

Now I'm standing there, feet stuck just like Bevin's. I don't know what to do. After a few seconds, the customers go back to their shopping. Claudia still has cold cloths on her eyes, but Bean leads her over to me like she's a blind woman and he's her Seeing Eye dog.

"Sorry, Luce," she whispers. "That was awkward."

"I know," I grumble.

"Bevin, may I have a word with you?" Claudia says, reaching out to grab her, since Claudia can't see a thing. Bean guides her over to Bevin and soon Bean is holding both of their hands, leading them into the Relaxation Room.

It's so ridiculous that it's funny, and I start to laugh. And then I start to cry. And then I'm laughing and crying at the same time. It reminds me of this song my mom wrote when she was in her acoustic-guitar-songwriting phase. She called it "How Can You Be Laughing When You're Crying?" It actually makes sense right now.

I overhear Claudia telling Bevin how wrong it was that she just did that, and Bean chimes in every few seconds, adding what he calls "the guy's perspective."

I plop down in the Turbo Massage Chair 7000 and turn on the massage button.

I bet Yamir will never talk to me again.

I'm missing the Skee-ball competition and I'll probably miss the movie too, not that I even wanted to see that dumb movie.

At least Claudia's looking out for me. That's one good thing.

Where did all of these makeup customers come from?" Grandma asks me, looking down at my appointment book as I'm setting up in one of the spa rooms. It occurred to me that I didn't need to keep doing makeup in the Relaxation Room now that the spa rooms are open. While I'm working, Anais, Gary, and Mom will be conducting a bunch more first-round interviews, since all the other candidates turned out to be horrendous.

"I had them scheduled," I tell her. "A few wedding trials, a few people getting their makeup done for that Connecticut Parks gala tonight."

Grandma nods. "That's great. Tell Anais so she knows and can greet people appropriately."

I sigh. "Grams, it's the same as it was before. They know I'm doing it. They made the appointments with me."

Grandma hugs me. "I know, I know, but we're a real-life spa now, and I want to make sure we're doing everything right." She pulls back from the hug and kisses me on the cheek.

"We're a real-life spa because you made us a real-life spa."

"Oh, Grams." I roll my eyes.

I don't get why she's so concerned with Anais. But I find her and tell her, and she says, "Oh, lovely. Let me make sure the water pitcher is out and the tea, so we can offer them stuff when they come in."

"Good idea."

It's so hot today that I turn the air-conditioning to sixty degrees and even put on the ceiling fan. You cannot have it so hot while doing makeup, or all the makeup will melt on the person's face and then drip down. It can be pretty disgusting.

I was a little concerned that Bevin might show up today, but so far I haven't seen her. After she blurted out everything to Yamir, I can't trust her at all, and especially not around clients.

As I'm waiting for my first customer, I adjust the lighting in the room and arrange all of the makeup on the silver makeup table. It feels so amazing to have these incredible supplies. The brushes are brand-new and perfect. The table is just the right height and there are so many light combinations, depending on the natural light and how the person's sitting.

Anais runs out to the grocery store around the corner and

picks up fresh flowers for the vase on the reception room table. She puts out the beautiful glass pitcher (it's from Tiffany's; she got it at an estate sale, and it was still bubble-wrapped!) and fills it with water and fruit slices.

Even though we're still weeks off from the grand opening, there's something about today that feels so important, so special. My first time doing makeup in the spa area! And it all looks so beautiful.

Anais takes a seat behind the reception desk and keeps looking at her watch.

"You have an interview soon, right?"

"I do." She smiles. "I think we'll work in the pharmacy office since you're in there today."

"I'm just in one treatment room," I tell her. "You can still use the spa office and the other rooms."

She nods. "OK. Thanks, Lucy."

Anais is wearing a pale pink linen dress, and she looks prettier than ever. Her hair is in a low bun and as I peek over her shoulder, I notice her writing something in the most beautiful handwriting I've ever seen, curly and straight up and down, and perfect.

I want her to like me. I want her to be impressed with me. But it seems like the more we work together, the more annoyed with me she gets.

It feels like she just wants me to disappear.

"Hello, I'm Bella. I have a ten o'clock interview," a woman says, walking in. Anais stands up to shake her hand and leads her to the pharmacy office.

"I'll be right with you," Anais says.

A few minutes later, my makeup appointment arrives.

"Hi, Tessa!" I say, walking over to her. She's on the board of the Connecticut Parks Association and she's the MC for the gala tonight. We had a whole long talk about the event over the phone when the date for the gala was set back in April.

"Lucy!" She hugs me.

"Hello, welcome," Anais says after we break our hug. "Would you care for some water? Tea?"

"I'd love some water, thanks," Tessa says. And then I'm just standing there, suddenly doing nothing.

Anais and Tessa start talking about local businesses going green, and Anais says, "We hope you enjoy your time at Pink and Green. Lucy's helping out for now, but in September, after the grand opening, we'll be fully staffed."

I look at Tessa, but she doesn't make eye contact with me. She's nodding at Anais and sipping her water.

I can't believe she just said that. Doesn't she realize that I was the one who scheduled Tessa's appointment? Now I know for sure what Anais thinks about me. I'm just here for the meantime. I'll be replaced eventually. She hasn't even seen what I can do yet.

When I first met Anais, I thought she was perfect, someone I really wanted to be like. Now I'm not so sure what's going on. But I can't let my bad mood affect my makeup treatment. Tessa came here expecting the best, and she will get better than the best. That's one thing I know I can control.

After Tessa finishes her water and her long chat with Anais, I guide her over to the treatment room. She hops up in the chair and puts her head back and I flick the switch to turn on the serene music. Claudia and I sampled all of these albums to find the perfect ones to play in the spa.

I used to play music while I did makeup in the Relaxation Room, but it was on this old boom box with a CD player and sometimes the tracks would skip, which didn't make for a very relaxing soundtrack.

I'm cleaning Tessa's face with a warm washcloth and I'm wondering if she's going to bring up anything about what Anais said about the real staff coming after the grand opening. Tessa called me after her neighbor told her about Old Mill Pharmacy and my amazing makeup work. Tessa knows all about the pharmacy and the grant and the spa opening. I kind of want her to say something, or ask me about what

Anais said so I can explain, or so I can feel better knowing that someone else realizes Anais is wrong.

But so far, she's been quiet with her eyes closed. She seems so relaxed, I don't want to disturb her. Maybe she'll say something when I'm done and she sees how great she looks.

I'm priming her face with cold cream and then I'll do a light foundation. I let the cold cream settle for a second and quickly glance at all the makeup on the tray so I can map it out in my mind. And that's when I hear someone calling me.

"Lucille! Lucille!"

Uh-oh. I thought Bevin was out for the day.

I'm wiping off the cold cream with a warm washcloth when the door to the treatment room slams open and Bevin barges through. "Lucille! I was worried sick. I thought something happened to you."

I quickly whisper in Bevin's ear, "I'm with a client. Can we please discuss whatever you need a little later on?"

She covers her mouth and then cracks up. "Come on. I know you think you're like a makeup artist or whatever, but you're just a kid like me."

Tessa's being really polite, just lying there, looking relaxed. But I bet this little back-and-forth between Bevin and me is starting to get annoying, and she doesn't want to wait all day to get her makeup done. I don't know how much longer she'll stay polite.

"Bevin, please leave."

She rolls her eyes. "I can do makeup just like you. I swear. Let me help!"

I bite the inside of my bottom lip; I don't know what to do. I can't let her help, but I also can't get into a fight in front of a customer. Grandma says that's a big no-no. It looks totally unprofessional.

"Just sit." I guide Bevin over to the chair in the corner. It's really there for customers to put their clothes and bags on, but in this case Tessa hung everything up on one of the hooks behind the door. I knew those hooks were a good idea.

"I can help. Really!" Bevin whispers.

I ignore her and go back to Tessa. I start dabbing on the foundation and carefully blending it. "What time is the gala?" I ask her.

"It starts at six," she says softly, definitely the tone of a relaxed person, so that's good. "But I need to be there at four thirty for pictures and chatting with the press and all of that."

I look at the fancy clock above the door. It's just about three, so we have plenty of time. The gala is at the nature conservancy ten minutes from here.

"OK, I just want to make sure none of your makeup melts. It's almost a hundred degrees today. Can you believe it?"

She shakes her head. "Too hot. When I was younger, summers in Connecticut, especially by the shoreline, were very cool. Some people didn't even have air-conditioning. Now, forget about it. You'd never survive."

After I'm done dabbing on the foundation, I get started on her eye makeup. She wants a very subtle look and I have the perfect color combination for her. I have a pale gray for the base of the eyelids and then a lighter color for the creases. And I've really mastered my skill at gel eyeliner.

"OK, can I at least do the blush and lipstick? Please?" Bevin walks over to us. Tessa keeps her eyes closed. I'm really not sure what she makes of this situation.

"Bevin," I say through my teeth. "Not now."

She keeps standing there while I'm finishing Tessa's eyes. Then I turn away for a second to put down the eye makeup and assess what I want to do for her lips. And that's when Bevin swoops in.

By the time I'm turned back to face Tessa, Bevin is brushing on some blush round and round in circles on her cheeks. "Bevin!" I yell. "Cheekbones! What are you doing?"

She waves me off. Tessa sits up for a second and looks at me, and I make an it's-all-going-to-be-OK face. I guess she believes me, because she lies back down.

"Voilà!" Bevin says a few seconds later, holding up a hand mirror for Tessa.

"You didn't do lips yet," I whisper. "Lips are the finishing touch."

"I know, but I wanted her to see a work in progress."

I've been looking at Bevin this whole time and I haven't gotten a good look at Tessa. So when she sits up, I see what Tessa is about to see in about three seconds.

Horror. She looks like she's in some kind of horror movie. And the worst part of it is that the awful blush work totally negates the wonders I did on Tessa's eyes.

"Uh, um," Tessa says, looking at herself in the mirror.

I stare at Bevin. Does she really think she did good work here? How did I let her do this? It's all my fault.

"I can fix it," I tell Tessa. "Just give me five minutes. I still have to do your lips."

"You hate it?" Bevin asks.

Tessa looks at me and then at Bevin and then back at me. "I have to go, girls. Thanks." She forces a smile. "I usually like to do my own lips anyway."

Tessa gets up, grabs her stuff, and leaves the spa area. I walk out too, leaving Bevin alone in the treatment room. I can't even look at her right now. That's how mad I am.

As Tessa's leaving the store, I hear her on the phone. "Can I get a rush appointment? Just makeup?"

Sheesh. She couldn't have waited to make that call until after she left the spa? I guess she didn't have time to waste.

"Why did Tessa look so upset when she left the spa?" Anais asks me, catching me totally off guard.

"Uh, she did?" I ask. I have no idea how to play this. I feel like any second, a bucket of water is going to fall on my head.

Anais nods. "Lucy, did something happen?"

Suddenly I feel like there was some kind of hidden camera in that spa room, and they were all spying on me that whole time. Could that be possible? I am so paranoid.

"It's not my fault, Anais." I start sniffling and then before I know it, I'm all-out crying. Anais leads me into the Relaxation Room and sits down next to me on the couch. "Bevin barged in, and then grabbed makeup off the tray while my back was turned. And she totally ruined Tessa's makeup. It needed to be redone."

"Lucy," Anais says in that stern tone that teachers use. "If you are going to be a responsible part of the spa staff, then you need to know how to handle these matters."

I look up at Anais. She seems about as comforting as a cold metal pipe. Why doesn't she care how upset I am?

"You can't be blaming others. OK?"

I start crying even harder, but Anais still doesn't really do much to comfort me.

"This is a place of business, and if we want to be taken seriously, we need to act professionally." She pauses. "I know it's your family's place and you've been able to do whatever you want around here, but we really want to up the ante on the spa end of things."

Anais pats me awkwardly on the shoulder and leaves the Relaxation Room. I want to go complain to Mom or Grandma, but that probably won't help me.

I want to yell at Bevin, but I doubt that will help me.

I sit down on the Turbo Massage Chair 7000 to process my thoughts. I have one more makeup appointment today and a few more this week. I turn on the massage settings and lean back and try to relax.

And that's when it hits me: Yelling at Bevin won't help. Complaining that I'm not involved in the spa won't help either. Yamir said I complain too much, and maybe I do. But there is one positive way I can help, and actually make a difference.

The ultimate makeover: Bevin.

She's a total disaster: She says things she shouldn't, she ruins makeup, her shoelaces are always untied, she gets food stuck in the corners of her mouth. She tries really hard, but she just needs some guidance.

I can be that guidance. I can show her how to act better in public, how to do makeup, how to be a good friend.

If I can't make a difference at the spa, I can make a difference in one person's life. I can give Bevin a makeover, but not just makeup and hair and whatever else I used to do around here. I can do more than that. A personal-improvement makeover.

The more I think about this, the more excited I get. I can hardly wait another second. I need to find Bevin. I need to start helping her. But I need to do it in the perfect way, so it's not too obvious, so she doesn't think it's weird and back away from me.

This is going to be my new project.

I've heard people say that if you save a life, you save the whole world. So does that mean that if you give one person a makeover, you make over the whole world too?

I think so. It sounds good, anyway.

11

Lucy's tip for a great summer:

Barbecue as often as you can. It doesn't need to be fancy. But you will need hot dogs. Otherwise, it's not a barbecue.

If I had looked at the Earth Club meeting schedule more closely, I would have made sure to return Yamir's text about that Skee-ball competition. Because as my luck would have it, we have an Earth Club meeting only a few days after Bevin's blurting-out episode, and now I actually have to see Yamir face-to-face.

I thought I'd be able to avoid him for a while since Sunny's at Indian Dance Camp this week, but I guess not. Now I have to go to Earth Club without Sunny to help me.

"That's gonna be so awkward," Bevin says to me as I'm getting ready to leave. "Though I said what I said for a reason. I thought he needed to know, because like he kind of ignores you most of the time, and he should treat you better."

This is my moment. This is the beginning of the make-over.

"Bevin, here's the thing," I say in my most gentle voice, patting the chair for her to sit down. "Sometimes we say things that need to be said, because we think they need to be said, but the truth is, if we think a moment before we say them, we realize it's best to stay quiet." I pause. "Do you understand?"

Her eyebrows are crinkled. She doesn't get it.

"Sorry." She puts her head down on the desk. "No one even wants me here."

Ugh. Now I need to cheer her up. I can't just let her go around feeling terrible and not needed. This is the first step to helping her.

"Bevin," I say. "Come on."

She keeps sitting there, with her head on the desk, her dirty-blondish hair spread around her like some kind of old-fashioned fan.

"It's true. I know you didn't want me here. Even my dad is too busy for me. He thought I would be with my mom, but she had to do some photography expedition in Senegal."

It's kind of hard to hear her because her head's down on the desk. If Anais sees this, she will not be pleased. I should tell her I understand about dads being too busy and dads moving away and all of that. But sometimes it's hard to admit you're suffering too. It's opening yourself up, knowing you'll never be able to close yourself again.

"And now I messed things up with you and your boy-friend."

"Bevin," I say again. "I don't even know if he's my boyfriend."

Her head jerks up. "See! Exactly why I had to say something. You don't even know. And you want him to be. And you're just letting the whole summer—the most romantic time of the year—pass by without knowing or not!"

"OK, Bevin." I fold my hands in my lap. "How would you like to spend the afternoon together?"

"I thought you had Earth Club," she says.

"It's optional." I smile. "And remember the other day when you were complimenting me on my clothes and I said how it's all about having staple items in your wardrobe?"

She nods.

"Well, I have an idea. Let's go shopping. We'll find you a few new things. We'll have lunch. We can even meet up with some friends of mine."

Her eyes bulge and she starts clapping. "Really? Really? Really? You mean that?"

"Shh." I put a finger to my lips. "I don't need everyone knowing I'm skipping Earth Club."

"Oh-kay," she mouths.

Claudia pops her head in after the interview she's conducting ends. "Ready, Luce?"

"Yup." I hop up from my chair and motion for Bevin to get up too. "Bevin's coming also. We're actually going to the mall for the Earth Club meeting today."

"Huh?" Claudia makes a face.

"Yup. We're making sure the food court is recycling all glass and plastic bottles." I look over at Bevin to make sure she stays quiet. Yes, it's a total lie, but it actually sounds like a good Earth Club project. I make a mental note to tell Mrs. Deleccio about it later.

Claudia and Bean drop us off at the mall's main entrance and I quickly look around to see if there's anyone I know nearby.

I'm half wishing that there is, and half wishing that there isn't.

Claudia waves good-bye as she drives away and then it's just Bevin and me.

I take a deep breath. This is really happening. A whole day alone with Bevin, working on her personality-improvement makeover.

"What should we do first?" she asks.

"Are you thirsty?" I ask her.

She shrugs. "I guess."

"Iced tea!" We walk through the mall to the food court and stop at the Beverage Bodega. It's a stand that only sells beverages—everything you can think of: milk shakes, coffee, soda, smoothies.

"When meeting new people, it's good to have a beverage in your hand," I tell Bevin. "That way if you can't think of something to say, you can take a sip while you think of it."

She nods.

"And this iced tea is so delicious, isn't it?"

"Best iced tea I've ever had." She smiles, and then slurps her drink loudly, gulping it all down and finishing with a huge burp.

My first instinct is to get all frustrated and yell at her, but that won't help. "You finished it in three seconds. Try to savor it. And also, maybe you don't want to burp so loud. In the future, take little sips, and make it last longer."

"OK," she says, and looks down at her feet. Her shoelaces are untied and one sock is higher than the other, like always. It's going to be a long day. "Lucy, why are you suddenly, like, hanging out with me and telling me all this stuff? Did my dad pay you to spend time with me or something?"

I laugh and then cover my mouth. "No!"

"Well, then, why?"

I sigh, take a sip of iced tea, and say, "Well, here's the thing, Bevin. I was lucky enough to have Claudia as my older sister to guide me through life. And you don't have an older sister. And since I'm three days older than you, I decided that because you're in Connecticut for the summer, I can at least provide you with a little big-sister guidance."

She sniffles, then reaches over to hug me. She hugs me so tight, I can't move, and here we are standing right in the middle of the food court hugging for what seems like three years. Finally she lets go.

"That is so nice, Lucy."

We spend the rest of the day shopping and picking up what I like to call *staples*: plain tees and capri pants and hoodies and little white sports socks that will always stay put.

"You have a lot of nice stuff," I tell Bevin while we're on line to pay. "But you just need things that go with everything else, so you can change it up sometimes. And also you need new socks."

She looks down at her feet and laughs. "Yeah, this isn't even a matching pair."

"I could tell."

By the time we're done shopping, it's too late to meet up with people, so I decide socializing Bevin will be our next project.

And the truth is, I'm not really sure who I could introduce her to, since Sunny's away and even when she's here, she's always busy with Evan, and everything is so awkward with Yamir and me.

I'm going to need to find temporary friends during this makeover process.

Later that night, my mind races with ways I can help Bevin, and I can't fall asleep. I decide that since I'm awake I can do some more research for Earth Club. I feel a little guilty that I bailed on the last meeting just to avoid Yamir.

As I'm researching, I come across all these Going Green community groups. They're basically groups of people who meet every month or so to discuss their Going Green progress. And then I come across all these other groups—restaurant owners' groups, gardeners' groups, vegan groups.

There's basically a group for anything and everything.

It's kind of amazing that the Internet can bring people together. I bet before the Internet, these people just had to do their own thing and worry about problems on their own. Maybe they knew a few people here or there and discussed issues with them. But they didn't have this wide-reaching support system, and now they do.

I wonder if there's an eco-spa owners' group!

If I found a group to join, it would be the perfect way to show Anais and Gary and Mom and Grandma that I know what I'm doing, that I'm really a part of things and an important member of the team.

I keep looking up eco-spa owners, spa owners' groups, small business owners, new business owners, all kinds of things, and then I narrow it down to Connecticut. It wouldn't make much sense to join a group in California, even though it would be kind of fun to go there!

I think I'm getting closer when I stumble upon a message board with business owners from the Newport area. That's only about an hour from here. Some of them talk about spas and salons, and they're going through a lot of the same issues we are.

More research leads me to discover that there's a southeastern Connecticut and Rhode Island small business owners' group that is actually meeting a few times this summer! The next meeting is pretty soon, and it's not even far away. It's at the Bayberry Cove Library.

Their website says they're a support group for people opening new businesses or expanding old ones. They share tips and advice on all sorts of issues that come up. I have to go. Grandma's too busy, and Mom wouldn't be interested. It's up to me.

This group might know things we don't about how to open a new business—they certainly know more than I know! But if I go, I could start to feel like I know what's going on. I could have something to contribute.

Plus, if I'm going to be a spa consultant when I grow up, it couldn't hurt to get started now.

I'm about to write in and say that I'll be coming, when I realize that these people could probably get arrested for talking to a thirteen-year-old online. We had this whole seminar about that in school this year. There are all kinds of cyber rules, and I really don't want to get these innocent people in trouble.

So I don't respond. I just e-mail myself the meeting time and some other information. There's no age requirement for a meeting like this. It's at a library and anyone can be at a library.

I'm so excited that I found this that I have even more trouble falling asleep.

12

Lucy's tip for becoming a better person:
Compliment others as often as you can.

A few days later I'm at the kitchen table thinking about how much Bevin has improved already. Her socks always match, her hair is neat, she wears the clear lip gloss I gave her, and she hasn't blurted out anything inappropriate since the Yamir incident.

I hate to be conceited, but it could be my influence. She's getting positive attention from me and it's going a long way.

We were hanging out at the mall food court the other day and we ran into some kids from Hebrew school. She was totally normal around them—for the most part. I mean, she did ask Elon Rosenberg ten times what his name was because she kept forgetting, but he seemed pretty understanding about it. I think she has a crush on him, but she hasn't mentioned it yet.

She only tripped once, and in all fairness, it was because

this guy left his tray on the floor next to the garbage can instead of putting it on the dirty-dishes cart.

She's really improving.

I'm feeling pretty pleased with myself and all of my hard work with Bevin as I sip Mom's fresh-squeezed OJ. And then my mom puts down the *New York Times* and stares at me.

"Lucy, I have to talk to you," she says. "It's about Dad."

My throat immediately tightens up. My feelings about my dad are always wobbly like a seesaw. I used to secretly wish every night before bed that he'd come back. Then, over time, I sort of just stopped wishing for that. We had a great time when we were together, and life was pretty OK when we were apart too. But sometimes I can miss him really bad, with no warning. And then I get mad at myself for missing him and wishing he'd come back. He left us, and we're fine without him, really. Plus, I don't want to wish for something that may never happen.

We never really talked about it, though. Until now.

"Is he sick? What's going on?"

My mom seems relatively calm. So why does she make everything sound so dramatic?

"He's fine, he's fine." She laughs, but it sounds a little forced. "I know you and Claudia have been wondering when he's coming this summer, and it's been up in the air."

I gulp the rest of the juice. "We know that."

"Right." She goes into the pantry and takes out a brown bag that's greasy on the sides. "Chocolate croissants." She puts the bag on the table and gives me one and takes one for herself. Since this is pretty much our second breakfast, she must be breaking some kind of bad news. "His contract with Oxford is still being worked out, and he doesn't have the time this year for his regular two-week stay."

See? Breaking bad news.

But at least I get a chocolate croissant.

"So when is he coming?" I ask after a bite.

"Well," she starts, and then picks a few pieces off hers. "Remember our friend Esme? She's the one who went backpacking across Africa and brought you back that handmade doll?"

"Yeah. I know. The wedding. You already discussed this, remember?" I don't mean to sound rude, but Mom can get lost on a tangent forever, and I don't understand what this has to do with Dad coming to Connecticut.

"Oh, right. So yeah, your dad wants to come for the wedding, and then he'll take you and Claudia somewhere for a few days either before or after. So you will get to see him."

She smiles and it seems like there's more to the story, stuff she's not telling me, but I can't figure out what it is. It's almost a mischievous smile, the kind of smile Claudia has when she's getting away with something she shouldn't. She had this smile when she told us Bean was staying for the summer.

"OK, so what's the big deal?" I ask.

"No big deal, I just wanted you to know." She looks down at her plate, but she's still got that smile.

As I'm putting the dishes in the dishwasher, it occurs to me that Mom is thinking something she's not saying. She's terrible at keeping secrets. And it seems like Dad is just squeezing in his visit with us because he's going to this wedding. I don't want to be a squeeze-in. I want to be a priority.

Grandma, Claudia, and Bean are already at the pharmacy. Mom goes down to do the laundry, and then when she's done we'll be heading over there too. I try to come up with a game plan for Bevin and me for the day, but I can't focus. I find myself wandering from room to room looking for something to do.

I decide to e-mail my dad. Maybe I just need to show him that I want to be a priority! I need to take action.

Dear Dad,
Mom said you're coming for Esme's wedding. That should be fun. I have ideas for our getaway. Maybe we can go to Cape Cod? Or Nantucket? People always say how amazing Nantucket is. Or we could even go to Fire

Island. My Earth Club teacher just went and it's so awesome. No cars! Let's come up with an awesome plan. You'll have to ask Claudia if Bean (her boyfriend) is coming. No, that's not his real name. Claudia will explain. Anyway, miss you! I'm excited for your visit.

Lots of love,

Lucy

A minute later, I get a reply.

Lucy dearest!

Fire Island sounds great. I knew you'd have a plan. The dates for my trip are still up in the air. I'll e-mail you my itinerary as soon as I have it. Do you like Bean? If you like him, I like him. But I love YOU! Let's Skype this week.

Dad

It's a short e-mail, but it does make me feel a little bit better. He replied quickly and he's excited about my plan. At least there's someone in this family who cares what I have to say!

Lucy's tip for a great summer:
Wear flip-flops every day.
Try not to ever wear real shoes.

Bevin's waiting for me in the Relaxation Room. She's wearing the jean shorts we bought on our first shopping trip and a ribbed black tank top. She has her white Converse on with the little ankle socks.

She looks perfect.

"Hi, Luce," she says. I notice right away that she's stopped calling me Lucille. The training is working. She gets it.

I sit down next to her and notice Bean and Claudia walking someone out of the spa area. It seems like I haven't seen them in days—they're always so busy working on things and not telling me what they're doing.

Whatever. I don't need them. I have my own project, and it's actually more important. I'm helping Bevin. When she gets back to school in September, no one will even recognize her, and they'll all be so amazed at how much she matured over the summer.

"So what are we doing today?" she asks me.

"That's a good question." I sit back on the couch and try to think of something. I need to start introducing Bevin to people. Hanging out with the Hebrew school kids was fine, but I don't know them well enough to hang out with them all the time. And hanging out with me alone isn't going to help her much when she gets back to school in the fall. But Sunny is going to a minor league baseball game with Evan and his friends. I think Yamir is going too. And truthfully, I'm not sure it would be a good idea for Bevin to hang out with them again anyway, after her blurting-out episode. She's better, but she's not perfect yet.

I try to think about where other people from school hang out in the summer. A lot of kids are away at camp, but I'm not really friends with those people anyway.

Then I remember Annabelle Wilson and her friends, and how they love to hang out on the boardwalk, get hot dogs for lunch at Hotdogger & Co., and try to sneak into the rooftop pool at the Allegria.

They call themselves AGE because their names are Annabelle, Georgina, and Eve. And they are so totally obnoxious, but they're perfect for Bevin's training! Georgina is the only one in the group that I like. But she's the kind of girl that everyone in every group likes.

"Go get a bathing suit, and meet me in front of the spa area," I tell her.

"Should I change now?" she asks.

"No, just bring flip-flops, a bathing suit, and sunscreen in a bag."

I run into the pharmacy office to find my bathing suit. Ever since I was little, I always kept an extra bathing suit at the pharmacy. You never know when you're going to take a spontaneous trip to the beach. It's just the way things work around here.

My mom and Anais are on speakerphone arguing with someone about their inspection forms, and Grandma's ordering supplies online. I try to be as quiet as possible, shuffling through the desk drawers looking for my bathing suit, but everyone shushes me anyway.

And the bathing suit is nowhere to be found.

There's only one thing I can do.

I tiptoe up the stairs to Bevin's apartment and knock on the door. Bevin comes out with a gym bag slung over her shoulder.

"Bevin, I'm so sorry to do this, but can I borrow one of the bathing suits we bought at the mall the other day?" I ask her in my nicest voice.

"You want to borrow something of mine?" She sounds shocked.

"I can't find my bathing suit." I shrug. "And there's no time to go back to my house and get a new one now, and there's no one to give us a ride. And those suits we bought you are really cute."

She's nodding really fast. "Sure! I'm wearing the pink one, but you can wear the turquoise-striped one."

"Thank you so much!" I don't need to worry about flip-flops since they're the only shoes I wear all summer long, and we can steal towels from the spa supply closet. Mom made a mistake with the ordering and they were final sale, so we have way more than we need anyway.

We walk over to the beach. It's hot, but there's a nice breeze and little humidity, so we're not sweating that much. That's a good thing. It's never good to be super sweaty when meeting new people.

On the way over, I tell Bevin that we'll probably see my friends from school there.

"Sunny?" she asks.

"No, Sunny has plans, but other people," I tell her. "So

just be chatty and friendly. If you see them picking at their nails, or looking off into the distance, it means you're talking too much."

"Really?" She seems more fascinated by this than insulted, so that's a good thing. I don't want to hurt her feelings, but I do have to be honest. Sometimes she really goes on and on forever.

Just as I suspected, the AGE girls are sitting on one of the benches, drinking sodas, with towels draped over their shoulders.

"Lucy!" Annabelle calls out. I've known her since nursery school, but we've never really been friends. She's perfect for Bevin's training.

"Hi guys, this is my family friend Bevin." I gently push her toward them, and she waves and says hi. "Her dad is helping with the opening of the spa, so they're staying in Connecticut for the summer."

"Oh, cool," Georgina says. "Where are you from?"

"Manhattan," Bevin tells them, and then looks at me. I guess she's worried about talking too much, but she can say more than one word.

"Really?" Eve yelps. She's the shortest person I know and has a really high-pitched squeaky voice. "That is *sooooo* cool."

"Yeah," Georgina adds. "You, like, live in the best city in the world."

"I guess." Bevin laughs. "It's not like I hang out with celebrities or anything."

"Not even a Real Housewife?" Annabelle laughs.

"Not really." Bevin shifts from foot to foot and I try as hard as I can to think of something else to say, a conversation Bevin can participate in, so we're not just standing here awkwardly.

"I'm gonna go get us a snack," I tell Bevin. Maybe it's too soon to leave her on her own with people she doesn't know, but it might be good for her to jump right in. Besides, I'm a little hungry, and sharing snacks always helps cover awkward silences.

I get an order of onion rings and some cut-up watermelon and figure it should hold us over until lunch.

When I get back, Bevin's sitting on the bench between Georgina and Annabelle. They don't even notice me standing there.

"Would you rather eat only lima beans and chocolate for the rest of your life or get to eat whatever you want but no chocolate for the rest of your life?" Annabelle asks.

"That's kind of a weird one," Georgina says.

"I'd have to say the second choice," Bevin adds.

"Can I exchange lima beans for asparagus, because I *looooove* asparagus?" Eve asks.

"This isn't even your question," Annabelle says to her. "And obviously not!"

This goes on and on for about five more minutes, and then they notice me.

"Bevin's really good at *Would you rather*," Annabelle says, grabbing an onion ring from me.

"That's why I brought her to hang out," I tell them. "I knew you'd appreciate her skills."

Bevin smiles and sits up straighter. It's the happiest I've ever seen the girl, and I've known her for a while.

We stay at the beach for the rest of the afternoon. AGE embraced Bevin much quicker than I thought they would, so I don't have much to do. But I can't complain—that was my goal in the first place.

At five P.M., I get a text from Sunny.

Where r u? stopped by pharmacy. Gma said u were wit bevin?

I decide to ignore it. The whole story's too long to explain over a text and I really can't sneak away and call her right now anyway.

"Are you guys staying for the hot-dog-eating contest?" Georgina asks.

"I totally forgot about that!" I yell, and then remember that Sunny and Evan had mentioned something about it earlier. Back when we all hung out.

"Let's stay," Bevin says, a whine in her voice like a little kid. "Please, please, please can we stay?"

Uh-oh.

I laugh to break the awkwardness. "Ha. Bevin, your little-kid imitation is really good." She looks confused for a second and then catches on.

"I've been working on it," she says. And then AGE laugh too, and I feel reassured that my work with Bevin is actually paying off.

I quickly text my mom that we're going to grab dinner on the boardwalk and that we'll be back at the pharmacy before closing.

People start coming and lining up outside of Hotdogger & Co. I doubt they're all participating; I think they just like to watch people stuff their faces.

We have a really good spot toward the front since we've basically been here all day.

We're watching the staff set up the tables and the big bins of hot dogs when I feel a tap on my shoulder.

"Lucy?"

I turn around. My heart is pounding because I obviously know that voice. I'd know it anywhere, even in a loud, screaming concert with a million people.

"Hi, Sun." I try to act calm even though I'm a total idiot—Sunny told me about this event weeks ago. I completely forgot she was coming, and I never texted her back.

But she's always busy with Evan. I doubt she even cares that I'm here.

"Who are you here with? I stopped by the pharmacy and then texted, to see if you wanted to come, and I got no response," she says, sounding befuddled.

"Oh, just Bevin and AGE." I point at them. They're watching us talk, and it's a little freaky.

I'm sure Sunny's confused since I don't usually hang out with them, but I can't explain with them listening in.

"Oh." She raises her eyebrows and stays silent for a few seconds. "Well, come on, let's go up front."

I turn around and look at Bevin and AGE, and then back at Sunny. Now I'm the confused one.

I laugh. "Sun, you're participating? We were planning on staying here and watching famous hot-dog eaters, like that guy who always does the Coney Island contest."

Sunny cracks up. "No. You and Yamir are participating!

Remember? We signed you guys up at my house that day after the Earth Club Earth Day party."

I try to think back, but I can barely remember anything from before we got the grant and started the construction, from before Sunny and Evan started going out, and before Claudia came home and Bevin moved to Connecticut. Everything happened so fast that it's all a blur.

"I think I'm going to beat my record," Yamir says, seemingly coming out of nowhere. "Last year I had eleven. I can totally do it."

Is this really happening?

"Last chance to sign up," a woman yells out to the crowd. "We had a few cancellations, so we have a few more spots!"

"Sunny, you can do it too." I pat her on the back, trying to inch her forward to sign up.

"Are you kidding?" She looks at me like I just told her to swim across the Atlantic Ocean. "I'm not doing it."

"You're not gonna bail—right, Luce-Juice?" Yamir grabs my hands, and then raises them in the air like we're at some kind of political rally or something. "Luce-Juice! Luce-Juice!"

I let go of his hands. "I guess not," I say quietly.

"You're in the contest?" Annabelle squeaks. "Is that why you've been hanging out here all day?"

"No, I forgot Sunny signed me up." I laugh, then look over at Bevin. She shouldn't enter this contest. She spits when she eats and gets food all over her face, and a hot-dog-eating contest isn't a good thing for her personality make-over.

To be honest, I'm a little embarrassed that I'm doing it.

Bevin goes to the bathroom with AGE and I'm left standing by myself for a minute, wondering if entering a hot-dog-eating contest is a huge game changer with Yamir. Maybe, if I do it, he won't see me in a girly way anymore. I'll just be some competitor, like one of the guys, and then we'll never go on a real date.

I tap him on the shoulder. "Yamir, I think I changed my mind. My stomach is kind of weird all of a sudden and—"

"Oh, come on!" he says. "You'll be great."

I tell myself that it's fine, that we're doing something together, that he wants me to be a part of it. So what that I forgot about it until now? Maybe it's better that I forgot, that way I wasn't nervous all day. I guess I was so busy thinking about Bevin that I wasn't thinking about myself.

The people who work at Hotdogger & Co. seat each of us at a little table with a plate overflowing with hot dogs. It's a no-buns kind of event and we can have as much water as we want.

"Don't fill up on water," Yamir whispers to me. "Just eat. Don't think."

The woman wearing a giant hot dog costume reads out the rules. There are fifteen people participating and what seems like a hundred spectators. Of our friends, Yamir and I are the only ones participating. Sunny, Evan, Clint, and Anthony are standing around us cheering, and so are Bevin and AGE.

"Go, Lucy! Go, Yamir! Go, Lucy and Yamir!" They keep saying it over and over again. It's a nice feeling when someone cheers for you.

The hot dog costume lady blows her whistle, and we all start eating.

It's weird to shove hot dogs in your mouth while people cheer for you, but then every few seconds, I look over at Yamir sitting next to me and he smiles this crooked smile because his mouth is full of hot dogs and it makes me laugh. And then I just keep eating. And for the first time in a while, I'm not thinking about the spa and Anais and all of that, I'm just thinking about eating hot dogs, and sitting next to Yamir, and Sunny and everyone cheering for us.

So I just keep eating and smiling and then before I know it, the hot dog lady is grabbing my arm and waving it in the air. "We have a wiener!" she yells. "Fifteen hot dogs!"

I can't believe I ate fifteen hot dogs. For the last few, I was just focusing on my plate and eating and thinking about Yamir and me. If we got married one day, we could tell everyone about this day and all the crazy things we did together.

I look down the row at my competition. It appears they all stopped eating a few seconds ago. I hadn't even noticed. Even Yamir is just sitting there, holding his stomach.

"What's your name?" hot dog lady whispers.

"Lucy." After I say it, my stomach starts to get funny and I wonder if drinking water will make it feel better or worse.

"Lucy here has just won unlimited hot dogs for an entire year!" the hot dog lady yells and hands me a giant check, but it doesn't really make sense, since there's no dollar amount on it. It just says UNLIMITED HOT DOGS FOR A YEAR. It doesn't even say dates or anything, but I guess they know when they're giving it to me.

"Yay, Lucy!" Sunny yells, and everyone starts cheering and it's all I can do not to throw up. Sunny squeezes her way to the front of the crowd so she can talk to me without anyone hearing. "When you've recovered, we have to talk."

"About?"

"About why you ditched me for AGE . . . and Bevin."

"Sunny, come on," I start, but then she gets a call from her mom and they need to figure out where they're meeting her, so she walks away to talk to her.

"You rocked that, Luce-Juice," Yamir says. "I'd kiss you right now, but we both ate a million hot dogs, so it would be kind of gross."

At first I don't process what he just said because I'm so focused on my insane thirst, and the fact that Sunny's really mad at me, and the fact that I just ate fifteen hot dogs. My mouth is too tired to say anything out loud.

Yamir just said he would kiss me. I wonder if he was serious.

"Lucy!" I hear Bevin yelling from the bench a few feet away from us. "Georgina's mom can drive us to the pharmacy! She'll be here in five minutes—come on."

I yell back OK, and then when I turn to say good-bye to Yamir and find Sunny, I see them already walking away, toward the parking lot.

Bevin arranged a ride home for us, with Georgina Emminson of all people, probably the most popular girl in our grade. Yamir said he'd kiss me, but we'd just eaten a million hot dogs. Sunny thinks I ditched her.

All of these things are bizarre, and I want to figure them out. But I don't know where to start.

I think about Bevin and I wonder if it's just all about leaving your comfort zone. I threw her in with strangers and she did fine. But when she hung around me and the spa, she was the most annoying girl in the world. Maybe people just need to shake things up every once in a while.

Maybe that's what it would be like if Dad came back to Connecticut for real. It would just shake things up. And maybe that would be good. Or maybe it would be bad. It's hard to say for sure, and in the meantime, it's a lot to worry about.

14

Lucy's tip for becoming a better person:
Never tell someone they look tired.
They don't want to hear it.

𝒜nais needs to leave town for a few days to handle all the filing for the spa inspections and certifications. Mom, Grandma, Anais, and Gary have been working on the paperwork for weeks now, and it always seems like they're tearing their hair out over it.

Morrie had to come in and sign some papers since he's the accountant and financial adviser. They've had to get forms notarized and go back and forth to the bank and city hall three million times.

It all seems really annoying and frustrating. Like if they forget to cross one *t*, it'll all fall apart. I hope not, but it seems that way.

So before Anais leaves she wants us all to have a meeting so we can catch each other up on what we've been doing. Unfortunately she's leaving by ten, so our meeting is happening at eight A.M.

We're all sitting in the Relaxation Room since none of the other meeting areas are big enough to hold all of us. But the Relaxation Room is the most calming, so it's obviously the best spot for an early-morning meeting.

"This is gonna be fast, right?" Bevin whispers in my ear.

I shrug. I don't even know why she's sitting here. She doesn't have to be. "I don't know. Why?"

"I told Annabelle we'd meet her at the pool in her neighborhood." She pauses. "You know where that is, right?"

"You made plans with Annabelle without me?" I ask. I can't tell if I'm annoyed or hurt or impressed. Hanging out with AGE was just supposed to be practice for Bevin. I don't really want to make a habit of it. They're super-popular, and they're not always the nicest girls.

"Well, I—"

"OK, thanks for meeting me so early," Anais interrupts. Claudia flicks Bean's shoulder because he's falling asleep on the couch with his head back and his mouth wide open. He jerks forward. "I'll be gone for a few days and I just want to make sure we're all on the same page."

Each week that Anais has been here, she's gotten progressively stricter and more stressed. Maybe it's harder work than she thought it was going to be, or maybe we're just hard to work with. Either way, her job is starting to seem like less fun than it was at first.

"Our website and e-mail addresses are all set up." She looks over at my mom. "Thank you to Jane for finding that wonderful web designer and for working with him on the layout. I've worked with him on all the technical stuff, and he's great."

"Oh, my pleasure. Seth's an old friend from college. He does great work. And would you believe his first career was veterinary work. Unbelievable." Grandma pats her leg and whispers something in her ear and then Mom stops talking.

"So the URL is pinkandgreenspa.com and it will be linked from the Old Mill Pharmacy site. I've made a few e-mail addresses and there's room to make more. So far we have info@pinkandgreenspa.com, appointments@pinkandgreenspa.com, and press@pinkandgreenspa.com. We need to make sure we're checking these at least once an hour in the coming weeks, so I've made it easy. The password for every e-mail is Desberg384. We can change it later, but that way it's easy and we know it so we can all check it and make sure everything is covered."

I'm so glad she just told everyone the password, because if she had done it in private and I was left out, I would have been so upset.

"We're still waiting on the shipment of brochures, business cards, and other marketing materials." Anais looks over at me. "Thanks to Lucy's friends and their family, we've secured a great price on printing."

I smile. It feels good to be thanked, even if it's just for knowing Sunny and the Ramals.

"We're still a little short-staffed, but Claudia and Bean will be continuing the interviews and demo procedures this week while I'm away." She looks down at her notebook. "Jane has to finish the last few supply orders. And then when I'm back, Doris and I need to finalize all the plans for the grand opening, if we want a booth on the street or how we want to approach it."

"A booth on the street could be great!" I exclaim. "We could have one of those portable massage chairs out there, and give free two-minute massages to bring people in."

Everyone's nodding. "That's an idea," Mom says.

"We could also sell some skin-care products in the booth," Claudia adds, "and take appointments."

Mom's phone starts ringing and she hops up from the couch. "I gotta take this, guys. It's Sam calling from London. Be right back."

Grandma puts her head back and closes her eyes for a second, like she's about to scream but trying to hold it in. I wonder why. Maybe she's mad at my dad for something, but I can't imagine what. She always seemed to like my dad, even now that they never see each other.

Mom closes the pharmacy office door to have the phone conversation with my dad. I would pay a million dollars—if I had a million dollars—to find out what that phone call is all about.

"OK, so I think we're set. Good work on everything, guys." Anais smiles. "We have a few weeks until the grand opening and I think we're in good shape. Cross your fingers that everything works out with the inspections."

I stand up and make an over-the-top crossing fingers gesture, but no one seems to find it funny. "I'll let you know when I get the final numbers on appointments from Sarabeth," I add, just so they take me seriously. "She said eight bridesmaids, but I want to make sure I know what each person is getting done."

"Thanks, Lucy." Anais gets up and straightens her flouncy skirt. "See you all in a few days."

Bevin and I are the first ones out of the meeting (except for my mom, who left early to take the call).

"I'm going to run an errand with my dad, and then he'll drop me off at Annabelle's pool. She texted me the address. Meet me there," Bevin says, more like a statement than a question.

"Um, OK." All I can think about right now is checking all the new e-mail addresses! It may be really pathetic, but it feels so official to have our own business e-mail accounts.

"I mean, you're not too busy for some swimming, right?" she continues.

I look at her, confused. She's asking me to go, but maybe that's just because she's being nice. Maybe this is the next step in her makeover, and she should go on her own. After all, it's not like Annabelle texted me about the plans—she texted Bevin.

"OK, have fun," I say, smiling. I decide to leave it open, and see if she presses the issue.

"OK." She makes a puckered kissy face. "Smooches."

So we still need to work on that obnoxious kissy face of hers.

Bevin heads out with Gary, and since my mom is in the pharmacy office, I sprint over to the spa reception area and sit down in the comfy rolling chair. I turn on the MacBook and follow the links to the Pink & Green e-mail.

I feel like I could stay in this seat forever. I'd love watching all the customers come in and out. I could always play online if I got bored. The computer is sparkly and shiny and superfast.

Unfortunately there isn't much e-mail to check. Just a

few registration sign-up things for Boat Fest, and some tips to enhance your e-mail and get the most out of your online experience.

Oh well. I'll keep checking, at least once an hour like Anais said.

While I'm at the computer, I check my personal e-mail, where there's a reminder that the southeastern Connecticut and Rhode Island small business owners' meeting is happening tonight! How did I not realize that? It's taking place at the Bayberry Cove Library, which is about four towns away from Old Mill. That's where Sunny's aunt and uncle and her cousin Asha live.

OK, Lucy, think. I need to figure out what I'm going to tell Mom and Grandma and Claudia, some reason why I need to go all the way to the Bayberry Cove Library. And now I don't even have to worry that Anais will be at the meeting because I know for sure she's out of town! The timing couldn't be more perfect.

My mom pops her head into the spa area. "So sorry to run out like this, Luce, but I have another meeting at the *Old Mill Observer*." She winks at me. "Top secret, but I think they're going to let me write some articles. Not really a staff writer, I won't have an office, but they're pleased with my writing."

"Mom!" I shout, and she shushes me. "That is so amazing! It's your dream!"

"I know," she whispers. "But let's keep it quiet. Nothing's certain yet, OK?

"I should be back later tonight. I have this meeting and then I'm going with one of the editors to this journalism and business conference," she tells me. "There's grilled chicken salad in the fridge for you." She leans over and kisses me on the cheek. "Make sure you're checking the e-mails while I'm gone."

I nod. This sneaking out to the meeting thing is going to be easier than I thought. It doesn't even seem like anyone's around. Claudia and Bean may be here, but they don't pay attention to me anyway.

And then I hear Grandma whistling.

OK, one tiny obstacle left.

"Lucy," she calls. "Come help me, please, doll."

I run over and find Grandma hovering over a box of washcloths. "Luce, Eli's in the spa area, helping to install that closet-organizer system. When he's done, I want you to arrange all these towels by size. Can you handle that?"

I nod. "Duh. Of course I can."

"Thanks, love." She gives me a hug.

"Oh, but, Grams, I need to go to the library tonight for

Earth Club research," I tell her. I wasn't even really planning what I was going to say; the lie is just coming out, flowing normally. "So I'll be leaving at six, OK?"

"What about dinner?" Grandma asks. "I don't want you skipping meals like your sister. You're still growing and you need to eat."

"Oh, don't worry, I'm going out for dinner with Sunny after," I tell her. Another lie.

"Well, let Claudia or me know if you need a ride, and please take this box over to the spa area. Eli should be done soon." Grandma ties her hair back in this pretty floral hair band. "Mr. Tuscano, I'm on my way to give you that prescription!" She jogs over to the prescription counter. I'm glad to have a grandma that can still jog, even if it only is a few feet.

I carry that box of washcloths over and Eli is still finishing organizing the closet. Claudia and Bean are conducting another interview and I don't want to disturb them. I step outside the building for a second and quickly call Sunny.

"Did you throw up?" she asks me before saying hello.

At first I'm confused and then I remember the hot-dog-eating contest. Wow, that seems like forever ago already. "No, not at all. I was fine!" I laugh. "Hope that's not even grosser."

"Well, you certainly impressed the boys," she says. "Yamir was telling my dad about it this morning. He was like 'isn't

that so awesome?' and 'she's so cool' and then when I caught
him and he noticed me, he started blushing. It was funny."

Yamir was bragging about me to his dad? Sure, it was only
about eating hot dogs, but that's still pretty cool.

"I need to ask you a favor," I tell her. "Please say yes. If
you're thinking about saying no, just remember all I did for
you by joining Earth Club and helping you with Evan and all
of that." I pause. "OK?"

"First of all we have to discuss you and Bevin becoming
BFFs with AGE," she starts.

"We aren't BFF," I say. "They're basically just people for
Bevin to hang out with so she can learn to be social. But I need
you to say you'll help me."

"Lucy! First of all, what a weird reason to hang out with
people. Second of all, I can't say yes if I don't know what it is.
What if you're asking me to jump into the river from a high
bridge or something?"

I groan. "It's nothing like that. I just need you to come
with me to Bayberry Cove Library tonight. You can sit and
read in the YA section while we're there, I just need you to
come with me so it doesn't look strange."

"Huh? Explain."

So I tell her all about the small business owners' group and
how I feel it's important for me to go. "I want to get advice on

how to be taken more seriously in the business," I add. "And they have meetings once a month, I think, and this one isn't too far away."

"But my aunt and uncle and Asha and Raj live in Bayberry Cove," she tells me. "So what if they see us?"

"Do they normally hang out at the library?" I laugh.

"No, they all have iPads and download like forty e-books a day, but that's a whole 'nother story." She sniffles; she always has summer allergies. "Fine, I'll go. But what should we say our reason for going is?"

I peek into the spa window to make sure Eli's still working on the closet. I don't want to shirk any responsibilities here. I need to make sure I unpack that box before I leave. "We'll say they have books and stuff we need for Earth Club that Old Mill and Waterside libraries don't have."

Sunny sniffles again. "OK, sure. It's twenty-five minutes away, though. My mom will probably just wait while we go in."

Darn. That won't work. "Here's an idea. I'll make Claudia and Bean drive us, and your mom can pick us up. We'll tell her a later time so she doesn't see the meeting in progress."

"Oh! I have an amazing idea. There's that famous lobster roll place a few blocks away," Sunny says. "Asha's taken me there a million times. We'll call when the meeting's over and tell my mom to meet us there and we'll get lobster rolls after the meeting!"

"Genius, Sunny!" I shout. "You always solve problems with food. I love it!"

She cracks up. "OK, I'm not gonna invite Yamir or Evan because then there's more of a chance of them spilling the beans. What time are we going?"

"Be ready at six. The meeting starts at seven."

"Got it," she says, then pauses. "You know we're making up this whole elaborate lie just so you can go to a business owners' meeting? That's really, really lame."

"Gee, thanks." She was being so nice up until now.

"I'm just saying. Usually teenagers make up this stuff to sneak out to concerts or to meet famous people or go to parties or something." She laughs. "But a discussion group? It's funny."

"Fine. It's funny." I'm not laughing.

"Don't take yourself so seriously, Luce." Sunny pauses and waits for me to say something. "Fine, whatever. See you at six."

I still don't understand why you need to go all the way to Bayberry Cove to do research, Lucy," Claudia says as I'm rushing her to leave. "We have computers, the Internet, databases, whatever, you don't need to go to a library so far away."

"They have a whole environmental Going Green section," I tell her.

"They do?" Bean asks. "That's pretty impressive."

"Let's just go. Come on. We're going to be late to pick up Sunny." I drop the subject because all I need is Bean coming in with me to peruse the section. Maybe I'm not as good a liar as I thought I was.

Claudia groans. "We've been busy here all day. We're not on call to be your chauffeur."

"Well, Grandma's busy, and Mom's busy," I say. "Besides,

you can go to Lobster Landing after you drop me off. Best lobster rolls in all of Connecticut, ten years in a row."

"Oh, yeah!" Claudia exclaims. "Bean, get ready. You've never had a lobster roll like the ones at Lobster Landing. It's right on the water and it's so nice."

"Bonus!" Bean high-fives me. "We get to chauffeur Lucy and Sunny and get lobster rolls. This is the best day of the summer so far."

I roll my eyes but eventually start laughing. Bean's not a bad guy. He's a little doofy, but he's funny sometimes, and he loves my sister, so I guess he can't be that awful.

We're in the car on the way to Sunny's house and I get a sinking-stomach feeling, similar to how I felt after I ate all the hot dogs. What if this is a huge mistake? I could be turned away from the meeting, or maybe someone there knows Mom or Grandma or even Anais. I should have thought this through. I need a wig or a hat or crazy glasses.

I need a full disguise.

"I'll be right back." I hop out of the car and go into Sunny's house. I don't wait for Claudia or Bean to ask me why I'm going in; I just go.

"Hello, Lucy darling," Mrs. Ramal says.

"Hi. Um, can I run upstairs? I need to get something from Sunny."

She nods, confused.

"Sunny!" I burst into her room. "I need a disguise. What if someone recognizes me?" I don't wait for a response. I just start rifling through her closet, looking at her hats and sweaters and anything I can find. "Do you have a wig?"

"Lucy." She puts her hand on my shoulder. "Calm down." She hands me her old glasses that had a very light prescription. "Wear these."

I put them on and I'm surprised at how cute I look in the wire frames.

"Even if I give you a hat, will you really wear it indoors?"

I shrug. "I don't know. I just think I should look a little different, a little unlike myself."

Sunny looks at her watch. "We need to go or you're going to be late." She's still looking through her closet. "I know! A sari!"

"Huh?"

"You're kind of tan now, so you can just look like a pale Indian girl." She finds the prettiest sari in her closet and hands it to me. It's pale pink and turquoise with little silver beading. It could probably pass as some kind of artsy sundress. "Go change."

I listen to her and when I come out of the bathroom, Sunny tells me how pretty I look.

"But won't your family wonder why I'm wearing this?" I ask.

She hesitates for a second. "Give me your clothes."

She runs back into the bathroom and puts on my jean cutoff shorts and my ribbed yellow tank top.

"We traded clothes! Perfect explanation!"

I don't have the heart to tell her it doesn't make sense really since she wasn't wearing the sari before. Sunny's trying so hard and not being mean; I can't ruin that. And we run out of the house so fast, no one really sees us. We just yell good-bye as we're out the door.

On the way over, I'm really, really nervous. I keep wanting to ask Sunny questions—like should I say my name is Sunny Ramal? Should I make up a new name? I thought I had this all planned out but now I'm not so sure. I worry that if I say my name is Lucy Desberg, someone will recognize it and figure me out.

"Why are you wearing that to go do research for Earth Club?" Claudia asks me after a few minutes. I wonder what took her so long. I guess she's been distracted by the book she's reading.

"I love wearing Sunny's clothes," I tell her, "and I rarely get to anymore."

"Oh-kay." Claudia drags out the word.

Bean is actually a very slow, cautious driver, or maybe it's just because he's driving Grandma's car and wants to be careful. Whatever it is, it feels like it's taking a billion years to get to the Bayberry Cove Library. And the longer it takes, the more nervous I get and the more I regret deciding to do this.

Sunny squeezes my hand. "You are acting so weird," she whispers.

After what feels like a two-hour drive, we finally get to the Bayberry Cove Library.

"So Sunny's mom is picking you up?" Claudia turns around from the front seat.

"Yup."

"If the line's really long at Lobster Landing, we can always come to the library after and wait for you to be done," she adds.

"No, no, that's OK," I say really fast.

Claudia crinkles her eyes at me. "You're odd, Lucy. But I love you anyway."

Sunny and I get out of the car and walk toward the double doors of the library. We watch Bean and Claudia drive away.

"Are you ready?" Sunny asks me.

"I don't know why I'm so nervous."

She shrugs. "You'll be fine." I clutch her arm, suddenly

feeling wobbly, and she widens her eyes at me and breathes through her nose. "Can you stop acting like this? You're driving me crazy."

"Sunny, you agreed to come. I need your help."

She ignores me.

"Should I make up a new name? Where should I say my spa is? I'm so scared. I don't want this to end up getting back to my mom or grandma or Anais. Then I'll really be in trouble." I sit down on the sidewalk outside of the library for a second. I need to think.

"Say your name is Lucy Ramal. Your spa is in New York City but you're back and forth to your summer home in Waterside, so you wanted to get some advice." Sunny blurts out this list as fast as she can. "No one will find you out."

"Maybe I should be Louise Ramal?"

"Fine." Sunny pats me on the back, but it's an impatient pat, not a nice one. "Now go. You're going to be late."

Lucy's tip for becoming a better person:
Always say "Thank you" when
someone holds a door for you.

"May I help you?" a woman at the reference desk asks me as I walk in. I guess I look lost. Sunny was planning to wait outside for a second or two and then come in so it didn't look suspicious.

"Oh, I'm here for the small business owners' group," I tell her, trying to sound as adult as possible.

"Sure, they're in the children's corner, in the back on the left-hand side." She smiles. "Beautiful sari, by the way."

"Thanks." I wonder if she thinks I'm Indian. I kind of hope so.

As I'm walking over, I feel my phone vibrating. I take it out because I think that it's Sunny, but when I look at it, it's Bevin calling.

I debate answering versus letting it go to voice mail but in the end, I decide to answer it.

"Lucy, I need your help," Bevin says as soon as I say hello.

"Can I call you back?" I whisper. "I'm at the library."

"What?" she yells.

"Never mind. Can I please call you back later?"

"I really need to talk to you," she says.

Out of the corner of my eye, I see the small business owners' group gathering. The meeting is going to start any minute. But Bevin needs me. I don't know what to do.

"I'm so sorry, Bevin, but I can't use cell phones in here. I promise to call back soon. Bye."

I hang up before she can say anything else. I feel bad, but I really don't have a choice. There's a huge sign with a cell phone in a red circle with a line through it.

I want to put Bevin's call and Sunny's weirdness out of my head, so I can focus on the task at hand: this meeting.

It's funny that this group is meeting in the children's section, but it makes sense since most little kids are home by now. The people sit in regular-sized chairs, with all of the little chairs stacked up in a corner.

"Hello, my name is Louise Ramal. I'm here for the meeting," I say to the lady standing up. Everyone else is sitting down. They all stare at me. I'm pretty sure one man is about to tell me to leave— he's got a scowl on his face like I've just interrupted his important conversation. I square my shoulders and try to look like Anais.

"Welcome. We'll be starting in just a minute." The lady smiles. At least she's nice. I let out a breath I didn't know I'd been holding. "Please fill out this contact information sheet. That way we'll be able to keep in touch, alert you to the next meetings, etc."

"OK."

I sit down on one of the chairs on the edge of the circle where there aren't any other people. I need space to fill out this form because I'm really not sure what to write. Out of the corner of my eye, I see Sunny coming in and talking to the same person at the reference desk. Then I see her walking over to the young adult section, which is very close to where our meeting is taking place. I hope she doesn't make faces at me and make me laugh. She looks grumpy, so I doubt she will.

This form is tricky because it asks for addresses of the business, phone numbers, and all that stuff. I decide to just write down my cell number and my e-mail and say that we're in the very beginning stages of opening our spa so I don't have contact info there yet.

That seems believable, I think.

Soon the lady collects the sheets and calls the meeting to order. There are about fifteen people here and they all look like my mom—natural, relaxed, attentive.

"Welcome to the third meeting of the southeastern Connecticut and Rhode Island small business owners' discussion group," the lady starts. "For those newcomers, my name is Ruthie, and my husband and I just sold the Utopia Body and Wellness Spa in Providence, Rhode Island. We're in the process of figuring out our next steps." She owned a spa! It's such a great coincidence I almost can't believe it. She could really help us out. She smiles and she's so calming that all of my nervousness just washes away. Even if I do get discovered and found out for being a liar, I doubt she would get mad at me. She's too chill. "Let's go around the circle and say our name and what type of business we're opening."

The lady next to me starts and then goes around the circle the other way, which means I'll be the last one to say my name.

Most of them are from Rhode Island, which puts me more at ease. There's less of a chance that they'll recognize me or know my mom or grandma.

"I'm Louise Ramal, and my family and I are in the beginning stages of opening a spa in Manhattan. We're back and forth to our summer home in Waterside, and I stumbled upon this meeting and figured I'd check it out." I giggle out of nervousness and hope that I didn't just ramble on for way too long. Everyone else's introductions were just four seconds each.

"Welcome, Louise," the moderator says. "It's good you're

here in the beginning stages since there's so much that goes into opening any type of business."

A lady across the circle from me raises her hand. "Louise, honey, are you here with a parent or something?" she asks, smiling but confused.

"Oh, right, I'm a kid." I laugh. "You probably noticed that. Well, um, my parents were here with me, and my grandfather was staying home with my younger brother, but then my brother got sick, so they went home, and I just decided to stay." I laugh again. I need to stop this nervous laugh. "So I'll just sit and listen. If that's, um, OK."

Ruthie nods. "Sure. We're happy to have you, Louise."

As I suspected, much of what is discussed is way over my head. Stuff about plumbing and construction and zoning and permits. They also talk about how to fire a frustrating employee and how to properly budget for the slow periods. I stay quiet most of the time, but jot down notes every few minutes. Some of what they're saying could be very helpful later on.

With about ten minutes left in the meeting, the only man here raises his hand. "I know we touched on this a little bit," he starts, and I try hard to remember his name and where he's from, but I'm drawing a blank. "I'm opening my second restaurant in a few months, same name and brand and everything, but I'm tripped up again on the inspection stuff. It seems Connecticut is much harder for inspections than Rhode Island, and I feel like all the paperwork is getting lost in the shuffle."

A few ladies give him answers that sound really complicated to me. They involve calling someone in Hartford and then making sure all of their yellow forms are filled out in triplicate, not to worry about the green forms, and then keeping copies of everything in a safety-deposit box.

At this point in the meeting it's hard for me to sit still. I can see Sunny in the section next to us looking at her watch every few seconds and groaning, and all I can think about are lobster rolls and root beers. And of course calling Bevin back. I can't even imagine what happened to her. She could have gone back to her old self by now; she could be saying embarrassing things about me to everyone in Old Mill. The longer I wait, the worse it can get.

I'm glad I came. But now I need the meeting to end.

A few minutes later, Ruthie thanks everyone for coming and people start to leave.

"Louise," Ruthie calls to me. "I just wanted to let you know that if your parents have any questions about the group, they can e-mail me."

"Oh, OK, thanks."

"And I hope your brother feels better." She smiles.

Is she onto me? I can't tell.

"Oh, thanks. You know kids, they always get fevers."

"Right."

I pretend to peruse the children's section for a few minutes and then I quietly walk over to Sunny.

"Can we go now?" she says immediately.

"How did I sound?" I ask. I kind of expect her to say something mean, since I made her wait and she's been in such a bad mood.

"Great."

"You were really listening?" I ask her. "You promise?"

"Totally." She smiles, and I'm so relieved. "So—lobster rolls?"

"You know it." We leave the library and walk the few blocks to Lobster Landing. We can smell the delicious salty sea air as we walk, and I just want to grab a blanket and lie down on the beach and stare out at the ocean and up at the sky and not think about anything else.

There's a line at Lobster Landing, of course. It's always packed, any time of the day.

"You owe me for tonight," Sunny says after we've been quiet for a few minutes.

"Huh?"

"Evan asked me to go to the beach with him. Doesn't that sound so romantic? But I had to tell him no so I could come with you." She glares at me.

I stay quiet for a few seconds. I'm not sure what she wants me to say. "Oh, well, thanks."

"That's it? Just thanks?"

"I don't know, Sunny. You didn't give me a kidney or anything." I roll my eyes. "Sorry you gave up a night with your boyfriend."

I wish this conversation had never started, because I'm getting a nervous feeling in my stomach, and it's going to ruin my whole lobster roll experience.

"You don't get it," Sunny says after another few minutes of silence. "You don't have a real boyfriend, so you don't get it."

When did Sunny get so mean?

"I'm not talking to you now," I tell her. "I just want to eat my lobster roll in peace. Tell your mom to come pick us up."

"And you only call me when you need me to help you. Hanging out with AGE? Not telling me? Spending so much time with Bevin?" She sniffles. "I don't get you anymore."

I don't say anything because we're at the front of the line. I order a Connecticut-style lobster roll, chips, a pickle, and a root beer. Sunny orders a Maine-style and a cream soda.

We sit at one of the white picnic tables right on the water.

Lights twinkle all around us and boats sway back and forth where they're docked. It would be a perfect Connecticut night except for the feeling like I have a knotted rope in my stomach.

"You don't have anything to say to the fact that you've basically been avoiding me all summer?" Sunny asks.

I put down my lobster roll and say, "Sunny, how can you say that? You've been with Evan all summer. You don't even want to hang out with me."

"You know that's not true." She leans forward onto the table and glares at me. "You make no effort. You wait for me to call you. And when I don't, you hang out with AGE."

"That was once. Sheesh."

"You know I'm right and you can't even admit it or say you're sorry," Sunny says. "Let's just not talk for a bit."

We eat our lobster rolls in silence and we might as well be eating lima beans—that's how depressing this feels.

I debate it over and over again in my head and then I realize I can't just let this go.

"Sunny, how can you say that I need to apologize when it was really mean of you to say that I owe you for tonight because you could have been with your boyfriend," I tell her. "Yes, you have a boyfriend, but you also have a best friend."

She looks at me and I can tell she's not sorry. "You sound like some kind of cheesy inspirational quote people put on

Facebook. And besides, you haven't been acting like a best friend."

I look down at my plate. I still have half a lobster roll and my chips, but I can't even eat them. And I can't just stay quiet either. "But, Sunny, saying I owe you and that you gave something up takes all the niceness out of what you did."

She rolls her eyes. "The world doesn't revolve around you, Lucy."

"I know," I mumble.

"I like helping you, but you can't expect that I'm always going to do it." Her phone vibrates on the table and she looks at it. "My mom will be here in five minutes. Finish eating, OK?"

"I'm not hungry."

"Lucy, come on. Stop being so sensitive."

"I'm not sensitive. You're mean."

"Fine. I'm mean." She stands up to throw away her garbage. "Then if I'm mean, I might as well tell you that Yamir doesn't really like you. He never really liked you. I overheard him on the phone with Clint the other day and he was talking about how that girl Arianna in his grade is really pretty."

I stand up to throw away my garbage and when I get back to the table, Sunny's already walking away, toward the street and her mom's car.

I can't believe she just said that.

I don't know how this night changed tone so fast. She was supportive about me wearing her sari, but after that she was totally different, like she flicked a switch.

Maybe it was out of line to ask her to hang out at the library while I had the meeting. Maybe I asked too much of her. But even so, she's my best friend, and that's what best friends do for each other. Right?

Lucy's tip for a great summer:

Spend a lot of time on a lounge chair.

©unny's mom notices something is up because she says "You two are very quiet" at least three times, but unlike my mom, she doesn't press it. She senses that we just want to be quiet and she lets it go.

We pull into my driveway and I realize that I'm going to have to say some kind of good-bye, and whatever I say is going to seem awkward.

I unbuckle my seat belt and say, "Thank you Mrs. Ramal. Bye, Sunny," and leave it at that.

I go over the day and night in my head and I can't figure out what set Sunny off. She's really that mad about me hanging out with AGE? She knows we don't even really like them. She knows I was just doing it to help Bevin. Doesn't she? And then I wonder if what she said about Yamir is true. I want to just come out and ask him, but I don't think I can.

I walk inside and my mom, grandma, and Claudia are all sitting in the living room.

This can't be good.

"Luce, come sit with us," Grandma says.

"Be right there," I yell back. I run upstairs and drop my bag and splash some cold water on my face. All I want to do right now is throw on my bathing suit and go for a night swim. We have lights out there, so it's safe, and I can just float around on my pink raft and process everything that has happened without anyone bothering me. I throw Sunny's sari in the corner of my room. I decide to put on my bathing suit now and grab a towel so I can go out and swim as soon as we're done talking. Then I can call Bevin back while relaxing on a lounge chair.

"What's up?" I say as soon as I'm sitting down on one of the living room armchairs. "Oh, Mom, how'd your *Old Mill Observer* meeting go?"

"It went well, Luce. Thanks." She smiles, but I can tell there's something hanging in the air here. I'm not exactly sure what it is.

I keep waiting for someone to say something. Then I try to convince myself that this weird feeling is all in my head. Maybe they're just sitting and relaxing and enjoying each other's company.

"Lucy, I just got off the phone with Gary," Grandma says.

"Apparently Bevin got stuck at Annabelle Wilson's house, and she hoped you were going to meet her, but you didn't, and Bevin got upset. I don't really know the whole story."

"What? No. Bevin's friends with them now. She was fine on her own. She said so herself."

"Why is Bevin friends with Annabelle Wilson?" Claudia asks. "Why doesn't she just hang out with you and Sunny?"

Claudia's the kind of older sister who really knows her little sister's friends. It's usually nice. But at a time like this, it would be easier if she didn't have a clue.

"We met them at the boardwalk one day and they hit it off. I was trying to help Bevin, you know, become a little bit more social, and like, you know, help her be a little more normal." I feel my cheeks getting hot. I don't even know what I'm saying anymore.

"I don't understand what's really going on here," Mom says. "Why is Bevin upset?"

"I have no idea, honestly," I tell them. "I'll call her. OK?"

"That's a good idea," Grandma says, sitting up straighter on the couch.

I can't believe this is happening. First Sunny yells at me and then tells me Yamir doesn't like me anymore, and now I'm in trouble for trying to help Bevin become a better version of herself.

"I'm going swimming," I tell them, and leave the living room. No one tries to stop me.

I hear mumbles and whispers as I'm walking out the back door to the deck, but I ignore them.

This has to be some kind of joke. Some kind of bad dream.

I throw my towel down on the lounge chair and cannonball off the diving board. I feel myself sinking down to the bottom of the pool and then I pop back up and jump onto my favorite pink raft.

I float and float and float and I keep telling myself to think because if I think hard enough, I can figure out what to tell Sunny and Bevin and my family. But nothing comes to me. I guess it's because I don't think any of what happened is my fault. But if I tell them that, it will sound defensive, like I'm blaming other people for my problems.

The worst part of it is, even with all of the drama with Sunny and the weirdness with this Bevin situation, I'm still thinking about what Sunny said about Yamir, and how he thought that girl Arianna was pretty.

I need to know if that's true. Because if Yamir doesn't like me anymore, then I can stop worrying about it. I definitely don't need something else to worry about, so it might be a relief.

I spend the next hour or so floating and then my mom

pops her head out. "Luce, it's almost eleven thirty. Come in, please. I don't like you out here while everyone else is asleep."

I get out of the pool, shower, and get into pajamas. I write three different e-mails to Yamir but I don't send any of them. I write out text message after text message but then click DIS-CARD after each one.

I don't know what to say, so I decide to just leave it as is for tonight. I'm too tired to deal with anything else.

I check my e-mail one more time before bed, thinking that maybe Sunny e-mailed me an apology or something, but I only have one e-mail in my in-box. It's from ruthie .wolland@gmail.com.

Hello Louise,

I just wanted to tell you it was a pleasure to meet you at tonight's gathering. I noticed you were very quiet, so please feel free to e-mail me any questions or concerns you may have. Our next meeting won't be until September since so many of us will be away in August.

Best wishes,

Ruthie

Well, that was nice. At least a grown-up stranger who thinks my name is Louise cares about my questions or concerns.

I've been putting it off all night, but after hours of tossing and turning, I decide that there's one thing I have to do.

I started Bevin on this path and I can't just abandon her now. She stays up late, so I know it's OK to text her.

Bevin, sorry I couldn't talk before. R U still up?

I stare at my phone waiting for a text back, but I don't get one.

Lucy's tip for becoming a better person:
Apologize when you know you need to, and even sometimes when you don't think you need to.

The next morning I sleep really late. When my eyes finally open, it's after ten.

I'm upstairs washing my face and getting dressed when I hear my phone ring. Maybe it's Sunny calling to apologize. I let it go to voice mail and then I wait and wait and wait for the message. Nothing. Finally I check my missed calls and see that it was Yamir.

Now I'm stuck in that weird place not knowing if I should call him back or just ignore it.

Ten minutes later, the phone rings again. It's Yamir.

"Hello."

"I thought you'd never answer," he says.

"Oh. Sorry." I laugh, but I have no idea why.

"Wanna come to Great Escape today? Me, Clint, Anthony, maybe Sunny and Evan are all going."

I don't know what to say. "Um, I really can't, Yamir. I feel like I need to be at the spa so people take me seriously."

Right after I say it, I regret it. I can go. I know I can. No one cares if I'm at the spa. No one wants me to be at the spa, even though I hate admitting that to myself.

"You never want to do anything anymore, Luce-Juice."

"Don't say that." I start doodling on my desk blotter. Sometimes it helps me think more clearly. My thoughts are spiraling around in my head and I feel like I don't have control over what I'm going to say next. "Anyway, I heard you think that girl Arianna is really pretty. Why don't you invite her to Great Escape?"

"Huh?"

"That's what Sunny said." I should stop talking. I know I should. But I can't. "She said you were talking to Clint about her."

"You're crazy, Lucy," Yamir says, all disgusted-sounding. "And anyway, I'm tired of asking you to do things and you saying no."

"That's not true. I did the hot-dog-eating contest."

"I gotta go. And we leave tomorrow to visit my cousins in L.A." I hear the dinging sounds of his video game starting up in the background. "So I guess I'll see you around."

He hangs up.

Maybe I have been saying no a lot, but not all the time. I did the hot-dog-eating contest. And the other things weren't my fault. I had Bevin to deal with and all the stuff at the spa. He should be able to understand that.

I take one more look in the mirror before I head downstairs and notice I have a billion new freckles on the bridge of my nose and on my cheeks. That's pretty much the best sign of a good summer, except so much of this summer hasn't been good at all. I don't get how that's possible, but it just seems to be the way it is.

"Ready to go?" Claudia asks me when I'm downstairs.

"Yup."

"What's wrong, Lucy?"

"Nothing. I'm fine."

Claudia walks closer to me. "Yeah, right. I know you. You're my little sister. I can tell how you're feeling. And you're definitely not fine."

"I'm fine!" I shout, and run outside.

I wait for them by the side of the car.

She's right. I'm not fine. I know I'm not fine. My best friend hates me and my almost-boyfriend doesn't want to be my almost-boyfriend anymore. Even my makeover project, Bevin, hasn't called me back. I'm not even allowed to help at the spa I helped create.

I am so not fine. And all I want is to be fine again. I just don't know how to get there.

When I get to the pharmacy, I try to just lie low and organize some shelves and stay out of everyone's way. I have to admit that I'm a little nervous about Bevin. If she hasn't called, she must be really upset, and if she's upset, Gary is too, and if I could make myself invisible right now, I would.

As soon as I hear the stairs from the upstairs apartment creaking, I make myself as busy as possible, taking all the shampoo bottles off the shelf and then putting them back up as neatly as I can.

"Lucy. We need to talk," Bevin says, standing behind me.

My project is backfiring. I'm regretting my decision to give Bevin a personality and life-skills makeover. Suddenly she's bold and confident and I'm about to be in huge trouble.

"OK, let's go over here, Bevin," I whisper, and guide her to the Relaxation Room. Unfortunately, there's a group of middle-aged ladies in there discussing the college application process. "Let's go outside. I changed my mind."

Once we're outside, I take a deep breath. "First of all, I'm really—"

Bevin interrupts me. "No, I talk first. You totally ditched me. I barely know Annabelle and them and I thought you were going to meet me," she yells. "And then they started prank-calling people in the grade, and they made me do it too. And I don't even know these people!"

People on the sidewalk are watching us have this conversation and I think it's bad for business. We need to look happy and relaxing.

"Bevin, I'm sorry, I thought you were OK to go on your own. And then I had to go to this meeting, and time got away from me."

"What meeting?"

Uh-oh. Suddenly I realize I shouldn't tell her about the business owners' group. I don't know how to get out of this one.

"Oh, just Earth Club stuff, really, no big deal."

"Yeah, that's another thing those girls were saying—you like projects. The way you made Sunny more confident when she liked Evan Mass, and how you're now obsessed with making the school green, and of course all the stuff with Old Mill Pharmacy. They said the only reason you're helping me is because I'm a project." She pauses and sniffles a bit. "Not because you really care about me."

My throat goes lumpy. "Bevin, that's not true at all. I . . . um . . . of course I care about you."

"Well, you say that now, but when I called you last night, you couldn't even talk to me, and it took you forever to call me back." She sniffles again. "Forget it, Lucy. I know the truth. You never liked me. You just needed a project because no one really wanted you involved in the spa opening."

Wow. That was harsh. I created a monster. I succeeded in turning Bevin confident and social, but now she's also really mean.

Bevin folds her arms across her chest. "Let's just take a break on the life makeover, OK? And maybe also a break from each other."

I don't respond.

"Bye, Lucy." She walks away before I have a chance to say anything else.

Lucy's tip for a great summer:

When it's too hot to be outside, go to the movies to be in the air-conditioning and get a supersized fountain soda.

The next few days feel like walking through cotton candy. The air is so sticky hot that it's hard to breathe or even be outside for a minute. The only way to stay outdoors is to stay in the pool the entire time.

Sunny and Yamir are off in Los Angeles. I haven't heard from them at all, except for a text from Sunny at the airport saying good-bye and that our favorite book series is front and center at the airport bookstore.

Gary signed Bevin up for some kind of sailing camp. Apparently he didn't want her hanging around the store so much. Which really means he didn't want her hanging around me so much.

I'm a pariah. No one wants to be near me. Sad, but true.

I guess the one needing a life makeover is me. And as soon as I figure out where to start, I will.

Anais is constantly running around dealing with the inspection. I thought it would have been dealt with already, but apparently not.

The funny thing is, all the people from that small business owners' group have been e-mailing nonstop about inspection problems. That woman Ruthie is apparently the guru and knows how to fix just about any inspection issue, though. So they're lucky to have her.

Some of the new spa employees have already started working, and they have a few appointments each day. It's more like an orientation, since the spa can't totally open until after the inspection is complete. They seem nice enough, but I don't really feel close to them yet.

Even though I was pretty much told to stay out of official spa business, I still check the e-mails a few times a day. When a new e-mail comes in I write the appointment down in the official appointment book and I send the customer a confirmation e-mail.

No one's asked who's doing it. Maybe they forget to check the e-mails. But I like doing it, and this way I'm at least doing something.

I've also been writing back and forth with Sarabeth, the stressed-out bride, making sure all of her appointments are in order. She has eight bridesmaids and they're all getting hair and makeup, plus her mom, her mother-in-law, and four grandmothers. That's a lot of appointments, so even if they're the only people who book for the grand opening, we're still in good shape.

"Yoo-hoo. Anyone here?" I hear someone saying. I don't recognize the voice right away.

I peek my head out from the spa reception area and see that it's Mayor Danes. His chief of staff, Amelia, is with him, wearing a pencil skirt and white blouse. It's really kind of amazing she's not sweating through it. I guess she's the kind of person who never sweats.

"Hi!" I say, and walk over to them.

"Oh, hello, Lucy!" Mayor Danes shakes my hand and I suddenly feel very official. "You're just the girl I wanted to see."

"I am?"

He nods. "Yessiree. I am working on the official press release for the grand opening. Can you believe it's in two weeks?"

I shake my head. I need to see a calendar. I wonder if we're really even ready to open this spa in two weeks.

"Well, I want to make sure I have everything correct, and I'd love to get a few quotes from you," he says. "Also, I know you're working on the Going Green proposal for the Old Mill School Board and I'd love to work that in." He smiles a big politician's smile.

"OK."

"I can't miss an opportunity to highlight our wonderful schools," he adds. "Amelia's going to record this so we have everything correct. Where should we go sit down?"

"Um." I look around. I don't see anyone. That hasn't happened in a long time. "Let's go to the spa office. It's all new and beautiful."

I'm surprised Mayor Danes didn't make this all official and set it up with Anais or my grandma in advance. I'm surprised he isn't asking to talk to them. But I'm not complaining!

We walk slowly into the spa area and I casually look around to make sure no one's there. But it's totally empty and quiet. I wonder if Anais called a special meeting and left me out on purpose. It sounds like I'm being paranoid, but that's totally something she would do.

I can't believe how amazing I thought she was in the beginning. She's one of those people who make a great first impression and that's it.

"Ready?" Mayor Danes asks Amelia.

"Yes, sir!" she says in a jokey voice. She always looks very official and serious, but she can be funny too. I like that. She hits the RECORD button on her iPad, and I start picking my cuticles out of nervousness.

"So," Mayor Danes starts. "I know the whole story behind this wonderful spa, but will you please refresh my memory?"

I smile. Mayor Danes is such a kind man. I bet he could be president if he wanted to. He'd get the Republicans and the Democrats to get along really well just because he's so nice. Sometimes I wonder if the secret to doing well in life is just being nice. Being nice and doing the right thing, and that's it.

Right then as I'm talking about the whole idea behind the spa and everything that happened, I realize that there are a few things I have to do. I need to be more like Mayor Danes. I need to always know the right thing, and if I don't know it, then I need to try to figure it out. Sometimes you need to be the bigger person and apologize even if you've been hurt too. Sometimes you need to really try to put yourself in someone else's position.

As soon as I'm done with this interview, I need to do the right thing.

"And tell me how the Earth Club at Old Mill Middle School influenced your work at your family's pharmacy," he says. One of his legs is crossed over the other and I notice that he has purple socks on.

He catches me staring at them and he says, "Oh, I always wear purple socks." He laughs. "You never noticed before?"

I shake my head.

"Yup. I made a bet with a student once. If he did his homework and got at least a B for the year, I'd wear purple socks every single day."

"Really?" I ask. "You were a teacher?"

He nods. "Yup. For ten years."

It makes sense that Mayor Danes was a teacher, because he really cares about people, especially kids. He thinks kids can do as much as adults can. "So I really started going to Earth Club because of my best friend, Sunny. Her mom made her go and she wanted me to go with her, and so I did and that changed everything."

I hope he doesn't include the mom-making-her-go part in the press release, but I can't exactly tell him what to include and what not to include. But as I'm talking, I realize that so much of what has happened at the pharmacy and with the spa is because of Sunny. Maybe she's right. Maybe I did take her for granted.

It's funny, but right now it feels like I just keep having epiphany after epiphany. It's like this conversation with Mayor Danes is shedding light on all these issues in my life.

I know he used to be a teacher, but maybe he used to be a psychologist too. Or maybe he's just a really good listener and he asks the right questions.

When we finish with the official interview part we sit talking, and he tells me all about his daughter who is a Rhodes scholar studying in London and his son who opened a gluten-free bakery in Seattle.

"I'm so proud of them," he says. "They're good kids. They really know—"

Our conversation is interrupted by shouts. Familiar-sounding shouts. My mom and grandma fighting. It's weird, though, because I haven't heard them yelling like this in a really long time.

"I told you to handle the paperwork," Grandma says. "I told you we needed an extra set of eyes!"

"I did! I did!" Mom's screaming and running behind Grandma as she walks through the pharmacy. Luckily I don't see any customers, since it's pretty early in the day.

"Jane! Doris!" I see Anais running behind them too, and without meaning to, I burst out laughing. It's ridiculous to see three grown woman running through the store like maniacs with their hands in the air. It's not like they have to chase the paperwork before it gets away.

"Um, maybe you should go," I whisper to Mayor Danes and Amelia. "I'm sure everything's fine, but you know how it is, it gets stressful when you're trying to open a business."

He nods. "OK, let's keep this as our secret. Not the press release, but that I witnessed all the screaming and running." He smiles. "I don't want to embarrass anyone."

See what I mean? He's so nice. He just does the right thing.

"We'll sneak out this side door," he whispers, and then gathers all his stuff. "See you soon, Lucy. And again, I'm so proud of you. And so impressed."

After they leave, I peek my head out from the spa area and see Mom, Grandma, Anais, and Gary lurking near the pharmacy office.

"Jane, you were the one who was responsible for dotting all the i's and crossing all the t's," Grandma says with her hands on her hips. "I am holding you responsible."

"Mom. Relax." My mom puts a hand on Grandma's shoulder. "I was looking it over, but these snafus happen all the time. Right, Anais?"

I'm having trouble getting the whole picture of their conversation, so I move out of the spa area and into the pharmacy. Anais has her arms across her chest. She's breathing heavily.

"They do happen all the time." She pauses and looks at the floor. "But I hate to tell you this, guys—the person I've been working with has left for vacation. It seems we're not going to have the paperwork in order to open Labor Day weekend."

"What?" Grandma says, more like an exclamation than a question.

"I'm so sorry. I'm so sorry." Anais is sniffling. "This is my fault. I should have stayed on top of it. I'm so sorry." Then she runs out of the pharmacy.

"Gary?" Grandma looks at him with her eyebrows raised. "Any ideas?"

He exhales out of the side of his mouth in this over-the-top exasperated way. "Dor, here's the thing. We can still do the ribbon cutting and the hoopla, and just postpone appointments."

Is he serious? What about Sarabeth? If we cancel, her mom will kill her. And it's her wedding day. That can't happen. I'm about to open my mouth to tell them that when I get a feeling like I should stay quiet. It seems my yelling will only make things worse.

Mom, Gary, and Grandma stand there looking at each other and I go back into the spa area. Anais told all the spa employees to take the rest of the day off since we didn't have any appointments and technically they're not legally allowed to work in the spa yet.

I go back to the computer to make sure Sarabeth didn't have any other questions. There's another appointment request from someone named Palmer Simone.

What a cool name. I open it up.

Hello! I know it's last-minute, but I'm in charge of the bachelorette/shower for my sister Walker. She, her six bridesmaids, and I are staying at the Old Mill Inn over Labor Day weekend. We'd love to get facials and massages at Pink & Green and bring in drinks and food. I'm wondering if it's possible for us to rent out the spa area for Saturday night. Let me know.

Thank you,

Palmer Simone

That would be great for business. And it wouldn't take away from other appointments since it's at night, but I can't answer her now because I don't know if we'll be allowed to do it. I'll keep the message as new and get back to her as soon as I can.

I click back over to my personal e-mail, where there are tons more back-and-forth discussion e-mails from the small business owners' group. I really don't have time to look at it now. But there's also an e-mail from my dad.

Hey Lu-ney Tune,

The countdown is on! Four days until I see you. I'm taking a cab from the airport and I'll pick you and Claud up at the house for a day of fun and surprises before the wedding. We got an e-mail last week. Get this—they're apparently only serving raw food for most of the wedding. Yuck. OK, love you.

See you soon.

Dad

A day of fun and surprises? Normally I'd go crazy trying to figure out what he's planning. I'd ask Sunny what she thinks and we'd come up with all these elaborate plans like a hot-air balloon ride to New York City and then a Broadway show and shopping spree at FAO Schwarz and sushi at Morimoto and a hot-air balloon ride back.

But I don't have time to come up with elaborate plans now. I have work to do. I have to figure out how I can get this spa opening back on track. I can't cancel on Sarabeth after we bonded on the Fourth of July and she confided in me. And the bachelorette party for Palmer's sister sounds amazing and fun. I want to make that happen.

I can't just sit at a computer and think. I need to literally be touching the keys or reading something. It helps my brain process. So I read articles online and check back through the spa e-mail to see if I've missed anything and then I go back to my personal e-mail to see if Yamir or Sunny e-mailed me anything from L.A.

Nothing in either account.

All I have to read is the boring business group e-mails about things I don't really understand. But I hate seeing all those new e-mails highlighted in my in-box. I like to have everything clean, showing that all is read and I don't have any new messages. So I click through them and skim them, looking for coupons and discounts that some of the businesses offer for group members and friends of group members. Maybe if the grand opening of our spa falls apart, I can send Sarabeth and Palmer to another spa in the group. I guess that wouldn't be the worst thing ever.

Outside in the pharmacy, I hear Grandma helping a customer with one of our custom gift baskets. The customer wants to take all these fancy bath products over to her friend who just had a baby.

Mom's on the phone in the pharmacy office. I can't hear everything she's saying, but it's probably about the inspection or a story for the *Old Mill Observer*. She takes her sort-of staff writer position very seriously, even though it's not even full-time.

I wonder if Anais is at her apartment now, packing up, ready to go somewhere else. Or what if she loses her job all together because she messed up everything for Pink & Green?

Yeah, she got a little crazy after a while, and she didn't

really want me involved with anything, but she's good at her job. I just wanted her to like me and to realize that I knew what I was talking about. I didn't want her to get fired.

I'm reading through more of the business owners' group e-mails, all this stuff about misfiled paperwork, and certain forms needing stamps, and other forms needing to be clipped and not stapled, and that's when it occurs to me. I don't know why it took so long. Sometimes forcing myself to figure things out isn't necessary when the answer is really right in front of me.

Sometimes if you just open your eyes and calm down, you realize all the resources you have right at your fingertips.

Lucy's tip for becoming a better person:
Find a role model. Or a few role models.

I've just had so many epiphanies, I almost
don't know what to do first.

"I'm going to do research for Earth Club," I call out
to the pharmacy as I'm leaving. I don't want to get into a
lengthy conversation with Mom and Grandma where they
ask where I'm going, so instead, I just run out of the store. If
they really need me or get worried, they can call me on my
cell phone.

It seems like God is looking out for me, because Ruthie
volunteers at the southeastern Connecticut food co-op a few
days a week, and this just so happens to be one of the days she's
there. I wonder if she knows my mom. My mom used to work
here back in the day before she got so fed up with the people.
All they did was sit around and talk about all these amazing
things they were doing, but they never actually did anything.

Instead of stocking shelves or bagging groceries, they'd just sit there talking about how amazing it is to use cloth diapers. Finally my mom got so mad she quit.

I wonder if Ruthie's one of those sit-around-and-talk-instead-of-doing people. I doubt it.

"Louise!" Ruthie yells as she sees me coming in. I guess she recognizes me even without the sari on. The co-op is walking distance from the pharmacy, but it's over a hundred degrees, so I'm dripping with sweat when I get there. "Let me get you some water."

It turns out Ruthie is one of the managers, so she's allowed to go in the back office and talk. She guides me there and hands me a jar, like an old cleaned-out pickle jar, full of water with a lemon slice. Some people love to use jars for glasses. It's kind of cool, and very green—reusing the jars is better than throwing them away!

"How can I help?" Ruthie pulls her frizzy gray curls into a tortoiseshell clip, which makes it look like she's ready for business.

I debated the whole way over whether or not I should tell Ruthie my real name and admit that I lied. I decided I had to come clean. I need real help here.

It was probably wrong of me to lie, but I hope Ruthie understands why I did it.

I tell her the whole story, about the pharmacy and the spa and Anais and the inspection.

She smiles this calming grown-up smile and sits back in her chair. "I know who you are, Lucy. I knew the whole time."

"Really?"

"Yes." She smiles. "Your mother and I go way back. She's a doll."

I should've figured, but somehow it was easier to be Louise Ramal for a little while. Sometimes you need to pretend a little bit to get where you want to be. It's like that saying: "Fake it till you make it." If you act like you belong, you will be treated that way. It doesn't really make sense, but it's just the way it is.

"Here's what you need to do," Ruthie says, leaning forward in her chair. "Go find Anais, get all the paperwork you can, every single thing even if you think it's not necessary, especially the forms from the inspector. Then come back here."

"Please don't call my mom or grandma," I say, suddenly worried. "I don't want to involve them. You'd think they'd believe me by now that I can handle things and help things, but for some reason they don't."

"Lucy, here's one thing you should remember," Ruthie says softly. "In some people's eyes, you will always be a kid. It's just how it is. And you will grow to appreciate it."

Ruthie's one of those people who has a calming presence.

She could be talking about the country's deficit and how much in debt we are to China, and it would seem calming.

"OK. I'll try to remember that."

"It's going to work out," she tells me.

I stand up. "Thank you so much."

"You're very welcome. Good luck."

It feels like a billion degrees, like I'm walking through a fire pit in a fur coat, but I start running anyway. Anais's apartment is about a mile from the co-op, but I can do it. I throw my backpack over my shoulders and put my hair up in a high bun and I run. I run and run and run and I'm huffing and puffing and worried I may pass out on the sidewalk, but I keep running. It feels good. I suddenly understand why people who love running talk about it all the time. It feels like I'm literally releasing all the stress and frustration into the air and it's leaving me and hopefully won't ever come back.

I finally get to Anais's apartment complex. Before I ring her bell, I go out on the beach and breathe in the salty sea air. There's something about ocean air that makes all of your problems seem small. The salty smell and the view of the ocean and the waves make every problem seem fixable. Everything can be solved, if you take a few minutes to look at the ocean before dealing with it.

I can't let any more time slip away, so I walk into Anais's

apartment building and tell the doorman that I know her and that I can just go up and ring the bell. I don't want the doorman to call up to her in case she doesn't let me up.

The doorman agrees and I go to the elevator and push floor number five, and then I walk to her apartment. I use the silver knocker, and after a few seconds, Anais comes to the door.

"Lucy," she says with a hint of surprise.

"Hi, Anais, I know you don't really like me, but can I come in for a minute? I think I can help."

She sighs. "I never said I didn't like you, Lucy."

I probably shouldn't have said that.

"Come in."

I walk in slowly, expecting to find boxes all over the place. But her apartment looks just as lovely as it did when I was there over the Fourth of July. Maybe she's not running away as fast as I thought she was.

"Would you like some lemonade? Water? It's so hot." Anais has a ceiling fan going and the door to the balcony open and it actually feels so lovely and cool. I can hear the ocean. If I were her, I'd sleep with the windows open every single night.

"Lemonade would be great," I tell her. When she's in the kitchen, I sit back on her couch and look out the window and

I imagine myself living here as a grown-up. I'd throw dinner parties and we'd play board games and go for late-night swims in the pool and the ocean.

"So," she says when she gets back to the couch with the lemonade.

"Here's the thing. I'll make it quick," I start, and then take a second to collect my thoughts. I don't want it to seem like I know better than Anais, because I obviously don't. I just know this one thing. "A few weeks ago I snuck out to this Connecticut and Rhode Island small business owners' meeting because . . . well, I just felt like I wanted to be a part of things, and I didn't know how to be. When I was there, I met this woman, Ruthie, who runs the group. She can handle any inspection problem, and so I came to talk to you and we can collect the papers, and um, she can help us." I decide it's time to stop talking. I've probably already said too much.

"Lucy, that's very sweet of you," she says, and I'm waiting for the "but," the reason why it won't work and I should give up trying right now.

"So you'll do it?" I ask.

"Do what?"

"I mean, um, you'll listen to me, and we can organize the paperwork and then go back to Ruthie and then, um, see what happens?" I'm rambling and can't seem to stop. Maybe it's the sugary lemonade going to my head, or the relaxing salty ocean air breeze.

"Sure. Whatever you think." Anais smiles. "Everything got crazy back there. I really love your family and your pharmacy and the spa, and I want things to work out for the grand opening Labor Day weekend. So if you know of a way to help, it can't hurt to try."

"Great!" I jump up and move to hug her, and it feels like such a relief that I didn't have to battle it out with her. She just listened to me, and believed me, and has faith that I can help.

It's that whole bring-your-own-chair philosophy. If you just go into it, and bring everything you've got, people will trust you eventually.

"We're going to need to go back to the spa, though, and grab all the files," Anais tells me. "I'm not sure what your mom or grandma will think."

It occurs to me that maybe Anais is nervous to see them after the whole argument. I'm nervous to see them too, and I haven't done anything wrong.

"You're right." I stop to think for a second, wondering if maybe they have plans and they'll be out somewhere. I doubt it. They rarely have plans.

I text Claudia to see what's going on at the store. I realize I didn't even see her before I left.

Hey claud. What r u up to?

A few seconds later, she texts me back.

Mom, Grandma and I r @ Sil's to look for a dress
4 Mom 4 Esme's wedding. U @ earth club still?

I totally forgot! Today was the big shopping day. My mom
hates shopping, so she had to make this whole big production
of scheduling a day when we could go with her to find a dress.
Sil's is this boutiquey shop in North Mill and it's the only
place my mom shops. I was supposed to go with them and
they must think I bailed for Earth Club. Oh well.

Yup. So sorry I forgot. Get Mom something
good! Xo

"OK, coast is clear," I tell Anais. "They're all out shopping. I guess Tory and Charise are covering the store. Who
knows where Gary is, but he's so oblivious, I bet he won't even
notice us in the spa getting the files."

"He is really oblivious, right?" Anais laughs. "I must've
asked him thirty times to go over all the order forms and
invoices and he was barely paying attention." She stops talk-

ing for a second, and dabs on some lip balm. "Not that I'm placing blame."

"Yeah, he's a scatterbrain. My mom is too. That's why they can't get along." I laugh. I don't know why I'm sharing these family secrets with Anais, but it seems like it's easing the tension.

"I think Gary's in love with your mom," Anais adds, and then covers her mouth. "Oops. I've said too much."

I crack up. "No, it's OK. It's never gonna happen. He's been in love with her for years. My dad's coming back in a few days and going to a wedding with my mom. They were invited separately; they're still good friends with this woman Esme they knew in college. She's seriously a crazy person, but they stay friends. I don't know why."

Anais nods. "My parents are divorced too. I get it."

"Oh, they're not divorced," I add. "Just separated. They get along. I've heard them on the phone and stuff."

Anais nods again. I know what she's thinking. That I have all this false hope and I should get over the idea that they're going to get back together. I've seen that nod and that expression from a million people before. I don't care, though. I still have hope. I think it can happen.

Lucy's tip for a great summer:

Walk along a boardwalk as often as you can.

$I'm\ glad\ you\ made\ up$ with Bevin," Anais says as we're in a cab on the way back to the pharmacy. Anais gets to take cabs back and forth since she doesn't have a car and her company pays all expenses. It's a really nice life, if you ask me.

"I didn't make up with her yet," I say, confused. "I've been planning out exactly what I want to say. I totally messed up."

"She told me you did." Anais gives me a crooked smile and I'm not really sure what it means. "She said you apologized and you went out for ice cream at 384 Sprinkles and then got manicures or something?"

I giggle nervously. "That sounds fun, but it didn't actually happen."

"The manicure part seemed a little iffy, since you guys practically live in a spa that just hired manicurists." Anais laughs too. Even this story is really funny, I'm not sure what I should do about it.

"She just wants to be your friend, Lucy," Anais adds after a few minutes of awkward silence with only the cab's eighties music station breaking the tension.

"Yeah. I know. I was actually starting to like her."

"I guess she made up that whole story because that's what she wishes would happen," Anais says. "But she'll be leaving soon anyway, to go back to Manhattan, right?"

I nod. "Yeah, I guess right after Labor Day."

"Today's the last day of her sailing camp," Anais tells me.

"I'll make up with her," I say. "For real this time."

The cab lets us out right in front of the pharmacy. Inside, I see Tory and Charise helping customers and everything going smoothly even without Grandma or Mom or me there. It's good to know we can all take a break once in a while and not have to worry.

We rush into the spa area and Anais goes straight to the pink filing cabinet behind the reception desk. All of the filing cabinets and supply cabinets are either pink or green, and some are pink-and-green striped. When I think about the time it took to order these supplies, it's amazing we got it done and with a few weeks to spare. The tables are covered with that soft paper, and the towels are rolled up neatly in baskets.

I want the grand opening to be now! I want to greet the customers and I want to welcome them and I want to hear all the compliments about how amazing Pink & Green is.

"Well, this is it." Anais shows me about four folders stuffed full of paper. "It's all organized by date. I have the sign-off from B. Bond, the inspector." She points to the signature and everything.

"If we have the sign-off, what happened? Why aren't we approved or whatever?"

Anais sighs. "Apparently it wasn't filed the right way, and we missed the person who does the filing because he's away the next two weeks." She rolls her eyes. "You'd think anyone could handle the filing, since it's the actual inspection that matters, but it's all red tape."

I still don't understand it, but Ruthie said she could help.

I sit at the spa reception desk while I'm waiting for Anais to finish gathering all the paperwork. I look at the beautiful Pink & Green notepad and business cards that just came in. I love the font on everything—curly and cute and feminine. Mom really did an amazing job with the branding. She even found these pink-and-green-striped gift bags so if people buy products to take home, they're carrying them in style. And the best part is that all our paper stuff is made out of recycled materials; even the gift bags are reusable. We're totally true to our eco-spa mission.

Anais comes back over to me with another folder. "E-mails back and forth," she says. She's wearing an ivory sundress and gold strappy sandals and, truthfully, she should've been the one to take Mom shopping. Anais has the best fashion sense out of any of us.

She's also probably right about Bevin. As soon as this whole inspection thing is taken care of, and Ruthie helps us, I'm going to smooth things over with Bevin.

Slowly but surely I'm checking things off my worry list. Soon all I'll have to worry about is Sunny and Yamir. But they're still in California, and I think a little time away will do all of us good. Besides, I can't fix everything at once!

Lucy's tip for becoming a better person:

Ask for help when you need it.

We're waiting for the cab to pick us up when my phone rings. I told Anais that we could walk to the food co-op from here, but she decided that it's way too hot to walk even a few inches. I pretty much agree with her, especially after running all the way to her apartment.

"Hello?" I say, worried that it's going to be Ruthie telling us not to even bother coming. The number on the caller ID came up as private.

"Luce! Guess what? Mom found an ah-may-zing dress!" Claudia shouts. "Come over here, now. Bean can pick you up!"

"Um." As nice as it is that Claudia thought to call me, I really can't just drop everything and go over there right now. "I can't, actually. But I am so so so so excited about Mom's dress. I'll see it later tonight."

"No. It's going to the tailor for alterations in an hour. You need to see it now."

She's acting a little crazy. "I can't, Claud. You know how important this school board proposal is." I pause and I hear voices in the background, but I can't tell who's talking. I didn't know Sil's was such a popular store. It always seemed like a weird combination of hippie and old lady to me.

"Lucy! Seriously. Just come. Bean will get you at school in ten minutes. Finish up." She's talking with a list of instructions and commands, not suggestions. She's talking like I don't have a choice.

"I can't. Also, my phone's dying. I gotta go. Love you."

I hang up and exhale and pray that Bean doesn't just show up at school.

"What was that all about?" Anais asks, startling me. For a second, I forgot she was even there.

"My sister was insisting that I go over to this boutique to see a dress my mom bought for that wedding this weekend." I brush some sweat off my forehead. "I don't get why it's such a big deal. It's not like it's her best friend's wedding or anything. They talk once a year."

Thinking about that makes me sad. What if that's what happens to Sunny and me one day? What if we become busy grown-ups who only have time to talk once a year? We talk pretty much once an hour now—or at least, we did before our fight—so it would really have to be seriously bad to turn into once a year. I try to brush that worry away. There's no way that will ever happen.

The cab pulls up and we get in, and thankfully the air-conditioning is going at its highest speed. It's a three-minute drive, so we're there in a flash and the driver doesn't even charge us. He drives Anais around all the time, so he says he'll get us on the next ride.

Claudia keeps calling me and I keep hitting IGNORE. I don't get it. It's like when she wants me, I have to be there in a second. But when she doesn't, or when she's busy with Bean or college, she totally forgets I exist. I wish we could find some kind of middle ground.

Also, it's really kind of sad that all Mom, Grandma, and Claudia care about is this dress when we have an inspection to worry about. They don't even care that the spa may not open, after all our hard work. It doesn't make sense.

Ruthie's waiting for us at the front of the co-op. She leads us toward the office. "Have a seat, ladies," she tells us. "I'm going to call my friend Patch and I think he'll know exactly what to do."

It's hard to believe I was just here a few hours earlier. It feels like that was weeks ago. It's only three o'clock, but it feels like midnight.

"Hey, Patch, it's Ruthie," she says into the phone. I like when people use the nickname Patch for guys named Patrick. It sounds so cute. "Yup, got another one. Uh-huh. I'll hold."

She puts the phone on speaker, sits back in her rolling chair, and says to us, "I see on your forms that it was Brandon Bond who did your inspection. He's an OK guy, but he's messed up the filing many times. That's why you're in trouble."

I wait for her to say more, but she doesn't. I wonder if our "trouble" is the kind of trouble that can be solved. Or not.

"After you talk to Patrick, what can we do? I mean, what's the next step?" Anais asks. "I've been in this business for fifteen years, opened spas in fifteen states, but I've never run into the kind of nitty-gritty I have here."

Ruthie nods. "I know. So many balls in the air." She types something into her computer and looks back at us.

"I didn't get the whole story here," Anais says. "Which spa is yours? Is it the Green Oasis in Ferry Port or the Dove and Canary in South Brookfield?"

Ruthie laughs. "Actually, we just sold our spa a few weeks ago. We're in the process of opening a bed-and-breakfast."

Anais nods, and Patrick comes back on the line. Ruthie picks up the phone and takes him off speaker.

"Right." She pauses. "Yes, they have." Pause again. "Yes, they have done everything, with ample time, every form is filled out in beautiful handwriting." She smiles at Anais. "I have it right here." Ruthie makes a face as if Patrick is talking too much, and she has her finger holding a spot on a piece of paper, like she doesn't want to lose what she was looking for. "Yes, it's dhg3727883mag." She takes a deep breath and gives us two thumbs-up. "Thank you so much, Patch. You always come through for me. But you need to talk to Brandon about why he's making so many mistakes." She claps quietly. "Right. OK, take care, Patch. Have a great rest of the summer."

Ruthie hangs up and exhales again. She goes to fill a few drinking jars with this organic sparkling apple juice. She hands a jar to Anais and one to me. "Cheers, ladies!" We clink jars. "You did it."

"You did it!" I yell. "Ruthie, you saved the day."

"Well, Louise Ramal, I think *you* saved the day."

I smile, and Anais looks at me, confused. I don't feel like explaining the whole name thing—that can be my private joke with Ruthie. I have a feeling we'll keep in touch.

We stay and chat with Ruthie for a few minutes, and then Ruthie has to go do a shift shelving produce. Anais wants to get back to the apartment and shower before meeting everyone back at the spa later this evening.

"Shouldn't you be getting to Sil's?" Anais asks.

"I doubt they're still there," I tell her. "I'll go back to the pharmacy and tidy the shelves and wait for them."

Anais calls the cab again (I swear, she refuses to walk anywhere, I don't get how she stays so thin), and the driver drops me off at the pharmacy before he drops her off at her apartment.

I walk in, and there's a line of customers behind the pharmacy counter. Charise is handling their purchases. Everyone seems happy, though, and a few people are waiting in the Relaxation Room. All the lights are off in the spa area. I wave hi to Charise and Tory and walk around making sure the shelves are nice and neat, the way Grandma likes them. Everything looks perfect.

But I don't see any of my family anywhere. They can't all still be at Sil's—it's not that big or interesting of a store. I decide to go to the pharmacy office to play on the computer until they get back. Maybe they went out for a snack.

As I get closer to the office, I hear voices—Mom's, Grandma's, Claudia's, and a male voice. It's hard to hear well with all the customers chatting and laughing, but I'm pretty sure it's not Bean's voice that I'm hearing.

I hurry back and push the door open.

"Luney-Tune!"

My dad is here! My dad is here!

Right then all of my doubts and anger and frustration melt away like the last few seconds of a lit candle. He's here and that's all that matters.

"I thought you weren't coming until tomorrow!" I yell, and run into him, practically knocking him down with the force of my hug.

"Surprise!"

"You're here. You're really here. Really and truly here."

"Yeah, Luce." Claudia hits my arm, while I'm still hugging Dad. "We wanted to surprise you at Sil's and all go out for lobster rolls and chowder for lunch, but you were not where you said you were."

Mom's smile quickly changes to a grimace, like she just remembered she was mad at me. "Yes, young lady. Where were you? Why did you lie?" She pats the chair next to her. "Sit. Then spill."

"And Lucy, I know you're happy your father is here, but this is a serious discussion," Grandma adds. "How can we trust you to work at the spa when we don't know where you are?"

I can't believe this is happening. Everyone's ruining my amazing moment with my dad. But I guess I can understand why. I was shady on the phone and then I stopped answering calls and texts. This is my chance to really live my do-the-right-thing philosophy. I was wrong and I need to own up to that.

"Nowhere. She's run away," Bean says, walking into the office.

And then he sees me. He raises a fist in the air. "There you are!" He's laughing, so I know he's not that mad. I don't think Bean really gets mad. "I thought you got hired as the entertainment on a cruise line! Or joined the circus! Or opened your own spa!" He winks at me. "I was worried sick!"

Everyone cracks up, and Dad says, "I like this guy."

I like him too. I just don't want to say it out loud.

"I was keeping my location a secret," I start.

"Of course you were," Grandma interrupts. "Always up to something, my granddaughter." She smiles, so I know she's not really mad. Just a little bit.

"I solved the problem with the inspection," I tell them.

"Lucy," my mom says in her what-have-you-done-now tone.

"No, really, I did," I say. "Ask Anais. It's a whole long story, but basically I know someone who knows someone at the state office who helped us. We passed the inspection with flying colors, the paperwork was just misfiled. It was a whole big misunderstanding. All someone named Brandon's fault."

Grandma looks confused. "But it's all set? Anais will tell me we're all set to open in a week?"

"Yup."

Dad high-fives me, and then everyone starts high-fiving.

"Lucy saved the day again," Claudia says.

"Seems to me Lucy's always the one who saves the day," Bean adds.

"I like you, Bean." I high-five him again.

It was the right time to say it out loud.

Lucy's tip for a great summer:
Build sand castles, but don't worry
if they get knocked down.

Claudia, Bean, Dad, and I spend all of Thursday together. We go out for the famous egg and cheese sandwiches at Amity Deli, right on the beach. And then we play in the sand for hours, like we did when we were little. Dad builds these intricate sand castles that have all these different chimneys and additions and even windows. We of course have lobster rolls for lunch and have a root-beer-drinking contest. Bean wins, but I came close. Bean drank ten huge cups of root beer. I had eight and a half.

And soon it's time for us to head back to the house so that Dad and Mom can leave for Esme's wedding. It's at this holistic yoga center in the middle of New Hampshire. They're both terrible with directions, so they'll probably get lost. It's a good thing they're leaving early, or they'd miss the wedding.

"We all have to do yoga tonight when we get there," Mom says, when we're back and sitting in the living room.

"Everyone?" Dad asks. "What if we don't even like yoga?"

"It's required," Mom says. "There's a whole schedule of activities."

"This is crazy," Dad says, and Mom shakes her head. They're complaining, but deep down they're excited to be going somewhere different together. I can just tell.

"Well, you kids have fun," Grandma says. "Tell Esme I say hello."

"Will do," Dad replies.

"But when you get back, it's crunch time." Grandma looks at Mom. "We'll have five days until the grand opening and that's it. We'll practically be sleeping at the store."

"Ma, we're not in bad shape," Mom tells Grandma. "Take a look around, everything's organized. We need to get in touch with Mayor Danes about the official ribbon cutting and all the hoopla, but as far as appointments and everything, we're doing great."

Grandma raises her eyebrows. "If you say so . . ."

"I say so!" I exclaim, and everyone laughs.

Soon Mom and Dad are off in Mom's old Volkswagen, heading toward New Hampshire. It's hard for me to believe that they're going away for a whole weekend together. Yeah, they weren't officially divorced, and they didn't fight a lot, but it's still weird. It's a good thing a lot of other people will be there. It would be super-awkward if they had to spend a whole weekend alone just the two of them.

In a way, I'm jealous that they're leaving, because I only got to see my dad for one full day and a little bit the night before. But in another way, I'm glad that my mom gets to spend time with him. It's hard to say. I guess that's what they mean by mixed feelings.

"So it's just us all weekend," Grandma says, with her feet up on the ottoman. "Bean, what's for dinner?"

"I was thinking Mexican—enchiladas, guacamole, margaritas."

"Sounds good," Grandma says. "Except the last part. No underage drinking in my house."

"Kidding, Doris, kidding."

Grandma smiles. "Make sure there's enough for six. I invited Gary and Bevin over." Grandma looks at me. "You haven't apologized, Lucy. I'm very grateful for your help with the inspection, but Bevin is waiting for an apology. It doesn't matter how good you are at solving problems and saving the day if you're not a nice person. Being nice is most important, you know."

If I had a dollar for every time Grandma has said that to me, I'd be able to buy a spa by myself.

"I know." I walk over and give Grandma a hug. She must've been out by the pool while we were out with Dad. She smells like sunscreen, and I love it. I wish everyone could smell like sunscreen all year long. "I've been planning out exactly what I want to say. I'm sorry it has taken so long."

I run upstairs and throw on my red-and-white polka-dot tankini, grab a towel out of the linen closet, and sprint down the stairs and out the back door to the pool. I set up my towel on the lounge chair, lie back, and take out my phone.

"Bevin?" I say, when I hear someone answer.

"Yeah?"

"Hi, it's Lucy."

"I know."

OK, so she's not going to make this easy for me. That's fine. I deserve it. She ruined my client's makeup way back in the beginning of summer, but I wasn't exactly welcoming to her either, and I waited so long to call and apologize. I've totally been avoiding her.

"Do you want to come swimming before dinner?" I ask.

"Maybe. I'm helping Anais put all of the appointments into the computer."

"Listen, Bevin, it shouldn't have taken me so long to call you. I'm really sorry." I stop to think for a second. "I know you think you were just another one of my projects, but it's not true."

She doesn't say anything and so I take that as a sign to go on. "I like you. I like the way you keep asking questions, like you really care about a person, and you're not just making conversation. I like the way you still fold over your anklet socks like a kid, but you can pull it off and make it look classy and cool. I like the way you're friendly and make people feel like they've known you forever even if they've just met you."

"That's not even true," she mumbles.

"Yes, it is," I tell her.

"You really think I have an easy time making friends?"

"Yes. I do." I clear my throat. "But you have to give yourself a chance. Don't think it's going to happen in five minutes, and don't assume that they're not going to like you, because they will."

"Really really?"

"Yes. Really really."

"Dad! Can I go over to Lucy's and swim?" she yells straight into the phone.

"Sure!" I hear Gary yell back.

"I'll be there in five minutes! Bye!" She hangs up, and I guess that means she accepted my apology.

I jump in the pool and float around, savoring these few minutes of quiet time before Bevin comes over.

As I'm floating, I think about Mom and Dad and the wedding, and the great day Claudia, Bean, and I had with Dad. I think about saving the day with Ruthie. I'm grateful to have a clear head now that I made peace with Bevin. I think about the grand opening and how amazing it's going to be, the ribbon cutting and Sarabeth and all her fancy friends and family getting ready for the wedding. I think about the news crews that will be there, and the paper, and all the boats on the water for Boat Fest.

But something still doesn't feel quite right. I've figured out a lot, but there're two other things I need to figure out.

And they're both named Ramal.

Lucy's tip for becoming a better person:
Be grateful for what you have.

$\mathcal{D}$inner with $\mathcal{B}$evin and $\mathcal{G}$ary ends up being pretty nice. Bean makes a Mexican feast and we sit at the table long after we've finished eating, just talking and laughing. And Bevin likes night swimming as much as I do, so we change back into our suits and race out to the pool for a late-night swim.

"You're so lucky to have a pool," she says.

"I know."

"You're so lucky that your parents get along even if they're not together," she says.

"I know."

"And Sunny's a pretty awesome best friend."

"I know."

She keeps listing a million other reasons I'm lucky: I have an older sister, my grandma doesn't need a wheelchair like hers does, I'm allowed to have soda in the house, all this stuff. And as she's talking, I realize that she's right. I really am lucky.

"You get to live in Manhattan, though," I tell her.

"True." She splashes me with water. "But I'd give that up for a private pool."

I splash her back. "Come visit whenever. But it's only open from May to September."

A little while later, Bevin and Gary go home to the pharmacy's upstairs apartment, and it feels funny that they'll be leaving soon and the apartment will be empty again. I wonder if anyone will ever live there in the future. Maybe Claudia and Bean, if they get married one day? That would be cute. I hope I get to be the maid of honor.

Thinking about Claudia's future wedding jogs my memory and I remember something I forgot to do! I'm such an idiot. I race upstairs to the computer. That girl Palmer who's planning her sister's bachelorette party—it's a week away! I totally forgot. I bet they booked another place.

I look through my e-mail and find hers and write her back.

Hello Palmer,

I am so sorry for my delay in responding. We would love to have the bachelorette party at our spa on Saturday evening. Please confirm that you'd still like to have it there.

Thank you,

Lucy Desberg

After I'm done taking care of official spa business, I go downstairs and find Claudia. It's not that late, and there's still something I have to do before tomorrow.

I tap Claudia on the shoulder. She and Bean are watching some documentary about New York City in the early 1900s, but she can be interrupted.

"Can you drive me to Sunny's?" I ask her.

"I thought Sunny was in L.A.," she responds. Sheesh, she has an amazing memory. She has so much going on, and yet she remembers every detail about my friends. That's a nice thing about older sisters.

"She is, but I need to do something."

Claudia looks at me all squinty-eyed and pauses the documentary. "What are you talking about, Lucy?"

"I need to go drop some stuff off. I just need a ride there."

"Claud, come on, let's take her." Bean smiles at me. "Live a little. A few minutes of breaking and entering never hurt anyone!"

He laughs, and I do too, but then I add, "It's not breaking and entering! I know where the key is!"

It only takes me a few minutes to do what I have to do while Bean and Claudia wait in the car.

I put the basket I made right in the middle of Sunny's bed. It's full of all her favorite stuff: pretzel M&M's, Red Hots, hot-dog-flavored potato chips, key-lime-pie-scented lip gloss, her favorite ultra-sheen shampoo, and a package of these new Hello Kitty note cards we just got in at the pharmacy.

I take out a separate card with two artsy-looking ice cream sundaes on the cover and write:

Dear Sunny,

I'm so sorry I have been such an annoying, selfish, weirdo grump this summer. I know this basket of some of your favorite stuff won't totally make up for it, but maybe it's a good start? I love you. I hope we're still BFFs.

A million hugs,

Lucy

25

Lucy's tip for a great summer:

Spend as much time with your friends as you can!

@My phone rings at seven A.M. the next morning. My eyes are still closed when I answer it, so I don't even see the caller ID.

"We're baaaaaaack," the voice on the other end sings through the phone.

"Sunny! Do you know what time it is?"

She laughs. "Not really. We took the red-eye. I'm all out of whack. Anyway, I couldn't wait any longer."

"For what?"

"To say thank you, duh, for the amazing basket! I love it! And I knew it was a good idea to tell you where we keep the extra key!"

"You're welcome," I mumble, still feeling sleepy. "I'm really sorry. I shouldn't have been so weird about hanging out with AGE, and the Bevin stuff, and leaving you out."

"I'm sorry too!" Sunny yells. "I'm sorry for what happened that day we snuck to Bayberry Cove Library. I'm sorry I said such mean things. And I was talking to Pindar about it, and she said I can't ditch my friends just because I have a boyfriend."

"You and Pindar are getting along again?" I ask. Pindar is Sunny's first cousin on her dad's side, the ones they were just visiting in L.A. She's sixteen and such a know-it-all. They usually fight.

"Yeah, we had the best time together. She's way better now."

"Well, that's good."

"I'm glad we've made up, Lucy. Of course we're still BFFs. I'll be over in forty-five minutes." I hear Yamir and Mr. Ramal arguing about something in the background. "I'm borrowing one of your bathing suits because mine are musty from being in our suitcases."

"OK, I'm going back to sleep until then."

It feels like only five minutes pass before the doorbell rings. I throw myself out of bed to let Sunny in. Grandma's reading the newspaper on the back porch and Bean and Claudia are at the table eating bowls of cereal. Sunny bounds in, practically jumping up and down.

"Sleepyhead! Wake up!"

"Shouldn't you be tired? It's only like six A.M. in Los Angeles right now."

"I'm hyped up! We have a week until the grand opening of Pink and Green."

I smile, and we traipse back up the stairs.

"Come on. Let's swim. And we have to talk," Sunny says when we're back in my room.

"We talked. We forgave each other. Remember?" I take my army-green one-piece out of the drawer and throw it at Sunny. "Here. Borrow this one. Green always looks good on you."

"We have to talk about something else," Sunny says, and goes into the bathroom to change. I run to Claudia's bathroom to brush my teeth and change into my bathing suit. When I get back, Sunny's sitting at my desk, spraying on sunscreen.

"It's about Yamir," she says. She raises her eyebrows up so high, they're practically touching her widow's peak. My heart starts pounding. I bet he fell in love with someone else in L.A. I bet Pindar knew the perfect girl for him. "He really likes you, Lucy. Can you just get it together?"

I try not to show my relief. "Get what together?"

"Just be normal around him." She raises her eyebrows at me again. "I know I was a freak when I started liking Evan, but you told me to stop being dumb, and I did, so I'm telling you the same thing now."

"How do you know he likes me?" I sit down on my bed. "What about that girl Arianna?"

"Oh, that." She pauses and makes a face like she feels bad. "I pretty much made that up because I was annoyed at you. I'm sorry. But he likes you. I overheard him talking to Vishal."

Vishal is their other cousin, Pindar's brother. He's Yamir's age.

"Sun, you're like a super-eavesdropper now!"

"Duh. Who do you think I learned it from?"

I slap her knee. "Fine. I'll try to be more normal around Yamir. But can we just discuss that he's been weird too? He's mean one day and nice the next and he invites me to things and then bails on other plans. Total mixed signals. Right? I think I once heard a song about that."

Sunny nods. "Boys are weird, Lucy. Haven't I said that a million times? That's why we need to stick together."

Sunny and I spend the rest of the day swimming, and she comes out for Chinese food with Grandma, Bean, Claudia, and me. We order Shirley Temples and share chicken chow fun. It feels like old times. Better than old times. She's back, and we've made up, and she told me Yamir likes me. She didn't even bring up Evan once in a way that seemed like she would rather be hanging out with him. We talked about him, but in a fun way.

"Remember what I said," Sunny tells me as we're waiting on the front porch for her mom to pick her up.

"OK. But I don't know what to do about it." I take a small sip of root beer float. Of course we stopped for Dairy Queen on the way home. It is summer, after all.

"Just be Lucy. Don't overthink it."

I'm half hoping Yamir will be in the car when Mrs. Ramal pulls up, but he isn't. Mrs. Ramal waves to me from the driver's seat, and Sunny walks over to the car.

Don't overthink it. I keep hearing that over and over in my head, but it almost seems like an oxymoron. How can you tell your brain not to think? You'd be thinking about not thinking. It's so mind-boggling that it makes me laugh.

I'm like a crazy lady sitting on the front porch drinking a root beer float, laughing by herself, but I don't really mind it.

Lucy's tip for becoming a better person:
Send thank-you notes! Real, handwritten ones.

Dear Lucy,

Thanks so much for getting back to me! We were looking into alternate plans, but the spa was still our first choice! We'll be there around 8 pm. We'd like manicures and pedicures and we'll bring in our own food and drinks. Please get back to me with the price.

Thank you,

Palmer

Grandma went to Block Island with Flo for the day, so I can't ask her the price for renting the spa. So instead, I call Anais and ask her. She's so excited that the spa has already been rented for an evening before it's even officially open that she's freaking out. "You set this up?" she asks.

"Well, I just responded to the spa e-mail," I tell her.

"Right. I guess I let that slip, after I had to fire our initial receptionist," she says.

"I didn't even know we had a receptionist," I reply, and then wish I hadn't said that. I don't want Anais to think I'm complaining about being left out again.

"Well, tell Palmer it's no charge to rent out the spa, just thirty-five dollars each for manicures and pedicures," Anais decides. "It's a nice little promotion since it's the first weekend and hopefully they'll tell others about it. Let me make sure Denise, Chloe, and Rebecca are all available. They're our best manicurists," she says. "Good work, Lucy."

"Thanks," I say, already typing back to Palmer.

After all of my computer work is done, I realize I forgot to do something very important. Something Mom taught Claudia and me about from a very early age: thank-you notes! I need to write a thank-you note to Ruthie, to thank her for all of her help with the inspection.

I dig around my desk for my best note card and settle on a red card with pencils on the front. I make it short and sweet: thanking her for her help, and encouraging her to come to the grand opening.

When Mom and Dad get back later that evening, they're cracking up as they're walking from the driveway to the house. I don't mean to be spying on them, but I can't help it; I'm on the couch and there's only the screen door between us.

"No one will believe us," Mom says.

"Nope."

"No one will ever understand how awful that was," Mom goes on.

"No, they won't." Dad laughs.

It's weird to see two people saying how awful something was but laughing about it at the same time. It's like they bonded over something horrible. It's pretty funny.

"How was it?" I ask as soon as they open the door.

"Awful," Mom says.

"Don't even ask." Dad laughs again.

"What? Why?" I don't understand how a wedding could really be that awful, but it doesn't seem like they had a fight or anything.

"Let's just put it this way," Mom starts. "We had to do this group chanting exercise to welcome them as husband and wife." She pauses for emphasis. "Then we had to weigh our food waste and participate in trust falls."

"OK, Jane." Dad puts a hand on her shoulder. "Lucy gets it."

Mom leans into him in an exasperated but humored

kind of way, and even though I'm curious about the rest of the wedding weekend, I think I'll wait until everyone else is there to hear it.

"Where's Claudia?" Dad asks.

"Probably in the pool. Where else?"

"Go get her," he says. "Please. And Grandma too."

"Grandma went to Block Island with Flo," I tell them. "She should be back by nine."

They look at each other in this way that seems as if they're speaking with their eyes. I haven't thought about this in so long, but now I remember it—they used to do this all the time when I was little, after I asked them if I could have ice cream or go to an amusement park, stuff like that.

"OK, well, go get Claudia," Dad says.

I practically have to drag Claudia and Bean in from the pool. They throw towels around themselves, but they're dripping water all over the house.

"What was so important?" Claudia asks. "Should we go change?"

"No. Sit." Mom pats the couch next to her.

"Mom, I'm dripping wet," Claudia says snottily.

"It's fine," Mom replies. "It's an old couch."

Bean sits in the leather arm chair, and I realize I'm not

disgusted by his feet. He actually has acceptable feet. His toenails aren't too long, and they're a pretty nice shape.

OK, Lucy, stop. Stop looking at Bean's feet.

"So, we have an announcement to make," Dad starts, and for some reason, my immediate thought is that we're getting a dog. I don't know why. "A lot has been going on for me professionally, and you know I never planned to stay in London forever . . ."

"Australia!" Claudia yells. "Please say Australia! I have always wanted to go to Australia!"

Sheesh, for a smart girl, she's really dumb. Why would we want our dad on the other side of the planet?

"No." Dad laughs. "Not Australia." He stops talking and gives us a look like he's waiting to see if we're ready. "Connecticut."

"What?" I yelp.

"I am now an associate professor of urban planning at Yale University." Dad smiles. "I start in a few weeks."

"Really?" I jump up and run over and hug him. "Really? Really?"

"Really! Really!"

He tells us all about wanting to move on from Oxford, and looking for new opportunities and the position opening up at Yale. He tells us how it's been his plan to come back to the United States all along, and when something opened up at Yale, it was like a dream come true.

"When did this happen?" Claudia asks.

"A month or so ago," Dad says. "That's why our plans kept changing, but I didn't want to tell any of you until it was final. The only one who knew was Grandma."

"Grandma?" I ask.

"Yes, I wanted her advice. She may not be my mother, but I really respect her." He smiles. "And I wanted to know if I could rent out the upstairs apartment until things got settled."

That makes sense. I don't know why I expected him to move back into the house and everything right away—that's just always how I pictured him here in Connecticut, I guess. But he and Mom have their own lives. It takes time for things to go back to the way they used to be, or go back to the way they're going to be, or whatever.

Maybe this is like a trial run to see if things can work out with him here. Maybe I can't totally feel like things are settled. He could leave again without warning. I just need to take it day by day.

I look at Claudia, who's smiling; and Mom, who's smiling; and Bean, who's smiling too.

"This calls for celebration!" I yell. "Ice cream sundaes, here we come!"

We all pile into the car. Bean, Claudia, and I sit in the backseat, and Dad drives. He even remembers how to get there. He remembers how to get everywhere around here. It's like he was meant to come back. He was always meant to come back.

The next week is a total whirlwind. I barely have time to just "be Lucy" like Sunny said because I barely have time to even see Yamir. We text back and forth a little bit, which is good and helps me not to overthink anything. He says he's planning to be at the grand opening and he's bringing Clint and Anthony, mostly because he heard that Leeoni's Pizza is having a table at Boat Fest right down the street from us, and it's their favorite.

I tell him Leeoni's is donating pizza for the grand opening and ribbon cutting and he texts me back that now he really has a reason to come.

I try not to get offended. Boys are just weird sometimes. I need to remind myself of that every day. Or maybe every hour.

Anais is busy every day doing final training for all the staff. She goes over how to talk to the guests, how to handle payment, tips, and greeting people in the reception area. Grandma and Mom have lunches with them too, officially welcoming them to the staff, and telling them the basics of how things work around here.

It's amazing that we now have nine new employees—four girls who do manicures, pedicures, massages, and hair blowouts and updos; three who do facials, makeup, and waxing; one who's our receptionist; and a guy who does all the upkeep, cleaning, stocking of towels, and stuff like that.

We are a fully operational spa!

I don't know if Anais said something to the staff, but they're all super-nice to me. Mara, who's one of the makeup artists, even invited me in early to show me a new shipment of makeup.

"You'll never believe the foundation," she tells me. "It's barely foundation. It's this liquid powder that goes on so smooth. Here. Sit down. I'll try it on you—not like you need it."

I hop up in our beautiful new makeup chair and Mara starts dabbing some on with one of those awesome triangular sponges. "I was so happy when I heard that the Earth Beauty line expanded into a whole new area of spa products—lotions, wax, toner. When I talked to Anais about the products you wanted to use, it was the only answer, and now we can have everything from one brand," Mara says as she's massaging in the foundation. I feel so relaxed.

"Yeah, it's the best makeup ever, and the fact that it's eco-friendly is like the icing on the cake," I say. "But now they have that higher-end line. Pure Magic. Is that what this is from?"

"Yup!" Mara hands me the mirror. "Take a look."

"Wow. So even. So smooth." I laugh. "I sound like a commercial."

Mara tells me all about her experience working at the high-end spas in Manhattan, and then wanting to move to a calmer, quieter place to raise her children. She has five-year-old twins. "It's so great here. Great schools, wonderful restaurants, a really nice tight-knit community."

"I know." I smile. "It's a great place to grow up."

After a few more hours at the spa, we all head home to rest and get ready for the big day tomorrow. It feels so weird to think that. *Tomorrow. Pink & Green is opening tomorrow.*

"I made a spaghetti feast," Bean tells all of us as we're relaxing on the deck by the pool. "I'm basically treating this grand opening weekend like a marathon, so we're doing a little carb-loading."

"Great. Just what I need." Grandma makes a face, then smiles at Bean. "I'm kidding. Thank you."

Bean finishes cooking and setting the table and tells us to be inside in about five minutes. It's going to be sad when

Bean and Claudia leave to go back to college, partly because Bean has been our cook this whole summer. He even does all the dishes. How are we ever going to go back to cooking and cleaning up for ourselves?

We all go inside and eat our spaghetti Bolognese and garlic bread and Caesar salad. Mom and Grandma have glasses of red wine. Claudia, Bean, and I have about a million glasses of Mom's mint iced tea. None of us will be able to sleep tonight. Dad had to go to Yale for the past few days to meet with some new colleagues, fill out forms, and sit in on some summer classes. But he'll be here tomorrow for the grand opening! And for the next few days while Bevin and Gary are still in the upstairs apartment, Dad's staying in our guest room.

After dinner, I call Sunny because she made me promise to call so that she could wish me good luck. Of course she'll be at the store bright and early tomorrow, but just in case I was busy, she wanted to wish me good luck in advance.

"So? You're ready?" she asks.

"I think so. I'm not the one doing all the hair and makeup for Sarabeth and her bridesmaids and moms and grandmas."

"You know what I mean, Luce." Sunny snorts. "So anyway, we'll all be there for the ribbon cutting—me, my parents, Evan, Yamir, I think Clint and Anthony too."

"Great." I'm hearing everything Sunny's saying, but I'm having trouble concentrating. I'm double-checking the spa e-mail, and my personal e-mail, and picking out different potential outfits for tomorrow.

"OK, so this is it. Tomorrow Pink and Green will be open. Everything you dreamed of will have come true!" Sunny yells into the phone.

"So amazing." I think about that, and I guess she's right. Even my dad's back, for now at least. It's hard to imagine what my life will be like without anything to worry about. Not that I'll know what that's like—there's still one big thing I have to figure out. And besides, new worries come around all the time. I used to be worried all the time about the pharmacy closing and having to sell the house, and then I was worried about my role in the spa this summer. Worrying is just a part of life.

"OK, g'night Luce. See you in the A.M.!"

"Night, Sunny."

I spend the next hour finding the perfect outfit: my frayed jean skirt and my gray ribbed tank top with my strappy black patent-leather sandals. Cute, comfy, sophisticated.

I hate to wash off the beautiful Pure Magic foundation that Mara applied before, but it's practically a law that you can't go to sleep with makeup on your face. I take one of the Earth Beauty makeup remover cloths and wipe away the foundation. It smells clean and it feels relaxing.

I go to sleep mostly free of worry, and filled with excitement and anticipation about tomorrow.

Lucy's tip for a great summer:

Wear vibrant colors and paint your toenails bright red.

Welcome! Welcome!" Mayor Danes is yelling into a megaphone. "You're all going to need to get close to your neighbors if you want to see the ribbon cutting. There are a lot of you here, and though the sidewalks on Ocean Street are wide, they're not quite wide enough for this crowd!"

I'm tempted to cover my ears because I'm so close to the megaphone and the volume is so high and Mayor Danes is yelling. But I don't. In a way, I like how loud it is. It feels big and important.

Amelia from Mayor Danes's office made a huge blowup of the press release and had it laminated and mounted on a stand outside the store. Every few seconds, someone else comes up to read the interview, and it feels pretty crazy that all of these people are reading about me.

The crowd stretches all the way down the sidewalk to Leeoni's Pizza and the Ocean View Diner and Millie's Antiques. And it stretches all the way down the other direction past the Red Cross office and the Old Mill Community Bank.

It feels a little like the ground breaking back in June, but bigger and more exciting. And Dad's here. He's standing right next to me, and he squeezes my hand, and whispers, "You did this!"

I smile. I did this. But others helped too—Morrie with the idea about Gary being an investor, and Gary finding Anais, and everything Mom put into the branding and the publicity, and Grandma being a steady force behind the prescription counter, realistic but encouraging.

"Are you ready to do the honors?" Mayor Danes turns his face toward me and away from the megaphone.

"Yes, but I want some people to help me." I look all around, then motion to Claudia and Bean to come up; we discussed it in advance that they'd help, but I didn't mention my other plan.

"Bevin?" I call. She's standing with her dad wearing some of the clothes we bought together. She looks up, confused. "Do you want to help cut the ribbon?"

Her eyes get huge and she runs up to me, and then the four of us stand there behind the big ribbon. I get to hold the scissors, and my hand is shaking a little bit. Finally I do it, and the ribbon falls to the ground and everyone starts cheering.

It's ten in the morning on a beautiful Saturday in August, and all of these people are so happy for us. Sarabeth and her friends and family will be here in an hour to primp before the wedding this evening. And then tonight Palmer and Walker will be enjoying an evening at Pink & Green.

The glass doors to Pink & Green are wide open, and people are coming in for a tour and for miniature pieces of Leeoni's donated pizzas. There's also mini spanakopita from Grecian Islands Restaurant around the corner and tea sand-wiches from Max's Café three blocks down. There are avo-cado rolls from Gari to keep with the green theme, and pink lemonade and strawberry milk shakes from 384 Sprinkles for the pink.

People are walking around, enjoying their food, talking to each other. Soon they'll leave the spa and enjoy the rest of Boat Fest and the other booths and events.

I'm sipping a glass of pink lemonade in the Relaxation Room and taking a moment of quiet for myself, just to sit back and appreciate everything, when I feel a tap on my shoul-der. I look to each side of me, and then turn around and look behind the couch.

It's Yamir.

"Hey, Luce-Juice."

"Hey."

I expect him to come and sit down with me, but he stays standing there, leaning over the top of the couch.

"So," he says.

"So."

"So now that Pink and Green is open, are you going to go back and be normal, fun Lucy again?"

"What's that supposed to mean?" I laugh.

"You know what I mean."

"Yamir, come sit, because it's really uncomfortable to keep turning my head this way to talk to you."

He gives me a crooked smile and comes to sit down.

I'm glad I asked him to sit, because my neck was starting to hurt, but now we're sitting on the couch together, alone in the Relaxation Room, and maybe it's the sourness of the lemonade, but my stomach feels like a washing machine.

"So if you go back to being normal Lucy again—"

"Wait. You're saying I used to be normal?"

He hits me on the arm. "You know what I mean."

He says that a lot. But I *do* kind of know what he means.

"If you go back to being Lucy again, and you have time for me, well, maybe we can be something . . . we can be, um, I don't know." He pauses and looks at me, and I think I know what he's getting at, but I don't know if I should say anything. "We can be . . . Lucy and Yamir."

I exhale and smile.

"I like that." I nod. "Lucy and Yamir."

"Good." He smiles, but not his crooked smile—his even, confident, self-assured smile.

"So I've only had about seventeen mini-slices of Leeoni's, which equals about one and a half real slices. Can we go get more?"

"Sure," I say.

We stand up, and as we're leaving the Relaxation Room, he grabs my hand.

We walk out through the pharmacy, still holding hands, and over to the entryway to Pink & Green.

There are people all around us—happy people, enjoying their time here. They're smiling and waving to me, and I smile back. Pink & Green sounded so great when it was just an idea I had a long time ago. Now it really exists, and it's better than I could have imagined. But right now I can only think about one thing: Lucy and Yamir.

I really like the sound of that.

Acknowledgments

Hugs, kisses, and oodles of thanks to:
Mom, Dad, Bubbie, Zeyda, Aunt Emily, Heidi, all the Rosenbergs near and far, the crew in Indiana, Libby Isaac, the BWL Library team, and everyone who has chosen to read my books.

To Ellie and Gracie, thanks for being such awesome fans! I can't wait to buy your books one day.

High fives and X's and O's for Jenny, Caroline, and Siobhan.

Alyssa, you continue to amaze me with your brilliance, honesty, sensitivity, and all-around awesomeness. If literary agenting was an Olympic sport, you would win gold every time.

Howard, Susan, Jason, Chad, Meagan, Mary Ann, Laura, Elisa, and everyone at Abrams, you are superstars. I am beyond grateful for everything that you do.

Maggie, I feel lucky every single day that you're on my team, reading my words and making each sentence better. I owe you a swimming pool of thanks.

Dave and Aleah, thanks for the love and support and for sharing vanilla milkshakes with me.

Read on for an excerpt from
Lisa Greenwald's newest book,

Welcome
to
Dog
Beach

On Seagate Island, there are three kinds of people: the lucky ones, the luckier ones, and the luckiest ones.

The lucky ones are the people who come for a weekend or maybe even a week. They stay at the Seagate Inn or they find a last-minute rental.

The luckier ones are the people who rent a house for the whole summer, Memorial Day to Labor Day. They usually come back summer after summer and stay in the same house.

And the luckiest ones are the people like me. I don't want to sound conceited—I'm grateful for how lucky I am. Because when it comes to Seagate Island, there's no doubt that I am the luckiest. I've spent every summer of my life on Seagate Island in my grandmother's house.

I was born at the end of May, so I spent my first three

months here. And I'll spend every summer here for the rest of my life. It's probably weird for me to think that far ahead, since I'm only eleven. But trust me—I will.

"Remy," I hear my mom calling from inside the house. I give her a few minutes to come outside and find me. It's kind of an unofficial house rule that if one of us is outside, the other one has to come out if they want to talk. No one should have to go inside to talk unless it's raining. On Seagate Island, our time outside by the sea is sacred. We've only been here for a week, and we have the whole summer stretched out in front of us, but we still don't take our outside time for granted.

I hear the quiet creak of the screen door, and then my mom pulls over the other wicker chair to sit next to me.

"Don't be mad, okay?" she asks, but it sounds more like a command than a question.

This can't be good.

"I just ran into Amber Seasons, and she's in a pickle," my mom starts. I wonder why people use the word *pickle* to mean a problem. In my mind, pickles are one of the most delicious foods. But I also get why people hate them. Bennett hates pickles. In fact, if he orders a hamburger and someone puts a pickle on his plate, he has to send the whole meal back. He feels bad about it, but he does it anyway. That's how much he hates pickles.

But Amber Seasons's being in a pickle isn't surprising. I've known her since I was born, pretty much, and she's always been in a pickle. She's fifteen years older than I am, and no matter what's going on, she always seems frazzled.

"What kind of pickle?" I ask.

"She offered to teach an art class for Seagate Seniors on Monday and Wednesday mornings at ten. But then her baby-sitter ended up staying in New Jersey for the summer, and now she needs someone to watch her son. She told me that's when he naps, so you'd just be sitting in her house every morning for a few hours."

I can't believe this is happening. This was going to be the first real summer that Micayla, Bennett, and I were allowed to roam free, all day, and do whatever we wanted.

In previous summers we were allowed to go off on our own, but only for a few hours at a time, and we needed to check in and always tell our parents where we were. But this summer was going to be different.

We're eleven now, going into sixth grade. That's middle school for Bennett and Micayla; it'll be the last year of elementary school for me.

And now I have to cut into that completely free time to watch Amber Seasons's son.

On the other hand, babysitting is kind of cool and something real teenagers do. I guess I'm older now and my mom thinks I'm more mature. I'm flattered that she thinks I can handle it.

"Please, Remy," my mom says. She's sitting on the wicker armchair with her head resting on her hands, and she looks pretty desperate. It's not even a favor for her, it's a favor for Amber Seasons, but I bet my mom already said that I'd do it. My mom has this weird thing about helping people solve their problems. She gets all jazzed up and has this intense, burning desire to help them, like she can't stop until she makes whatever situation they're in a little better. Helping other people makes her happier than anything else.

"Fine." I sigh, all defeated, but knowing I would never get out of it. "Maybe Micayla and Bennett can come with me some mornings?"

My mom considers that for a moment. "Well, you can certainly talk to Amber and ask her if it's okay."

She goes inside to finish getting ready for her afternoon swimming session, and I sit back in my chair and think. How bad will it really be? It's only a few hours two mornings a week.

My mom always says how good it makes her feel when she helps other people. So maybe I'll be like that too. I'll help Amber, and then I'll feel better. About everything.

Being sad on Seagate is kind of an oxymoron. The two things don't go together at all. But this year is different. I'm sad on Seagate, and I can't seem to help it.

"I got you two scoops," Micayla tells me when she walks through the house and finds me on the back porch. That's another thing about Seagate—no one locks their doors, and we all just barge into each other's homes. It can be awkward sometimes, like when I saw Bennett's mom getting out of the shower, but she had a towel on, and we just laughed about it. But the rest of the time it feels like the whole island's our home.

The turquoise ice cream cups from Sundae Best, Seagate Island's oldest and best ice cream shop, somehow make the ice cream taste even more delicious. I always get espresso cookie, and Micayla always gets cherry chip. When it comes to ice cream, we are as different as can be. But when it comes to almost everything else, we're pretty much the same.

Well, except that I'm white and she's black. And then there's also the difference of our hair—she wears it in braids year-round, and I have thin, straight, boring, not-quite-blonde and not-quite-brown hair that barely stays in an elastic band. Hers always looks good, even after she's just woken up.

Her parents are both from St. Lucia, in the Caribbean. They moved to the United States when they were kids but didn't meet until college. They have amazing accents, and when we're a little bit older, they're going to take me with them when they go back to visit Micayla's grandma in St. Lucia.

We take our ice cream cups and walk down the wooden stairs of my deck to the beach. Even though I do this at least ten times a day, I feel lucky every single time. On Seagate, the beach is my backyard, and I'm pretty sure there is nothing better than that in the whole world.

Sometimes we don't even bother with towels or chairs—we just sit down on the sand. We dig our feet in as far as they will go and we eat our ice cream. Our plan is to meet up with Bennett when he's done playing Ping-Pong with his dad, and then we'll decide what to do for the rest of the day.

"I hope this will cheer you up," Micayla says, burrowing through her ice cream cup for a chunk of chocolate. "I've never seen you sad on Seagate before."

She's right about that. But she's also never really seen me anywhere else, except for the time her dad brought her to New York City for a last-minute meeting. Her mom had flown to St. Lucia to visit Micayla's grandma, and Micayla couldn't stay home alone. So Micayla came to New York and we spent the day together. I don't think I was sad that day, so she's never really seen me sad anywhere, not just on Seagate. But I know what she means.

"I'm happy to be here. I just keep picturing Danish running on the beach . . . And his dog bed is still upstairs. I wish my parents would just throw it out, but I think they're too sad to do it. And the Pooch Parade during Seagate Halloween will be so horrible without him."

"I know," she says, not looking at me. "Well, maybe we can figure out something else to do during the Pooch Parade."

It's probably weird that it's not even July yet and I'm already thinking about Seagate Halloween, which takes place over Labor Day weekend. But it's one of the biggest traditions of the summer—everyone participates. Seagate Halloween is exactly the same every year, and that's the way I like it.

Bennett dresses up as Harvey from Sundae Best. He wears his shorts really high and a Seagate baseball cap. Micayla dresses up as a mermaid, like the statue you see when you first get off the ferry. I dress up as a beach pail. My mom makes me a new costume every year out of painted cardboard, and it comes out awesome every time. And the best part was that Danish would dress up as the shovel! We'd get the biggest sand shovel we could find and strap it to his back, and I'd carry him, so we looked like a perfect pair— beach pail and sand shovel. So happy together.

We've been on Seagate Island for a week, and I've been partially sad the whole time. Happy to be here, but sad without Danish. I don't want to be sad here. It's my most favorite place in the universe. But I can't seem to help it.

Danish was my grandma's dog, so for many years I only ever saw him on Seagate. Our house here was Grandma's house. When she died three years ago, we got Danish and the house, although it always seemed like they were partially ours to begin with.

During the summer, Danish slept in my bed. He spent all day with Micayla, Bennett, and me. Everyone thought he was my dog. And the house—well, the house felt like ours too. The yellow room with the canopy bed was mine. No one else slept there. Mom and Dad had the room around the corner with the blue-and-ivory-striped wallpaper. And Grandma's room was at the end of the hallway. She had her own bathroom, but she'd let us use it.

All year she'd be busy on Seagate, volunteering at the elementary school to help the kids with math, setting up the concert schedule for the summer, taking Danish to Dog Beach even when it was a little bit cold outside. Even though I knew all that, I always imagined her waiting patiently for us to come back for the summer. We'd come for weekends sometimes, but that didn't really count. Summer was summer.

Summer was when we were all together. Grandma would make her famous corn chowder. Mom would set up her easel on the back deck and paint landscapes of the ocean, and Dad would try to play Ping-Pong with everyone on the island at least once.

After Grandma died, we were all really sad. We couldn't imagine being on Seagate without her. But when we came back that next summer, being there was more comforting than we expected it to be. Everyone wanted to tell us stories about Grandma. Dad did some work on the house to spruce it up a little bit, and Mom organized a special concert in Grandma's memory. Now the annual concert series is known as the Sally Bell Seagate Concert Calendar.

Danish died this past December. It was sudden, and I don't really like to even think about it. All winter and spring, I kept hoping that being back on Seagate would be comforting, the way it was after Grandma died. But so far, it's not. So far, I just miss him. It was always Micayla, Bennett, and me—with Danish running along with us.

A key member of our crew is missing.

"I have to tell you something," Micayla and I say at the exact same time, and then we both burst into laughter.

"You first," I say. She probably has more exciting news than my babysitting job.

"Avery Sanders has a boyfriend," Micayla tells me.

"Yeah?" I ask. "She didn't mention it to me when I saw her at Pastrami on Rye the other night."

"Just saw her at Sundae Best. She was going on and on about it. She said this new kid moved to Seagate in the middle of the year. And he's, like, a real-life boyfriend."

I look at Micayla, surprised. "I wonder why she didn't tell me before."

Avery Sanders is a friend of ours, but not a best friend. She moved to Seagate four years ago, and she lives here year-round. She's the type of friend that we never really call to make plans, but if we run into each other, we'll hang out.

She's nice, but she's one of those girls who seemed like a teenager when we were, like, nine, and she'd always say that Bennett was my boyfriend, even when I didn't really know what a boyfriend was.

The past few times I talked to her, she told me that she was bored with Seagate and that it has really changed since she moved here.

I always listened to what she said, even though none of it made sense. How could Seagate be boring? And how could it change? Seagate will always be perfect, and summer after summer, it always stays the same. That's the beauty of it.

"I think her grandparents live here year-round now too," Micayla tells me. "That's what my mom said."

Actually, that's another group of lucky people on Seagate—the year-rounders. I always wonder if that makes them luckier than the luckiest or somewhere in between. On the one hand, they never have to leave Seagate. But on the other hand, they have to see almost everyone else leave. And they don't get that amazing anticipation—the excited, heart-bursting feeling of coming back.

"What did you have to tell me?" Micayla asks.

I explain the whole pickle situation with Amber Seasons.

"That's cool," Micayla says. "It's, like, your first real job."

"You think?"

"Yeah, for sure." She digs deep in her cup for the last little bit of ice cream. "And it's only a few hours. You won't miss anything."

"I guess."

Micayla gives me her please-cheer-up smile again and taps my leg. "Come on. Let's go meet Bennett at Ping-Pong. Bennett always makes you laugh after five minutes."

She's right about that.

About the Author

Lisa Greenwald works in the library at the Birch Wathen Lenox School on the Upper East Side of Manhattan. She is a graduate of the New School's MFA program in writing for children. She lives with her husband and daughter in Brooklyn, New York.

Read all of the
Pink & Green series!

Book One:
My Life in Pink & Green
By Lisa Greenwald

Book Two:
My Summer in Pink & Green
By Lisa Greenwald

Amulet Books
An imprint of ABRAMS
WWW.AMULETBOOKS.COM

SEND AUTHOR FAN MAIL TO:
Amulet Books, Att: Marketing, 115 West 18th Street, New York, NY 100
Or e-mail marketing@abramsbooks.com. All mail will be forwarded

Available Fall 2014

Pink & Green

Is the

More from Lisa Greenwald!

FROM THE AUTHOR OF *MY LIFE IN PINK & GREEN*

LISA GREENWALD

Sweet Treats & Secret Crushes

Amulet Books
An imprint of ABRAMS
WWW.AMULETBOOKS.COM

SEND AUTHOR FAN MAIL TO:
Amulet Books, Att: Marketing, 115 West 18th Street, New York, NY 100
Or e-mail marketing@abramsbooks.com. All mail will be forwarded

FROM THE AUTHOR OF *MY LIFE IN PINK & GREEN*

LISA GREENWALD

Reel Life
STARRING US